STO

DO NOT REMOVE
CARDS FROM POCKET

7/1/94

The Specter of Capitalism
And the Promise of a
Classless Society

The Specter of Capitalism
And the Promise of a
Classless Society

DONALD WEISS

Humanities Press International, Inc.
New Jersey ▼ London

First published 1993 by Humanities Press International, Inc.,
Atlantic Highlands, New Jersey 07716, and
3 Henrietta Street, Covent Garden, London WC2E 8LU

© 1993 by Donald Weiss

Library of Congress Cataloging-in-Publication Data
Weiss, Donald (Donald David)
    The specter of capitalism and the promise of a classless society /
Donald Weiss.
        p.   cm.
    Includes bibliographical reference and index.
    ISBN 0-391-03752-8
    1. Economic development—Effect of education on.   2. Capitalism.
3. Marxian economics.   4. Philosophy, Marxist.   5. Social classes.
6. Social structure.   7. Post-communism.   8. Philosophy.
9. Social sciences.   I. Title.
HD75.7.W45   1992
335.4—dc20   91-45221
                        CIP

A catalog record for this book is available from the British Library.

Printed in the United States of America

*To my parents, who gave me ideals,
and words, in the first place:
Helene Miller Weiss, in memoriam,
and Arthur E. Weiss*

Contents

Preface

Communism is dead. But so is capitalism in its classical form. Despite the shallow "we-have-won" propaganda so frequently heard in the West these days, the truth embodied in contemporary world events is a good deal more subtle. Each system embodies a crucial truth the other must learn.

The two most significant revolutionary ideals of the modern epoch can both be satisfied. We can and should have the benefits of capitalism. But we can and should also attempt to realize the Marxian dream of a classless society.

We must understand where Marx went wrong. In thinking that the world was about to pass beyond its present "development" phase, Marx indeed betrayed the Hegelian "dialectical" philosophy in which his own work is supposedly rooted.

But we must also see where Marx was right. Here we Westerners must pay special attention. The rational trajectory of educational practices, in advanced "mixed" economies, tends toward "Formative Parity": allocation of formative benefits in accord with talent and need. And this turns out to be the key to the fulfillment of Marx's fondest dream: the overthrow of classes.

Given the pace of world events, it may seem odd that I could so quickly have finished a complex theoretical work on so "hot" a topic. But these issues have been on my mind—and, in various stages of development, on my word processor—for about a decade.

I have, since the mid-1980s, used versions of this text in my classes on Marxism. Many of my students have assisted in the evolution of the final product in both technical and substantive ways.

World events gave me the impetus to complete what I had long since begun, and a recent sabbatical gave me the time.

Most of my earlier publications, especially during the 1970s, were sympathetic to "democratic" and "critical" versions of Marxism. Like so many of my fellows, I have, since those days, been forced to reconsider some of what I once took for granted.

I would, for reasons the text makes plain, no longer call myself a Marxist at all. But I remain convinced that there is a rational kernel that must be extricated from the orthodox Marxian husk—a truth the world has not yet fully absorbed.

I can bring to this discussion no more than my own training and experience allow. I am a philosophy professor, and you should not be shocked if sometimes I write like one. I am comforted that Marx, too, got his doctorate in philosophy, and would have made for himself a fine university career had he not been the nineteenth century's most prominent firebrand.

Philosophers who think about economics are in the same no-one's-land as economists who think philosophically. The peril in my own case is that as an economist I am an amateur. I have never been paid a dime for plotting a supply curve on a blackboard.

I console myself with the faith, no doubt self-serving, that some good may come of a philosophical interrogation of fundamental economic categories like capital, the division of labor, and social classes.

I owe thanks to too many students to name, but I must mention Louis Agresta's fine copyediting and Susan Goldbaum's help with the index. Colleagues have been helpful too: Dennis Schmidt and Leon Goldstein deserve specific mention.

Two sabbatical leaves, in 1982 and 1989, have been devoted to the project, for which I am grateful to the State University of New York. Thanks are also due the Rabinowitz Foundation, a grant from which, back in the 1970s, allowed me to write the ancestral texts from which the present version is descended; and to Keith Ashfield, Karen Starks, Olivia Pittet, and Rebecca Hogancamp of Humanities Press. I must also mention the late William Schuman, whose intellectual provocation over lunch one day in 1976 convinced me that somebody had to write a book of this kind.

Special thanks go to Arthur Weiss and Barbara Pfeffer Weiss, who turned over their beach house at Oxnard, California, to me and my word processor in the spring of 1989. It was under those benign and quiet conditions that the first complete draft was composed.

I owe thanks for the kind of support that is beyond measure to my wife, Kathleen Ferro Weiss, and to my son, Joshua Samuel Weiss. Similar heartfelt thanks go out to Andrew Stuart Weiss, Jane Weiss Sturman, Leon Sturman, Marie Ferro Zarakov, Eric Zarakov, Stephen and Toni Ferro, and to my friends Michael McKimmy, Robert Kalb, Chip Uhe, Jeanne Constable, and Valerie and Frederick Hotchkiss.

The birth of a daughter, Helene Marie Weiss, during the very last stages of writing, has been a spiritual gift likewise beyond estimation.

Prelude
Is Marxism Dead?

1. The Utopian Prospect

Have the schemes of emancipation proposed by social philosophers contributed much to human history? Some would say: most of these ivory-tower proposals are impossible—hence worthless.

That may be an understatement. Others would say: the world would have been a far better place if not a single utopian dream had ever disturbed a savant's sleep. For such schemes are, unfortunately, sometimes far worse than merely useless. Just because they *are* unrealizable, the price we pay in their futile pursuit—in lives lost and economies ruined—can be incalculable.

In short: impossible goals can inspire very possible forms of terror. When it comes to the day-to-day welfare of the ordinary folk of this planet, there may be nothing more hazardous than the attempt to force reality, hard and inscrutable as it is, to measure up to pretty ideas.

During two hundred years of revolutionary theory and practice, we have heard our most celebrated social and political thinkers call for the overthrow of classes, of war, of poverty, of differences between the sexes, of exploitation, of the mediation of money, of crime, of punishment, of state authority, of degrading labor, of "alienation" of every kind.

Some of these goals are attainable. Some are not. Some have been proposed prematurely. Some, we may be sure, should never have been proposed at all.

2. The Decline of the East

What, in this context, are we to say of communism? It is time for a settling of accounts.

The facts that prompt the question are salient enough. Today, a fault-line runs eastward from the rubble of the Berlin Wall, producing fissures and quakes in every part of the communist landscape. In Germany, Poland, Hungary, Bulgaria, Romania, Czechoslovakia, the Baltic states—in Mother Russia herself—the social and economic edifice constructed by Marx and Lenin is in ruins.

These events apparently demonstrate the irresistibility of our own political and economic system. They seem to refute a pivotal aspect of Karl Marx's understanding of modern history: that the market mode of production is destined to die out. The bourgeois system, it seems, is with us to stay.

But this conclusion is, in fact, only a half truth. Even if recent events convince us that communism, as such, is a failed idea, they do not support the unqualified pronouncement that "we have won and they have lost." There is a baby here we should be careful not to throw out with the bathwater—a basic aspect of Marxian revolutionism worth salvaging.

The Marxian quest to dismantle the market system is an irredeemable shambles. But what if, despite the manifest failure of classical Marxism, there are equally weighty deficiencies in the Western economic model as well? What if the "communist" ideal represents a needed corrective to these failings? Perhaps, once the dust has settled, we will have learned as much from them as they have from us. Victory may belong to neither side—or to both.

The "communist" idea worth salvaging is that a classless society, in the best sense of the term, not only is desirable but is becoming increasingly feasible. Marx was wrong in considering capitalism obsolescent, but right in thinking class distinctions moribund. The abolition of classes is indeed necessary for the most efficient operation of capitalism in an advanced setting.

Social classes have, of course, been the earmark of the only form of capitalism the world has so far known. But it is possible that, now at long last, the two most significant revolutionary ideals of the modern epoch can be conjointly satisfied. We can have the benefits of the "individualistic" modern market society, at the same time as we fulfill the Marxian dream of the "communal" classless society.

3. The Specter of Communism?

On the eve of the revolutions of 1848, in the opening sentence of *The Manifesto of the Communist Party*, Marx and Engels penned a pronouncement that would ring down through a century and a half of revolution and counter-revolution: "A specter is haunting Europe—the specter of communism."

Indeed the whole world has been haunted since those days—though not in the sense the founders of communism intended.

Marx and Engels, after all, allied themselves with this "specter." What they meant was: the doomed reactionaries are tormented by the nascent spirit of communist emancipation.

Today, Marxism, if spectral at all, is the tormented shade of an exhausted form of revolutionism.

And if, on the eve of the Third Millennium, we find ourselves haunted in a more positive sense—by a vision of real liberation—then *that* specter is of a classless capitalism: a society whose likes the world has not yet seen.

Introduction
Technological Emancipation:
Its Importance and Its Limits

1. Varieties of Contemporary Interpretation

The apparent decomposition of communism is, of course, subject to varying interpretations. Our own thesis will come into sharper focus if we take a moment to situate our view within the spectrum of positions currently dominant.

A. We need not spend much time on the familiar "we have won" posture taken by uncritical apologists of Western capitalism: by the ubiquitous Jeane Kirkpatrick, for example, who makes the bold and unqualified assertion that "socialism has no credible defenders" and that "what has happened is a clear victory for the traditional principles on which Western democracies are based."[1] Mainline periodicals in the West have indeed fallen over themselves in an orgy of self-congratulation on this point, making it seem as if "capitalism" had emerged victorious.

The truth is a good deal more complex and ambiguous. For, of course, our system is not capitalism pure and simple, but rather a mixed economy having a good many "socialized" aspects and components. Addressing "friends in Eastern Europe," one commentator notes:

> If the mixed economies are a far cry from the centralized systems you wish to dismantle, they are also very far from the classic . . . model of a self-regulating market economy. If you wish to look to the most advanced economies for guidance, then, you should not . . . be misled by dogma about "free markets." Although the economies of these countries are often described as "free market" systems, they are not. [They] are mixtures of markets (themselves of enormous variety) and deliberately imposed government interventions (also of incredible variety).[2]

In a similar vein, a noted Polish journalist bluntly asserts: "it was the socialists, the enemies of God and capital, who, as both reformists and revolutionaries, turned out to be the agents of change that gave birth to the West as it is today."[3]

Classical capitalism has long been as dead as Marley. It has been revolutionized, utterly, by means of "socialization." If the proponents of capitalism are right in insisting on the need for the market, it seems equally true that a sound modern economy must be built on a foundation of far-reaching privileges guaranteed as everyone's "socialized" birthright.

The we-have-won mentality seems founded on some willful forgetfulness. Whereas in the 1930s a dyed-in-the-wool Republican would not be caught dead favoring "socialist" programs like social security, medicaid, unemployment insurance, and so forth, the world a half century later is so different that even conservatives—those who are honest and conscious, anyway—are obliged to praise the labor movement for "saving capitalism."[4] They are forced to admit that our system might well have blown itself apart if it had not found ways of ensuring minimum life standards for the entire population: a socialized "safety net," as it has been called.

It makes for a strange retrospect. For most of the century before the New Deal, and in many quarters even after that, the conservative wing of American capitalism waged war against such "communist" tendencies as trade unionism and indeed the entire panoply of welfare rights. Through arduous struggle against such resistance—against the cruelty and wastefulness of capitalism in its earlier, less fettered form—reformers forced the incorporation, one by one, of "socialist" planks into the "capitalist" platform. We reached the point, finally, at which these rights had been absorbed into everybody's bones and sinews. Today they are taken for granted, even by conservatives.

Now, at long last, having been dragged kicking and screaming into acceptance of these "un-American" ideas, capitalism's propagandists have the effrontery to turn around and inform the world—that "we have won"!

B. A diametrically opposed viewpoint is that taken by remaining elements of the hard-line communist left. The Trotskyist Fourth International, for example, has been insisting for the better part of a century that "Stalinist bureaucracy" must be overthrown if the working class is to consummate a socialist revolution. Events in Eastern Europe are accordingly interpreted.

The working class was the most powerful social component of the mass movements which brought down the Stalinist regimes throughout Eastern Europe [in the fall of 1989]. . . .
But these movements were politically dominated by petty bourgeois forces, encouraged by the Stalinists and subservient to imperialist interests, who seized the political initiative. These elements transformed the

overthrow of the Stalinist police dictatorships into a general onslaught on the social conquests [made by] the working class . . . over the last forty years, [gains] indissolubly bound up with the nationalized property and planned economies which existed, despite the distortions introduced by the parasitic Stalinist bureaucracy.

   The East German workers . . . are beginning to shake off the illusions in the rosy future under capitalism peddled by the petty-bourgeois democrats and the Stalinists. . . .[5]

This approach identifies the Stalinist bureaucracy, and not the planned economy as such, as the real villain in the piece. Recent events are taken to prove the continued importance of "the struggle for world socialist revolution, the abolition of capitalist private property . . . and the establishment of a rationally planned economy on a world scale."[6]

Marx, if he could witness contemporary events, might draw much the same conclusion. Our own reply to this orthodox Marxian interpretation will be developed at some length in Part One. Despite the undoubted importance of the "socialist" component of advanced economies, we will find that Marx himself erred in considering the market an obsolescent aspect of production.

   This by itself is hardly news. It has long been the dominant view in the West, and it is already becoming prevalent in the East.

   But one striking fact has not been recognized at all: that a vindication of market relations is supplied by basic aspects of Marx's own reasoning. The need for the market is implicit in Marx's treatment of scarcity—though, fatefully enough, he does not see the implication. Marxian economic theory founders on this irony: Marx himself does not take sufficiently to heart his own "dialectical" insight that scarcity cannot be eliminated because human demand always outstrips any age's ability to satisfy it.

   The consequences of this apparently innocent premise are far-reaching. The dialectical recurrence of scarcity implies that economic "development" is itself incessant. It follows, on Marx's own principles, that capitalism is not the temporary phenomenon, destined to "wither away," that communist theory says it is. These themes will be considered presently.

   C. Our own view falls within the (itself broad) category of the "revisionist," social democratic left. The market, though it will continue to prove useful, must operate within a framework of ground-rules ensuring strong universal—"socialized"—human rights.

   In recent years, this tendency has often been labeled "market socialism."[7] Market socialists depart from the Marxian model by virtue of their concession, or insistence, that planned economies are, even if administered with honesty and thoroughness, typically inferior to the market system as a mechanism of social distribution and investment. They are willing to accept some of the standard theoretical objections to planned economies. But they reject the apparent implication: that the essential objectives of socialism are beyond reach. They argue that it is necessary to draw a sharp distinction between socialism as *means* and as *end*.[8]

True, classical Marxism made the mistake of thinking that the means of production had to be publicly or communally managed. But that does not mean that we cannot have the "end-states" which socialists have always advocated: the abolition of exploitation, the achievement of a meaningfully equalitarian society. We can have these results if the economy is constrained by a legal framework which rules out the exploitative abuses of laissez-faire capitalism. In such a legally constrained market system, companies would be required to distribute wages and salaries more nearly in accord with the quantity and quality of work actually contributed. We can guarantee a more or less equalitarian result by means of market methods, but at the same time eliminate the obnoxious aspects of profiteering.

The problem is that this social democratic view is today in danger of losing its nerve—or at least its distinctness. For once we admit that we need *both* the market *and* socialized guarantees, it may seem as if it is merely the familiar "liberal"—welfare statist—viewpoint that emerges victorious. If liberals, as much as so-called "social democrats," insist that brutally productive capitalism must meet economically sluggish socialism somewhere in the middle—as one form or another of "mixed economy"—then what is the difference between them?

Shouldn't we drop "socialist" pretenses and simply identify this third category as "welfare-state liberalism"—and be done with it?

The problem can be seen in a socialist "Credo" published recently by Michael Walzer, one of the most thoughtful social democrats of recent decades:

> The socialist creed can be summed up in three principles. First, that political society should be open and accessible to all. No one should be excluded from political participation, from democratic power-sharing, because of class, race, religion, or gender.
> Second, that the economy should also be open and accessible to all its members. Economic power should be shared by the same people who share political power. This second principle by no means rules out market relations; it only rules out what might be called market imperialism—the conversion of private wealth into political influence and social privilege.
> Third, that the members of political society and economy are collec-

tively responsible for each other's welfare. Citizens and workers have claims, always partial, on the resources of the whole society.[9]

There is, from the standard liberal viewpoint, nothing objectionable in this broad expression of democratic conviction. These three principles are all axiomatic in the ideology of the welfare state. But if the liberal can embrace what Walzer denotes by the word "socialism," one wonders if this word, however much we still wish to utter it, retains more than the vaguest resonances of its older, more robust meaning. Again we ask: what remains distinctive about democratic "socialism"?

Walzer says no one should be excluded for reasons of "class, race, religion, or gender." His use of the first of these terms seems curious, indeed discordant, in a Credo still wishing to claim a "socialist" pedigree. The formulation seems to presume the continued existence of classes, with the proviso that they not be used as grounds—any more than race, religion, and gender—for anybody's exclusion from the political and economic process.

Walzer's formulation thus makes it seem as if the struggle against classes is not merely to be prolonged, but to be abandoned entirely. It is this that seems to remove the last plank definitive of the socialist platform—its very point of distinction from welfare-state liberalism.[10] For if classes are to be retained, what more can a guarantee of economic "inclusion" signify than the "equality of opportunity" upon which liberal theorists have always insisted?

2. The "End of History"?

This atrophy of a sense of class conflict may also partly explain why some mainstream Western theorists, trying to draw conclusions from communism's apparent demise, have begun to wonder if the epoch of world revolutionism itself is over. Perhaps the most celebrated instance of this is Francis Fukuyama's 1989 essay, "The End of History?"[11] Fukuyama dares to speculate that social history is approaching its apogee in the modern liberal capitalist state—that is, *in us*.

The author admits the idea is "highly speculative."[12] Critics have concurred. One calls it "a weird thesis, utterly speculative and impossible to prove."[13]

From our own perspective, that such a "weird" thesis has been taken so seriously by so many, means that many of our intellectuals are suffering an acute failure of historical imagination.

The brunt[14] of Fukuyama's argument is that our own system has quite simply run out of worthy dialectical adversaries. This is because communism, our one remaining powerful opponent after the (apparent) fall of fascism, seems finally to have been beaten, leaving our own system in (apparently) sole possession of the field.

The class problem remains the pivotal site of contention. In order to sustain his claim that the revolutionary era is over, Fukuyama must argue that the central "contradiction" identified by communist theory—class struggle—is no longer a contradiction at all. So charming is Fukuyama's treatment of this matter, that we should pay him the courtesy of complete quotation:

> Marx, speaking Hegel's language, asserted that liberal society contained a fundamental contradiction that could not be resolved within its context, that between capital and labor, and this contradiction has constituted the chief accusation against liberalism ever since. But surely, the class issue has actually been successfully resolved in the West. As Kojève (among others) noted, the egalitarianism of modern America represents the essential achievement of the classless society envisioned by Marx. This is not to say that there are not rich people in the United States, or that the gap between them has not grown in recent years. But the root causes of economic inequality do not have to do with the underlying legal and social structure of our society, which remains fundamentally egalitarian and moderately redistributionist, so much as with the cultural and social characteristics of the groups that make it up, which are in turn the historical legacy of premodern conditions. Thus black poverty in the United States is not the inherent product of liberalism, but is rather the "legacy of slavery and racism" which persisted long after the formal abolition of slavery.[15]

"Surely" the class issue has actually been successfully resolved in the West! This astonishing claim is significant, not because it is even faintly plausible, but because it represents, to a frightening degree, prevalent learned opinion in the West.

Some of Fukuyama's critics do express reservations at such a nonchalant treatment of the class issue.[16] But the criticism so far has been casual and mild. And no wonder. To grasp the ineptitude of "Endism,"[17] one would have to step outside the conventional wisdom and look at things from the viewpoint of another "paradigm" of social relations—one that is qualitatively distinct, not only from classical communism, but also from bourgeois democracy.

We recall Fukuyama's blithe words: our form of society is "fundamentally egalitarian and mildly redistributionist." If we ask how this nebulous claim can be squared with the undeniable facts—which he simultaneously concedes—that "there are rich people and poor people in the United States" and that "the gap between them has grown in recent years," he replies that our skepticism misses the point: "the basic *principles* of the liberal democratic state could not be improved upon."[18]

The emphasis on "principles" is his own. The point seems to be: the problem is not with the principles themselves that have historically become manifest in the modern liberal state, but rather with the simple fact that these principles have not, as Fukuyama says, been "spatially" extended to all peoples in all lands.

Fukuyama cannot imagine any "principles" that are qualitative leaps higher than those now realized in modern bourgeois democracy. This failure of imagination is most clearly seen in his banal notion of what the end of "class society" might be all about.

Or perhaps we should call it a "non-notion," since he tells us precious little about classlessness that carries beyond the reader's willingness to nod sleepily at the tired associations of a term—hardly explicated by the author—like "egalitarianism." Fukuyama's idea of égalité, by his own insistence, conveys little more than what would occur to a French revolutionary at the barricades. Napoleon's victory at the Battle of Jena, he tells us, "marked the end of history because it was at that point that the *vanguard of humanity* . . . actualized the principles of the French revolution."[19]

All that Fukuyama says by way of explication of this "principle" of "egalitarianism" held by the "vanguard" of that time is that "the state that emerges at the end of history is liberal insofar as it recognizes and protects through a system of law man's universal right to freedom, and democratic insofar as it exists only with the consent of the governed."[20]

Those who have been waiting patiently for a more concrete rendering of these abstractions must turn away disappointed. Is Fukuyama aware how many crucial distinctions are simply ignored on this level of vague and pious generality? Alas, he leaves us to fill in the blanks ourselves.

Fukuyama bases his thesis, he tells us, on André Kojève's reading of Hegel. And a somewhat one-sided reading it is—for, though aspects of Hegel's philosophy do sometimes incline him to the view that social history is reaching fulfillment in his time,[21] the enduring Hegelian legacy is the notion that qualitative changes in culture and society go on ad infinitum.[22]

Even if Hegel does occasionally write as though the "Absolute" is becoming incarnate in the modern world, his subtle and paradoxical "Absolute" is nothing more nor less than self-conscious realization that dialectical dynamism is a logical requirement—is universal, necessary, and incessant. The Hegelian philosophy itself asserts that any advances made by a given social order will generate their own "contradictions" which, when resolved, condition in turn a leap to a dialectically higher system, thus setting the stage for problems which themselves are of a new order.

Thus any suggestion by Hegel himself that there is an "end of history" seems at variance with the basic drift of his own dialectical logic.[23] Engels made a pithy summation of this point as long ago as 1878:

> The Hegelian system, in itself, was a colossal miscarriage—but it was also the last of its kind. It was suffering, in fact, from an internal and incurable contradiction. Upon the one hand, its essential proposition was . . . that human history is a process of evolution, which, by its very nature, cannot find its intellectual final term in the discovery of any so-called final truth. But, on the other hand, it laid claim to being the very essence of this absolute truth. A system of natural and historical knowledge, embracing everything, and final for all time, is a contradiction to the fundamental law of dialectic reasoning.[24]

But, though invoking such abstract dialectical considerations against Endism may seem methodologically sound, we must not rest our case (as do those who have dared to criticize Endism at all[25]) on the vague idea that Fukuyama is foolish to suppose that history will ever stop still. For in that event, our own dialectical bias would amount to little more than a priori dogmatism: "Things have always changed; so they must keep on changing; so our culture just *can't* be the final word in social history."

To rebut the "end-of-history" thesis convincingly, we must refute it concretely. And to do that, we must specify *what it is* about our own culture that—despite its manifest accomplishments—sets the stage for even farther-reaching revolutions to come.

Lacking this, any rejection of Endism would be little more than bluster—as in the case of the critic in the popular press who dismisses Fukuyama with a sneer: "Any freshman history student should be able to criticize [Fukuyama's] article on the ground that historical forces and the people who shape them are more complex, irrational and unpredictable than the theory allows."[26] Absent a specific critique of the social status quo, appeals to "what any freshman knows" are sophomoric.

For "surely" Fukuyama does not, in calling current bourgeois democracy "egalitarian," mean that "fundamental" agreement has been reached on the "principle" that all our citizens ought to be guaranteed material benefits in strict accord with their talents, all the way up to adulthood. No doubt he would find such "socialism" a violation of the "freedom" for which the French revolutionaries were fighting.

It is indeed such a violation. It is just the sort of violation that we enemies of the class system *ought* to intend. It is a denial of the *bourgeois* conception of the proper scope of equality: of the idea that equality means only the equal right to take one's chances in the unrestrained and unconstrained marketplace, "let the chips fall where they may."

Though such a denial of our system's conception of equality seems a "violation of freedom" from the bourgeois point of view, it is not a diminution of freedom *tout court*. On the contrary: the abolition of class, in the radical sense to be proposed here, is the condition of augmented freedom—even (or especially) in the sense relevant to the marketplace society, capitalism.

Here we encounter an aspect of Marxism that remains sound—even if, as I will hold, it must be dissociated from the chimerical communist idea that the market is on the way to being abolished.

We will have to draw a basic distinction. If we may use the word "bourgeois" to refer specifically to the class-divided form of the market society, I think we must conclude, pro Marx, that the bourgeois order is a passing phase of social history. But if we use "capitalist" to refer to the market form of society in general, we should conclude, contra Marx, that the capitalist system is with us to stay.

This twofold idea will sound odd, even paradoxical, at this juncture. A central task of this book is to clarify and defend it.

To summarize: in order to dispel Endist speculation once and for all, we must provide a tangible sense of what historical developments—qualitative leaps—have yet to be taken. And to do that, we must frame in sharp terms the real challenge of classlessness.

Fukuyama, like just about everybody else these days, is right in judging communism a failure. But he utterly fails—like just about everybody else— to see what this means: that a far-reaching social "synthesis" is underway, the terms of which will carry us far beyond the wildest imagination of anyone who confesses to the bold, and quite mad, conviction that "the class issue has actually been successfully resolved in the West."

Such a goal would carry us far beyond the "principles" operative in the present system. Such a "principle" of classlessness is much more radical than the "mildly redistributive" bourgeois conceptions Fukuyama and other bourgeois apologists have in mind.

This idea of a truly "classless society" will at first seem wildly utopian. And that is just the point: it is not an ideal that is as yet broadly endorsed or accepted, much less approximated, in today's world. It is an ideal which, could we achieve it, would carry us a quantum leap beyond any sort of "egalitarianism" officially recognized in our culture.

Just because it seems scandalously "utopian" in the eyes of that world, and yet at the same time (as I will argue) stands as a feasible goal for human society in the years to come, this idea of classlessness shows just why there is need for a transformation—both feasible and revolutionary—of contemporary society. That would be enough to show that the present version of Western culture cannot possibly be "the end of history."

The Endist thesis can make sense only to those who fail to grasp that "capitalism" itself can reach full flower only when a radical equality—or, as I prefer to call it, parity—of benefit is extended to all our children up to the point at which they are to enter the market as fully fledged competitors in their own right.

It is possible for Fukuyama to speculate that the "principles" of the West are the culmination of history, and for his critics to find this thesis fascinating (even if vexing), only because they have no intimation of the emancipatory steps their own children may be destined to take.

3. The Ideal of Formative Parity

Neither Walzer nor Fukuyama retains a lively sense of the "class problem" as a still largely unsolved item on the revolutionary agenda. It is not hard to locate the source of the problem.

For, from the perspective of the "paradigm" of political economy that has been dominant for the past two centuries, once one grants the continuing need for a market system, one must concede that some semblance of social classes must likewise endure.

It follows that if we do wish to salvage the noblest ideal of socialism, that of the classless society, this very paradigm must be called into question. The objectives of Social Democracy can be distinguished from those of pragmatic liberalism only if it is possible for us to advocate a form of economy which—however much it continues to rest on market principles—is also predicated upon the abolition of class.[27]

Some have come to praise Marx; others (more lately) to bury him. A third voice has only begun to make itself heard. What we need—to vary Marx's own trope on Hegel—is to extricate the "rational kernel" from the orthodox Marxian husk.

For, as I will maintain, a truly classless society, in the most useful sense of the term, is achieved only when society's rules effectively guarantee that all our children are given, throughout the entirety of their minority years, material benefits in proportion to their ability. This would, in the phraseology I will adopt, be nothing less than society's pledge that there be "parity" of treatment for all, regardless of the position of their parents, throughout the duration of the "formative" period of acculturation and education.

Such "Formative Parity" may be the prospect of our own age. Capitalism gives very significant scope to private appropriation; and this, when properly constrained and restrained, is a quite reasonable dimension of adult economic behavior. Nonetheless, in an advanced technological setting, it is at long last possible for the economy also to become responsive to socialism's most urgent demand: that human beings be nurtured and prepared for adult interaction, while still children, by being given formative advantages commensurate with their potential to benefit from them.

The institution of Formative Parity would, to an unprecedented degree, diminish the import of inheritable advantages to the point of only incidental significance. It would insulate our children from the economic vicissitudes of the parental generation. It would thus ensure that economic competition occurred on an essentially "level playing surface."

Unlike Walzer's "socialist" Credo, this conception goes far beyond the mixed-economy priorities of modern liberalism. The main objective of liberal measures is to soften the blow of capitalism through deft placement of "safety nets," so that, for example, our worst-off citizens can be prevented from starving or bleeding to death. Such stratagems, important as they are, are "socialistic" only in a minimal sense. And nobody any longer doubts that they are consistent with the operation of the market.

By contrast, abolishing classes is a "socialistic" priority in a robust sense. And it is not at all obvious that it can occur where capital still holds sway.

This ideal of classlessness, in the sense of Formative Parity, is the one remaining legacy of "socialism" that can carry real weight in the contemporary world. Exploration of the trajectory of technological development will show that the centerpiece of Marxian aspiration, the establishment of a classless society, may be a goal both worthy and feasible.

4. Marx Versus the Classical Defense of Capitalism

Marx himself believes that we can achieve classlessness only if we abolish the market. And he regards this act of abolition as becoming, in the fullness of time, a quite reasonable prospect. The first major objective of this book is to examine—and explode—the Marxian assumptions underlying this conviction.

But Marx can be decisively refuted only if we do battle with him on his own soil. This requires digging a stratum or two deeper than the proponents of the "Classical Defense" of capitalism typically do.

I use the term "Classical Defense" to refer to the economic arguments—championed in recent decades by economists like Friedrich Hayek and Milton Friedman—designed to show that the allocative mechanism of the market is a far more efficient means of satisfaction of human need than methods of centralized socialist planning can ever hope to be.

While the Classical Defense does go a long way toward explaining the failure of the Eastern European version of the socialist experiment, it does not probe deeply enough to address the issues that exercised the founder of communism. The entire discussion has been conducted as if "communism" were merely a contemporaneous rival to the market system. This is no doubt a fruitful approach if we are concerned with exposing the shortcomings of such planned economies. But it does not, by itself, refute Marx, whose conception has a quite different logic.

For Marx considered communism the appropriate economic system for a very different world: the dawning world of radical technological emancipation. "Communism," in his sense, becomes increasingly relevant and irresistible only insofar as production has been radically transformed by automation.

Proponents of the Classical Defense make the historically unrestricted claim that only the market system can automatically recirculate the power of social investment itself into the hands of those who have in the previous round of investment most efficiently satisfied social demand. Such a mechanism, they believe, gives us a better "decision procedure" than any central committee, no matter how thoughtful and honest, could ever provide.

Marx, by contrast, endorses capitalism in a historically qualified sense: as relevant during the period in which scientific production has not yet been consolidated. Noncompetitive schemes cannot be as efficient as capitalism until the industrial creativity of the species has reached the dependable form of a science. Till then, the various procapitalist arguments of the Classical Defense are largely correct. They lose their force only insofar as the conditions for scientific social planning do evolve.

Thus Marx is an orthodox apologist for bourgeois methods, insofar as we are dealing with societies not yet fully developed. Only after our Promethean quest has been consolidated does it prove feasible (and irresistible) for us to dispense with market methods *tout court*. During capitalism's heyday, this threshold has not yet been crossed: production is not yet amenable to the "scientific management" which socialist proponents of planned economies propose. During such a phase, the typical "bourgeois objections" to planned economies, lodged by what we have called the Classical Defense, would be supported by Marx himself.

Marx confronted classical political economy in the work of Smith, Ricardo, et al. This tradition is still with us today; and Marx would, no doubt, respond to the objections to planned economies offered by the "Austrian School" of Ludwig von Mises and Friedrich A. Hayek, or by the "Chicago School" led by Milton Friedman, with the very same systematic ambivalence he directed toward the political economists dominant in his own period.

A. The Austrian School Insofar as underdevelopment is presumed, it is probably safe to say that Marx would endorse the idea that planned econo-mies can neither gather nor process information as effectively as the market mechanism of price.

Mises[28] argues, in this vein, that no central agency is capable of aggregat-ing all the data on which decisions about allocation and production have to be based: so heterogeneous and unwieldy would be the data, that there would be no way to process these into a finite and manageable set of social instructions. And Hayek[29] goes a step further, maintaining that not only (as with Mises) could no central planning agency ever *process* all the relevant data; it could not even *know* them: the immediate, hunch-ridden "data" of individual experience can never be adequately translated into explicit, discursive concepts which could serve as an information base for central social planning.

On this basis, the Austrian argument proceeds: production must be decentralized; but this implies, in turn, the need for some means of coor-dination among local productive units so that overall output roughly cor-responds to overall social need; but no method of mutually adjusting production and need can do *this* nearly so effectively as the automatic homeostasis of supply and demand of the competitive market. No political procedure could replace the competitive market as a way of instantly translating an incredible welter of local data into a shorthand signal that both conveys and motivates the need for adjustments elsewhere in the macrosystem, so that gluts and shortages can be avoided. As Hayek says:

> [B]ecause all the details of the changes constantly affecting the conditions of demand and supply of the different commodities can never be fully known, or quickly enough be collected and disseminated, by any one center, what is required is some apparatus of registration which automati-cally records all the relevant effects of individual actions and whose indications are at the same time the resultant of, and the guide for, all the individual decisions.
>   This is precisely what the price system does under competition, and which no other system even promises to accomplish.[30]

The pretense made by economic planners is that we can know what the most useful allocations of resources will be. We should, Hayek argues, substitute for such knowledge-claims the pragmatic conviction that, when we are in the essentially unpredictable domain of industrial creativity itself, the competitive model, at its best, is better than the central planning model, at its best.

What would Marx say in reply? No doubt he would regard this nexus of arguments as pertinent to the period of development—but only to that period. His response to the Austrian theorists would, I think, run somewhat as follows:

"Your claim is correct insofar as it can be translated into the historically more modest contention that no society till now could dispense with the market and, still and all, effectively cope with the myriad sources and flows of information that characterize any advanced economy. But the paradigm of information gathering and processing that you assume is true only for a limited prescientific epoch. When scientific management at last becomes possible, capitalism's comparative irrationalities—especially the anarchy of decentralized, individualistic production—come to outweigh whatever advantages it once enjoyed. In this dialectical sense, you are wrong to presume that scientific solutions will never be achieved which can render the market mechanism obsolete."

B. *The Chicago School*   If the Austrian critique concerns *information*, that lodged by the Chicago theorists has more to do with *motivation*. On this accounting, the prime virtue of the market system is that it permits and promotes adventurous and innovative risk-taking in a way that state socialism does not. While no doubt people can, under communism, be somewhat motivated by prospective glory—fame and social recognition—there are good reasons for thinking that this would induce little more than the minimal risk-taking we have seen in the East for the past half century—with the accompanying economic stagnation.[31]

According to Milton Friedman's vivid statement of this point, a market system can entice investors to make 10-to-1 gambles on the prospect of 100-to-1 returns on investment; while planned economies, which lack such incentive, induce economic strategists to "play it safe, to undertake investments that are almost certain to yield returns . . . [T]hat is the reasonable . . . way [for such managers] to behave. For society as a whole, however, [it] is the road to stagnation and rigidity, and that in fact has been the outcome in collectivist societies."[32] In domains which are typified by unpredictability, the risk-taking inherent in social experimentation seems to require a social structure conducive to wager-like "speculative" vying on the part of those with different investment ideas.

What would Marx say to this? We may imagine his reply:

"No doubt you are right that risk-taking can be properly motivated only by the prospect of capital gain. This remains the case during that entire period in which scientific planning is not yet possible, and in which social investment is, necessarily, a crapshoot. But when society comes to be established on a scientific basis, this entire wager-like dimension of human existence—on which the Chicago argument rests—itself becomes obsolete."

Who is right, Marx or his critics? Though Marx's replies may ultimately be inadequate, the controversy cannot be easily resolved. One might be tempted to say that Marx stands refuted by the apparent collapse of the economy of Eastern Europe, but we have seen that Marxists have their own way of reading these events.

One might add that the dispute between Marx and bourgeois political economy has, in its essentials, been raging since Marx's own time—with neither side showing much tendency to be affected by the other. Rather we have an orgy of special pleading and onus shifting on both sides. Each is only too pleased with its own data, its own criteria of relevance, its own arguments. One might therefore suspect that we have here a fundamental "paradigm conflict"—a dispute that can never be mediated.

But this may be an overstatement. Something akin to mediation might be achieved—though on a somewhat theoretical level. We might get the Marxians to question their own approach, if we could succeed in showing them that this approach is at variance with the best aspects of the dialectical theory in which Marxism supposedly is rooted. This defines my strategy in the chapters that follow.

5. Confronting Marxism in its Own Terms

We have seen that the Classical Defense does not come to grips with the futuristic scenario projected by Marx's theory. It does not grapple with his conviction that the technological revolution of the modern age finally eliminates our need for money-accounting, the coercion of labor, and capitalist speculation.

Marx's Prometheanism leads him to expect communism to appear in the infrastructurally advanced sectors of the world which have already passed through a capitalist phase of industrial development: places like England and the United States, and not rural backwaters like the Russia of 1917 or the China of 1949.

That self-styled "communist" revolutions actually did first occur in the latter locales does not prove Marx wrong—so much as force us to ask if these upheavals have really been communist at all, in Marx's ambitious sense of the term.

The Marxian argument must be evaluated on its own terms. This will have two essential benefits.

In the first place, it will provide a firmer foundation for the Classical Defense's arguments in defense of market methods. For only if we critically encounter Marx's futuristic conception of communism will we be able to ascertain the fundamental point of invalidity of Marxian economic theory:

the proposition that alienated labor can be reduced to marginal significance. Only when that proposition is exploded, will we feel confident that the calculi of market rationality, presumed by the Classical Defense, will continue to apply to economies of the future.

The second benefit works to the advantage of socialist ideals. Marx's attention to the implications of developing technology gives us the best means of appreciating, and extricating, the still-sound premise imbedded in his otherwise flawed theory: the historical transiency of the mental-manual division of labor. I will argue that the phenomenon underlying classes—the division of work between literate and nonliterate functions—is, unlike the market, of merely temporary historical significance. It is this fact that sustains the promise basic to socialist aspiration: the possibility of a classless society.

I am suggesting, in effect, that standard economic theory needs to be supplemented by a reconsideration of the underpinnings of economics as such. Every introductory textbook tells us that "economics deals with the allocation of scarce resources." Economists take this presumption of scarcity as their point of departure, and it is certainly reasonable for them to do so. But sometimes points of departure must become points of inquiry. It becomes necessary to look into the grounds of such alleged scarcity, to ask if it is a temporary or permanent feature of social life, and to draw the appropriate conclusions.

Disciplinary distinctions are notoriously hard to draw, but, given my own training, I prefer to think of the latter, "deeper" sort of inquiry as philosophical rather than strictly economic in character. It is here perhaps worth reminding ourselves that Marx earned his Ph.D. in philosophy (Jena, 1841), rejected the need for markets on the basis of a critical revision of Hegel's doctrine of "alienation," and arrived at his critique of political economy by giving a new twist to the philosophical communism of Ludwig Feuerbach. Though this did necessitate a lengthy excursus into economic theory, Marx always maintained that economics itself, as we know it, pertains to the specific and transient "bourgeois" portion of history—the period in which human emancipation is not yet possible, because technology is not yet fully developed.

In an April 1851 letter to Engels, Marx bluntly expressed the hope that "in five weeks I will be through with the whole economic shit."[33] In this, he was overly optimistic—indeed by years and years: the creation of Marxian economics exhausted much of the remainder of his life. Marx did not die an old man; and if he had lived longer, he no doubt would have tried to reintegrate his economic writings with the philosophical inquiry concerning "alienation" that originally motivated them.[34]

Few contemporary economists feel the need to study philosophy. For most purposes, it is probably just as well that they do not. But sometimes more fundamental purposes must supervene. When it comes to the issue of "capitalism versus communism," a crucial dimension of inquiry must take place on the level of the "philosophy of economics" or (if you will) "metaeconomics."

However much our conclusions may differ from Marx's, we cannot be secure about them unless they are the product of a dialogue that takes place on the very same metaeconomic plane of abstraction.

6. The Methodological Limits of this Study

The result of our inquiry into Marx's Promethean quest will not be favorable to all of his most cherished theses. The idea of overcoming alienated labor leads into a blind alley, and this casts radical doubt (as I will argue) on the idea that society might transcend the need for market methods.

But this does not mean that an emphasis on technological emancipation is misplaced in principle. I will argue, to the contrary, the centerpiece of Marxian aspiration, the classless society, may be feasible for roughly the same reasons Marx thought it was.

Thus, despite our sometimes profound differences with Marx, we remain faithful to his project to this extent: we agree that one pervasive dimension of our species's emancipation—the abolition of classes—depends on the continued rationalization of technology.

To be sure, many readers will find this very idea of technological emancipation naive and dangerous. Many today have grown wary of the tendency—all too common in the nineteenth century—to deify the "instrumental reason" at the basis of science and technology. (Indeed, as we will see in Chapter 6.4, many have begun to suspect that it is this sort of scientific "reductionism" that lies at the basis of our species's perilous relation to the nonhuman "environment.")

Those who are called "postmodernists," especially, can no longer allow the scientific-technical "language game"[35] to be exalted above all other ways of talking about the world: treated as the means by which "reality" as it is "in itself" is revealed. That language must rather be demoted to one among the limitless tongues we might, for various purposes, wish to speak.

From this perspective we can see that one of the big problems with Marx is that he is indeed too "scientistic" for our postmodern tastes: he does advertise the dialectic of technology and the division of labor as *the* key to human freedom. He does not content himself with the more modest claim that these factors make up one important moment of historical analysis.

For Marx, technological emancipation is equivalent to emancipation in toto. It is not as if the dynamics of religion or gender—considered as semiautonomous domains of development—might be equally worthy domains to explore. Marx rather treats the constellation of technology and division of labor—constituting the "mode of production"—as the "base," relegating the allegedly *non*-basal aspects of culture as elements of a "superstructure" that is itself largely or entirely passive, inefficacious, or at most ancillary.

In these postmodern times, even those most sympathetic to the Marxian project tend to adopt a more open and pluralistic approach to social change. The very language of "base" and "superstructure" has fallen into disrepute. As, for example, Laclau and Mouffe[36] have argued in their internal critique of classical socialist strategy, economic class struggle may be a valid aspect of revolutionary critique, but it is not the only valid one. The emancipation of women, for example, is as "basic" or "basal" a historical event as Marx's projected proletarian revolution.

But none of this can be taken to invalidate the claim that technological emancipation, within its own limits, remains a fertile field of inquiry. The trouble with Marx's emphasis on technological emancipation is not that this approach is fruitless, but that it obscures the fact that other sorts of fruit also deserve to be savored.

Marx does give us a method of inquiry, and some very powerful social-scientific postulates, which permit us to gain insight into the relation between evolving technology and evolving social division of labor. The presumption underlying this book is that the technical-economic moment remains *an* important dimension of revolutionary potential, even if not the one and only. One can focus on the still-unrealized potential for an emancipated form of labor, based in a highly developed infrastructure, without discrediting other revolutionary foci.

I do not think there are any good *arguments* for the continued revolutionary potential of a technical approach. The temptation to invent such arguments should be resisted. "Arguments" in favor of technological emancipation will be found compelling only by those who already inhabit cultures that have long since committed themselves to that very project. (As usual, argument is persuasive only where it is superfluous.)

Thus one might think it possible to prove that there is something "inevitable" about our culture's stress on technological emancipation—as if it were a necessary truth that all cultures must accord technical intelligence the central place in their value scheme that ours does.

But this would be an extravagant claim. We have learned enough history, and enough anthropology, to discredit such claims of "inevitability." We can, for example, well imagine cultures that show very little interest in methods of technology and much interest in (say) methods of personal salvation. Technological advances might occur in such a culture, but they would be desultory and haphazard, the more or less passive ("epiphenomenal") resultants of developments occurring in the religious arena. *Explicit* and *systematic* privileging of the technical would be lacking.

Medieval culture was, to a large degree, nontechnological in this sense. Europe's love affair with technology, far from being an expression of something necessary and universal, is a contingent phenomenon of rather recent vintage.

But if argument is not possible, it is also hardly necessary. The importance of technological emancipation may be "proved" merely by appeal to the simple—and yet I think profound—truism that technological civilization cannot doubt the indispensability of its own peculiar genius. It is enough to confess that the science-technology nexus is one of the main pillars on which our own world is built.

We cannot imagine living without the fruits of instrumental rationality— without cars or planes or refrigerators or TVs or word processors or scientific medicine. Nor can *we* imagine how such wealth could be satisfactorily produced without using high-tech methods and the rigorous science these methods presuppose.

It is one thing to reflect on roads not taken: to speculate that Europe could, way back when, have taken a very different turn. It is quite another thing to suggest that we might—given the road we *have* taken—now be able to resist talking about possible ways of organizing our productive lives more efficiently. Discourse that focuses on technology and the division of labor may be dispensable in principle, but it is no longer dispensable by us.

Since this particular study does fall within the bounds of "technical intelligence," it will have a Marxian aroma. We retain Marx's methodological assumption that at least *some* systematic aspects of human emancipation do depend upon the gradual mastery and regularization of productive technique. *Some* of society's most important liberatory prospects are those made possible by its maturing industrial intelligence.

In pressing this strategy, we adopt the methodological resolve to resist moralizing: we will not base our reflections on what seems humane or right, but try instead to develop harder-boiled arguments to show that a classless society is in the interests of a more efficient economy.

In the same methodological vein, we will even adopt as our own the (in itself oversimple) economistic maxim that we should implement social reforms in order to "maximize productivity." For Marx, this criterion—which we may dub the "Productivity Principle"[37]—was virtually axiomatic. For us, it is only strategic. We do not assume that economic efficiency is the only relevant standard of social evaluation.

There may indeed be good reasons of an ethical kind, or of a kind rooted in a Habermasian analysis of communicative action, for attempting to get rid of classes. But arguments of this sort will themselves have a firmer basis if the ideals in question can be justified, not only on noneconomic grounds, but on the basis of a hard-boiled calculation of productivity alone.

In our culture, technological argumentation really does hold a privileged place. If, then, we can establish that the classless society is a reasonable objective even from that cold-blooded perspective, we will be hard put to imagine what remaining objections there could be to such an ideal.

Economic analysis is not the only hilltop looking over Jordan. And the classless society is not the only land of milk and honey. There is no theory that can claim primacy of place, no practice that is once and for all, no revolution to end all revolutions.

But these truths reflect no discredit on our own specific purposes here: to salvage some of the unredeemed potential of Karl Marx's technological-economic view of human emancipation. This approach still contains the key to a fundamental insight: that there are specific kinds of irrationality that can be eliminated only when a certain level of technology has come into being.

7. The Project

In Part One of this study, we consider two different ways in which the Marxist might defend the view that capitalism must rationally culminate in a society sans class, sans money, sans "alienated labor."

Chapters 1 and 2 deal with Marx's Promethean conception of emancipation from "alienated labor": the gradual overcoming of the drudgery and coercion typifying "the Division of Labor" in Marx's sense of the term. Chapter 3 concerns a different (but equally Marxian) conception: that what constitutes "alienated labor," and needs to be overthrown, is the subjection of working people to an exploitative, expropriative ruling class.

In both cases, Marx's argument is a failure: his conviction that alienated labor is historically transient is at odds with a credible "dialectical" view of history. We are led to adopt a "neo-Hegelian" perspective from which we can see that the social problematic is always being "sublimated" from one level to the next, never strictly eliminated. This gives us good cause to suspect that market relations have an enduring logic that escapes Marxian "science."

We now make an about-face. In Part Two we find that the persistence of development, and hence of the market, does not imply that Marx's quest is misconceived through and through. Marx is right to speculate that the overcoming of social classes can be the coming epoch's technological achievement.

The argument I develop here is not strictly "Marxian," since it rests on the retention of private appropriation and the market. But it is "Marxesque" in insisting that it is possible for us to erode the basic social discrepancies in wealth and power which constitute the core of "class."

Chapter 4 is largely devoted to defining and explicating the objective of the classless society. Privilege, in some form or other, seems inherent in social existence. But class, understood as disparity (literally: lack of parity) in the formative wealth into which children are born, is not.

This opens up enough logical space for the following radical claim: that the guaranteed "social minimum" standard of existence may, in coming years, improve to such a degree that social classes as we have known them may pass from the scene. This would indeed result in a more efficient use of human resources than is possible in a class-divided society. It follows that, as society becomes more and more productive, formative disparities—rooted in the need for a distinction between the more and the less literate—become increasingly obsolescent.

Finally it becomes feasible to prepare our children for adult life in a way that is at least roughly in accord with their talents. Only then does adult competition become fully rationalized.

In Chapters 5 and 6 we examine the specific means by which this prima facie ideal may be a realistic prospect. Our position is rooted in a dialectical study of the economic trajectory of the history of education. The first major step in the direction of the abolition of classes was the great revolution in public education that swept the advanced sectors of the world in the nineteenth century. This revolution established the economic desirability of a universally educated populace as a fundamental social principle.

But though the beginning of this revolutionary transformation was all but unthinkable without public education, the revolution cannot consummate in the classless society unless there is a movement, in our time, in the direction of a stipend (or "voucher") system in a privatized context. Only when all people are entitled to choose from a broad spectrum of formative options do they have a meaningful chance to obtain an education that really is commensurate with their very particular needs and talents. And only then do we overcome the form of alienation or disaffection most characteristic of our time: that of social classes.

The argument, taken as a whole, entails a radical revision of the way we usually think of the apparent antithesis between "capitalism" and "communism." The priorities of the two systems turn out to be reconcilable at the advanced level of industrial development that the species is now approaching.

This point is taken up in the Conclusion to this study. We must ultimately ask why, given the ultimate reconcilability of these two systems, they have been such stern antagonists for so much of recent history. We find that such opposition is rooted in the limitations of our own period, an epoch which we optimists may wish to regard as a "transitional phase": a time in which Formative Parity necessarily appears as a rational objective, but in which capitalism is not yet mature enough to realize it.

Notes

1. Kirkpatrick, Jeane, "Time to Criticize U.S. Critics," syndicated column of 22 July 1990.
2. Dahl, Robert, "Social Reality & 'Free Markets,'" *Dissent*, vol. 37, no. 2 (Spring 1990), p. 226. The first sentence of this quotation serves as a section title, and so is italicized in the original.
3. Surdykowski, Jerzy, "What Does the Left Have to Offer?" *Dissent*, vol. 37, no. 2 (Sping 1990), p. 203.
4. Will, George, nationally syndicated newspaper column of 16 November 1989.
5. "Strikes Sweep East Germany," by the editorial board of *Bulletin*, the weekly organ of the Central Committee of the Workers League, 6 July 1990, p. 20. The Workers League is perhaps the "purest" example of Marxian-Leninist orthodoxy extant today.
6. Ibid., p. 20.
7. Two very recent anthologies, both of excellent quality, fall within this genre: Paul, Ellen Frankel, et al., eds., *Socialism*; and Le Grand, Julian, and Estrin, Saul, *Market Socialism*.
8. See the introductory essay by Estrin and Le Grand to their volume, *Market Socialism*, pp. 1–24, for a clear exposition of this distinction.
9. Walzer, Michael, "A Credo for This Moment," reprinted from the London *Sunday Correspondent* in *Dissent*, vol. 37, no. 2 (Spring 1990), p. 160.
10. I am quite certain that this is not Walzer's actual intent. He would probably

insist that the overcoming of classes remains a worthy goal. Even so, his Credo does seem to show that this objective has, even in the hands of some of the best social democrats, lately dropped beneath the horizon. Hardly ever is it explicitly articulated as a relevant and reasonable objective for the modern period. A basic aim of the present essay is to bring this objective back into view.

11. Fukuyama, Francis, "The End of History?" *The National Interest*, no. 16 (Summer 1989), pp. 3–18.

12. Fukuyama as quoted in Alter, Jonathan, "The Intellectual Hula Hoop," *Newsweek*, 9 October 1989, p. 39.

13. Atlas, James, "What Is Fukuyama Saying," *The New York Times Magazine*, 22 October 1989, p. 42.

14. Though Fukuyama's main claim seems to be that the central problems of social organization—including that of class—have, in the main, been solved in the history of the West, his argument has a pessimistic finale which seems to veer off in a different direction. In the very last paragraph of his piece he tells us that "the end of history will be a very sad time. . . . In the post-historical period there will be neither art nor philosophy, just the perpetual caretaking of the museum of human history. . . . Perhaps this very prospect of centuries of boredom at the end of history will serve to get history started once again."

   But if indeed the "end of history" is—as Fukuyama himself says—the end of "daring, courage, imagination, and idealism," why in the world would the human species be satisfied with such a banalization of its existence? Here Fukuyama's conception of our modern bureaucratic-technological-consumerist society comes surprisingly close to the view of some of our era's anti-utopians. It turns out, by the end of his essay, that saying history is over is not quite the same as saying it *ought* to be. It is but a step from Fukuyama's fears of a future of boredom, to the conclusion drawn by the likes of Orwell and Marcuse: that the "end of history," if such a thing were to be reached, would be due to the repressively totalizing, or—why not say it?—*totalitarian* power of the all-encompassing late-industrial leviathan.

   Nineteenth-century dialecticians like Hegel and Marx tended to believe that irrational forces could not hold out indefinitely against the march of Reason, while some twentieth-century dialecticians like Marcuse (and others of the Frankfurt School) have increasingly worried about the possibility that dialectical progress might be "contained."

   If *that* were all Fukuyama meant, then his claim would not be that our own system is the last word in social *rationality*, but rather that it is no longer clear that we will be able to overcome the irrational. His "we have won" bravura would in that case turn out to be little more than upbeat packaging for a pessimistic, anti-utopian product.

15. Fukuyama, "The End of History?" p. 9.

16. Gertrude Himmelfarb wonders if "the poverty of the underclass in general . . . is not the relic of an old problem, qualitatively and quantitatively . . . different from the old" (*The National Interest*, no. 16 [Summer 1989], p. 26).

   Pierre Hassner (*The National Interest*, no. 16 [Summer 1989], p. 23) has similar doubts: "Fukuyama recognizes the persistence of war and poverty outside the West but tends to dismiss them as irrelevant since they do not concern the great developed nations which are stepping out of history. But can the latter remain unaffected? Or, rather, do we not have growing evidence of the increasing intolerance caused by the shock of cultures and the overcrowding of the planet? . . .

"Are not the homeless refugee and the homeless drug addict the inseparable companions of the materialistic consumer?"

17. This term has actually gained some currency in recent popular periodicals.
18. Fukuyama, "The End of History?" p. 5.
19. Ibid., p. 5.
20. Ibid., p. 5.
21. Of course, as Fukuyama knows, and Kojève knew, Hegel himself did not *quite* say that the World Spirit is rolling irresistibly toward consummation in bourgeois democracy: not only is his predominant tendency that of an open-ended dialecticism; it should be noted that Hegel's ideal social order was a bit different from the bourgeois democratic model. Among other small points of note, Hegel was a monarchist.
22. At the end of *The Philosophy of History* (trans. Sibree [New York: 1956]), Hegel says, quite cautiously: "This is the point which consciousness has attained" (p. 456). This seems hardly the language one would use if one thought that consciousness had reached its absolute culmination. And in a famous passage at the end of the Introduction to the same work, Hegel speculates that the highest stage of history thus far attained—the Northern European—will be eclipsed by something further: "America is . . . the land of the future, where, in the ages that lie before us, the burden of the World's History shall reveal itself . . ." (p. 86). Such passages are always quoted, and for good reason, by those who see the Hegelian dialectic as essentially open and ongoing.
23. This is the most vexed subject in all Hegel interpretation, and deserves far lengthier treatment than I can give it here. Suffice it to say: Hegel seems to have tended, in his more or less *official* moments, to the view that his conceptual presentation of dialectical logic was fully formed and adequate—even though the *content* of that very logic indicates that every existent thing, every system, must fall into dialectical contradiction and hence be itself "sublated" into some further form in a process that goes on *sans cesse*. "Conservative" Hegelians have always inclined to the "official" version, while "radicals"—like Feuerbach and the young Marx—have tended to the view that the inner message of the Logic is that even the Hegelian philosophy itself is subject to just such sublation. I do not try to mask the fact that some of my own sympathies—and the point here is philosophical as well as political—are on the radical side. It is not surprising that Hegel himself seems, at various junctures, drawn both ways on the subject. Fukuyama's interpretation, on the other hand, seems monochromatically "conservative."
24. Engels, Friedrich, *Anti-Dühring* (Moscow: 1954), p. 39.

Of course, it remains an open question—one that will be explored in this study—to what extent Marx himself is guilty of such a counterdialectical absolutism, this time in the form of a millennial version of "communism" as the "end of history."

The "fundamental law" referred to by Engels should not, in any event, sound strange to our ears. It is at least arguable that we Americans are, in our own unself-conscious way, born dialecticians: that we are so inured to the idea—the ideology—of incessant progress, that we are innately mistrustful of any proclamation that the final form of *anything* is at hand.

If that point is granted, we would have to say that the idea that the Spirit of the West is the Absolute, and hence the culmination of history, seems contrary to the incessantly revolutionary Spirit of the West!

25. Pierre Hassner (*The National Interest*, no. 16 [Summer 1989], p. 24), for example, bases his confidence that Endism is wrong on a vague "belief in the complexity of human nature and in the notion that fundamental dimensions of the human soul can be repressed for whole periods but not eradicated forever."

Gertrude Himmelfarb (*The National Interest*, no. 16 [Summer 1989], p. 26) takes a related but slightly different dialectical tack. She reminds us that Hegel's famous adage that "the owl of minerva spreads it wings only with the falling of dusk" means that philosophy has only retrospective, but not prospective, significance: "We know, at best, only what was, not what will be. The optimists among us may take comfort in [Hegel's] adage; the pessimists may find it cause for anxiety. But both must take cognizance of a future of which we know only that it is unknowable." From this perspective, "Endism" is an empty exercise because we cannot, in principle, ever know what coming years have in store.

26. Alter, Jonathan, *Newsweek*, 9 October 1989, p. 39.

27. I strongly suspect that hard-line Marxists would disdainfully dismiss this objective, thus stated, as "petty bourgeois." The works of Marx and Engels are indeed full of disparagement of the mentality of the small "shopkeeper" who would like to see the inequities of the world eliminated in the context of a "fair" form of market competition. I do not mind the epithet: the failure of hard-line communism itself forces us to ask if such "petty bourgeois" dreams are not, Marxian disparagement notwithstanding, the most reasonable and balanced that our age has produced.

28. Mises, Ludwig von, "Economic Calculation in the Socialist Commonwealth," in *Collectivist Economic Planning*, ed. Hayek, Friedrich (New York: 1967), pp. 85–130.

29. Hayek has been the most persistent—and probably the philosophically most interesting—critic of planned economies. His *The Road to Serfdom* (Chicago: 1944) is today hardly dated, and remains the best introduction to the subject. Specialists will want to read Part 2 of *The Essence of Hayek*, ed. Nishiyama, Chiaki, and Leube, Kurt R. (Stanford: 1984). Variations on this same theme will also be familiar to readers of Milton Friedman; see for example his "Market Mechanisms and Economic Planning," in *The Essence of Friedman*, ed. Leube, Kurt R. (Stanford: 1987), pp. 18–35. The main opponent of von Mises and Hayek in the original "Calculation Debate" was Oskar Lange; see his "On the Economic Theory of Socialism," reprinted in Lippincott, Benjamin, ed., *On the Economic Theory of Socialism* (New York: 1964).

30. Hayek, Friedrich A., *The Road to Serfdom*, p. 49.

31. Important aspects of this approach go back to the celebrated arguments of the Chicago economist Frank Knight. See his *Risk, Uncertainty and Profit*, Reprints of Scarce Tracts of London School of Economics and Political Science, no. 16 (1933). But my own understanding of this approach has been more directly influenced by Thomas Sowell's *Knowledge and Decisions* (New York: 1980).

32. See Friedman, Milton, "Market Mechanisms and Central Planning," reprinted in *The Essence of Friedman* (Stanford: 1987), pp. 27–28, for a full paraphrase of Sowell's argument, which reads as follows:

> . . . A person has an idea which, in his best judgment, has only one chance in ten of being successful. If successful, however, the financial return in the form of the value of the extra product produced or of the saving in production expenses would be, let us say, a hundred times the cost of introducing the idea.

It is clearly desirable that this activity be taken. It is a good bet. If many such bets are taken, the end-result will be highly favorable. . . .

In a market system in which the individual who makes the decision to undertake that venture receives all or a large fraction of the additional returns, he has an incentive to undertake it. He knows that there are nine chances out of ten that he will lose his money; yet the gain he will receive in the one case out of ten . . . is big enough to justify taking the risk.

Consider the same situation in a state-run enterprise. How can the manager of that enterprise persuade the people under whom he works that the odds and potential returns are what he believes them to be? . . . In addition, the reward structure is likely to be very different. If the venture is successful, he will no doubt receive some extra compensation; he may . . . receive honors, become a hero of the nation. If, however, [it] is a failure, as it will be in nine cases out of ten, he will almost surely be reprimanded and may lose his position. . . . The reward in the case of success does not compensate for the loss in case of failure. His tendency is to . . . play it safe, to undertake investments that are almost certain to yield returns . . . [T]hat is the reasonable . . . way [for such managers] to behave. For society as a whole, however, [it] is the road to stagnation and rigidity, and that in fact has been the outcome in collectivist societies.

33. "Ich bin so weit, dass ich in 5 Wochen mit der ganzen ökonomischen Scheisse fertig bin." Marx, Letter to Engels of 2 April 1851, in the Marx-Engels *Werke*, vol. 27 (Berlin: 1965), p. 228.
34. A sound and brief exposition of this point can be found in the "Introduction" by David McLellan to his translation of excerpts from Marx's *Grundrisse* (New York: 1971), pp. 1–15. McLellan shows convincingly the wrongheadedness of the view that Marx abandoned his preoccupation with the alienation problem after his youthful Feuerbachian period had ended.
35. This coinage by Ludwig Wittgenstein has long since passed into general currency.
36. Laclau, Ernesto, and Mouffe, Chantal, *Hegemony and Socialist Strategy* (London: 1985).
37. This criterion is, as all economists know, not univocal; nor is it easy to explicate in technical detail. Difficulties and perplexities abound concerning the very measurement of national product. One may be thankful that it is the economist's job to agonize over these issues. It is not our problem here. It will be enough for us to assume that, technical clarifications aside, the idea of "maximizing productivity" is at least intuitively clear—and also that there can be no real question of a society departing very far from that demand.

PART ONE:
Down from Utopia

1
Beyond the Coercion of Labor:
Toward the Inner Sanctum
of Marxian Communism

1. Marx's Attack on the Coercion of Labor

Over the winter of 1845–46, Marx and Engels, living in exile in Brussels, composed *The German Ideology*. Marx, recalling this period many years later, tells us that the collaborative venture was written "in order to settle accounts with our erstwhile philosophical conscience. The resolve was carried out in the form of a criticism of post-Hegelian philosophy."[1]

Though the manuscript was delivered to the publisher, political repression by the Prussian government did not, in Marx's words, "allow of its being printed. We abandoned the manuscript to the gnawing criticism of the mice all the more willingly as we had served our main purpose—self-clarification."[2] The work—which had indeed been partly devoured by rodents—did not actually see the light of day until 1932.

Part One of this long manuscript, written by Marx himself, is devoted to the most comprehensive and detailed presentation of "the materialist conception of history" ever to come from the pen of communism's founders.[3] This portion of the text has generally been regarded by interpreters and critics as the birthplace of mature "Historical Materialism." Gone, at least for the most part, are the Hegelian turns of phrase that still lingered in the inspiring but transitional *Economic and Philosophical Manuscripts* of 1844. Abandoning the apparatus of idealist philosophy altogether, Marx now seeks to provide a firm, social-scientific basis for his research into the evolution of economic forms. "Empirical observation must in each separate instance bring out empirically, and without any mystification and speculation, the connection of the social and political structure with production."[4]

It is noteworthy that this work does seem to have such a sober and nonspeculative aspect. For there seems little that is modest about one of the central themes of the manuscript: that a primary objective of communism is "the abolition of the division of labor."[5]

This seems outlandish: as if Marx were proposing that all semblance of human specialization must go by the board.

And indeed, Marx does sometimes write as if this were precisely what he does have in mind. He occasionally flirts with the idea that communism will, in his words, open up "the possibility of the universal development of individuals." This, he says, is a virtual requirement of the production process under the advanced industrial conditions that the bourgeois order has itself produced. That system has, in Marx's words, "developed to a totality" the human productive powers:

> The appropriation of these forces [by the proletariat] is itself nothing more than the development of the individual capacities corresponding to the material instruments of production. The appropriation of a totality of instruments of production is, for this very reason, the development of a totality of capacities in the individuals themselves.[6]

Such universality would be in stark contrast to the stupefying narrowness of individual existence under capitalism. Marx does not mince words:

> What characterizes the division of labor inside modern society is that it engenders specialized functions, specialists, and with them craft-idiocy.[7]

Marx made these remarks in the 1840s. But such bold phrasemaking does not only characterize his youth. We see the same idea, in virtually the same words, in the unquestionably "mature" *Grundrisse*. There, Marx tells us that the advanced technology produced by capitalism now makes possible a society predicated upon "the richest development of the individual"[8]—a world typified by

> universal development of the productive forces—and wealth in general . . . [This] basis offers the possibility of the universal development of the individuals. . . . The universality of the individual is not [as in earlier society] thought or imagined, but is the universality of his real and ideal relationships.[9]

Again we say: this seems preposterous. Does Marx seriously envision a world populated by universally skilled Leonardo-like polymaths? It makes sense to say that we ought to abolish *extreme* forms of the division of labor—that is, make people *less* specialized than they are at present—but no sense at all to say that we might eliminate specialization as such. The idea of a literally "universal" human being is the veriest economic nonsense. Indeed, Leonardo himself was not, strictly speaking, a "universal man." Though his skills were both broad and deep when compared to those of the ordinary soul, these were, and could be, only a minuscule fraction of the expertise realized throughout society as a whole.

If Marx were proposing such literal universality of the individual powers, we could reject his conception out of hand. But when we turn to his most celebrated pronouncement on the division of labor, we see that his predominant thought is a bit more subtle—and not nearly so farfetched. This famous passage deserves quotation at some length:

> . . . [T]he division of labor offers us the primary example[10] of how, as long as man remains in natural society, that is, as long as a cleavage exists between the particular and the common interest, as long, therefore, as activity is not voluntarily, but naturally, divided, man's own deed becomes an alien power opposed to him, which enslaves him instead of being controlled by him. For as soon as the distribution [i.e., division] of labor comes into being, each man has a particular, exclusive sphere of activity, which is forced upon him and from which he cannot escape. He is a hunter, a fisherman, a shepherd or a critical critic, and must remain so if he does not want to lose his means of livelihood; while in a communist society, where nobody has one exclusive sphere of activity but each can become accomplished in any branch he wishes, . . . it [is] possible for me to do one thing today and another tomorrow, to hunt in the morning, fish in the afternoon, rear cattle in the evening, just as I have a mind, without ever becoming hunter, fisherman, shepherd or critic.[11]

On this understanding, the achievement of communism would *not* involve the "abolition of the division of labor" in the utopian sense one might have attached to those words. What Marx actually says here is that people in the communist future will have *unrestricted mobility* when it comes to choosing, and changing, their life-activity. The intended contrast is that between the unfreedom of those in precommunist society, and the freedom of each, under communism, "to become accomplished" in whatever field he "has a mind" to.

I do believe that this is the meaning that Marx, in his more circumspect moments, attaches to the "abolition of the division of labor." But in that case one wants to say that his choice of terminology is a little misleading. One might more precisely put it: Marx does not (as would be wildly implausible) actually question the *division* of labor—that is, society's need for a variety of productive specializations—but "only"[12] the *coercion* of labor. (I will myself keep to this more careful usage in the sequel.)

Marx's complaint does not concern the fact that I tend to be good at one productive task, you at another. Nobody feels this, by itself, to be objectionable. I may decide to become a mechanic, a lawyer, a pro tennis player, or a philosophy professor; I may be "a hunter, a fisherman, a shepherd, or a critical critic"; but, whatever I become, I cannot but be "specialized." And indeed there is evidence enough that Marx thought the increasing differentiation of the human powers an ever more salient and demanding aspect of the production process as history advances.[13]

The trouble with social "division" is not *difference*—the fact that you realize one possibility for human existence, while I realize another. Social difference, in itself, is more than just benign; it is the very lifeblood of human existence. The core of "alienation" consists rather in the fact that society constrains us to do what we would not, if fully free, choose to do. Just as Marx says:

> This fixation of social activity, this consolidation of what we ourselves produce into an objective power above us, growing out of our control, thwarting our expectations, bringing to naught our calculations, is one of the chief factors in historical development till now.[14]

Marx's complaint, thus understood, comes down to this: people lack the freedom to devote their productive hours however they wish. They are required, by the rules of society, to remain stuck within this or that sphere of activity, whether they like it or not.

Under the current social dispensation, that is what it means to say that something is my "occupation": it is something I am forced to do if I want to get by, or even survive. It is this coercive "fixation of social activity"[15] to particular occupational niches that must come to an end.

2. Beyond Economic "Punishment"

Though not the same as the abolition of the division of labor, the elimination of the coercion of labor seems almost as wild a notion. Does Marx mean seriously to propose that we might have a form of society which permitted people to do whatever they please, whenever they please? Surely such a world would instantly degenerate in an orgy of dilettantism and sloth! If people are not *made* to do socially useful things, if they are not *forced* to focus their attention on some particular discipline, won't they end up having no socially useful competence at all? And wouldn't such an economy fall apart?

Marx and Engels consider the assumption at work here—that, under communism, "all work will cease, and universal laziness will overtake us"[16]—as worthy only of disdain. Allow me to epitomize the Marxian position by putting an imaginary soliloquy in Marx's mouth:

> You suppose that the coordination of people's plans and activities is incompatible with the communist idea of freedom. You assume that, since human affairs would be hopelessly disorganized if society did not have some sort of unified means of planning, it somehow follows that the coercion of the individual by society is inevitable. You are certain that the claims of society must confront the individual as a denial of desire, as something externally imposed. You think there is something about

"human nature" that prevents people from directly desiring the mutual, orderly arrangement of their plans and projects.

These are just the bogus assumptions that flourish in the society of the marketplace. Such a society is founded upon antagonistic relations among people, and thus requires an ideology that deifies just such antagonism. Under capitalism, adversary relations among people must appear normal or inevitable. So as long as this system prevails, there will be no end to "theories" that "explain" why it is impossible for people to have an inherent interest in social cooperation.

We communists have never made any secret of the fact that we regard such bourgeois ideas as scientifically defenseless. Let there be no ambiguity about this: the achievement of communism requires the communalization of the human spirit, the inculcation in our children of directly cooperative needs and desires, the abolition of the apparently "necessary connection" between social existence and coercion. And we maintain that there is nothing in "human nature" to prevent such an achievement.

And so we communists make the twofold claim: in a free society, people will indeed be allowed to pursue their labors however they want; but their wants, now communalized, will include a desire for the mutual adjustment of their activities, so that the free enjoyment of each may at the same time be a contribution to the well-being of all.[17]

Marx's own call for the birth of a directly communal human existence ranged over an entire career, and was eloquent and intoxicating enough to become the leading revolutionary idea of the modern world.

But we ourselves must ask: what would labor be if it existed in uncoerced form? Is such an objective attainable? Is it desirable? Would its attainment, if such were possible, heal the rift "between the particular and the common interest," as Marx says it would?

It is clear that Marx himself is committed to a quite radical understanding of what it would mean for society to transcend the coercion of labor. Student nonpareil of economic history that he is, Marx's gaze penetrates the veneer of social relations and sees such coercion even when it is not superficially obvious. Typically, it is obvious only in historical retrospect—and the more so, the further back we look. Consider the sequence of main economic forms.

In the case of the slave system, coercion is, to us, as plain as could be.

With feudalism, which (for all its unfreedom) is after all governed by the mutuality of a service contract between lord and serf, force seems a little abated—though it remains quite strong in the eyes of us twentieth-century *bourgeois*, especially in view of the serf's "attachment to the land": his lack of the right to sell his labor power when and where he chooses.

So it is that, when we finally reach capitalism, coercion is, to *us*, not evident at all. Is not every human being entitled to enter the adult economic fray? And is not every individual free to associate with, and affiliate with, whomever she pleases? Where is the coercion here?

Marx, stripping the mask from bourgeois ideology, replies: the bogus appearance of freedom under capitalism is a result of the fact that force is no longer directly—politically—imposed; but labor is not really free so long as the economy is structured so that "each man has a particular, exclusive sphere of activity, which is forced upon him and from which he cannot escape."[18]

But what does this "inability to escape" itself consist in? What is the force of the word "force"?

We already know Marx's reply: force obtains, and a person is unfree, insofar as he must remain trapped in a specialized trade at pain of "losing his means of livelihood."

The point is not that, under capitalism, you cannot physically get up and walk out of your job as an accountant or mechanic and go off and spend the next five years wandering the countryside, or philosophizing, or writing sonnets. The point is that you can do this only at pain of *economic punishment*.

Many people, in the austere and cruel circumstances of Marx's own time, could leave their jobs only at the risk of literal starvation. It would, in this context, be a bad joke—but the kind characteristic (in Marx's view) of bourgeois ideology—to tell us that, after all, the worker "is free" because he has a complete legal right to sell his services wherever and whenever he chooses.

It would be reasonable to retort: I am free in *that* sense even while the bandit threatens me at gunpoint: I can do it—if I am willing to pay the price. Even in the strictest legal contexts, a person is regarded as uncoerced, as truly free, *only if no threat attaches to noncompliance*.

Once we look at matters from this Marxian perspective, it seems clear that any régime that enforces outcomes by means of economic incentives *is* (insofar) punitive in character.

In prebourgeois societies, such threats took direct, even directly political, form.

In early industrial capitalism, where the alternative to work might be starvation, the threat was still fairly plain.

Under welfare capitalism, in which minimum standards of nourishment and health are (at least supposedly) guaranteed, the coercion, though more subtle, is still quite real: those who (as we say) "drop out" must suffer some significant economic hardship, relative to the standards of their time, insofar as what they do is not deemed a contribution to social productivity.

Marx believes that social evolution has not reached its climax as long as the threat of such punishment does exist. Real and complete victory over forced labor, the victory communists stand for, must involve the overthrow of economic coercion as such.

This comes to pass only under communism. The path to that consummating stage of social relations is long and arduous, and communism is not fully established until the revolutionary struggles of the present have been completed. Nonetheless, economic development finally does reach the point at which all people are equally free to work whenever and however they please: a point at which no penalties attach to your measurable success in your chosen livelihood.[19]

Under communism, you might in good faith judge badly what your strengths are. You might not actually be much good at writing sonnets: it might be a waste of time to pursue Keatsian truth and beauty. Even so, you would not be economically punished for your miscalculation: there would be nobody standing behind you, measuring your performance—gauging it with reference to a wage. You would, no matter what the outcome, be allowed, like everybody else, to draw upon the social wealth commensurately with your actual requirements:

> In a higher phase of communist society, after the enslaving subordination of the individual to the division of labor, and therewith also the antithesis between mental and physical labor, has vanished; after labor has become not only a means of life but life's prime want; after the productive forces have also increased with the all-round development of the individual, and all the springs of cooperative wealth flow more abundantly— only then can the narrow horizon of bourgeois right be crossed and society inscribe on its banner: From each according to his ability, to each according to his needs![20]

3. The Dialectics of Scarcity

We see that economic punishment, hence the coercion of labor, exists insofar as the economy is structured in accordance with a system of incentives. The question we must now face is: what would lead anyone to think that society would *ever* outgrow its need for incentives?

One wants to reply: society has every right to use material incentives in order to coax into existence whatever pattern of productive behavior is appropriate to its needs. We are justified in rewarding people for moving in desirable directions within the social division of labor. It is good policy to correlate "wages" with productivity—hence rational for any society to impose what Marx would see as "economic punishment" on those who pay too little regard to the requirements of labor. As the economics textbooks say: incentive systems make sense as long as "scarcity" remains a fact of life.

But does this last remark contain a clue to the way out of the difficulty? Is Marx assuming that communism is the social form suited to a world beyond the limitations of scarcity?

Such a quick and simple solution will not do. For Marx himself—to his credit—does not naively suppose that "scarcity" itself can be eliminated. Thus in *The German Ideology* he says that the satisfaction of one level of need always "leads to new needs,"[21]—a conception that is even more clearly articulated by the mature Marx in the first volume of *Capital*, where he asserts:

> the number and extent . . . [of the workers'] necessary wants, as also the modes of satisfying them, are themselves the product of historical development, and depend therefore to a great extent on the degree of the civilization of a country.[22]

This would seem to imply that needs multiply insofar as we improve the means of fulfilling them—in a process that is in principle endless. The same understanding is implicit in Marx's remark that

> at the dawn of civilization the productiveness acquired by labor is small, but so too are the wants which develop with and by the means of satisfying them.[23]

In a word: the more we get, the more we want. In this historically relative sense, the best things in life must always be in short supply.

Marx's historically relative notion of scarcity must be sharply distinguished from Malthusian pessimism: it has nothing to do with the idea that the degree of human advancement has any inherent limits.[24] Far to the contrary, Marx assumes that there is no productive problem to which a solution cannot ultimately be found. Whereas (for example) Malthus thinks there are natural limits on how much food can be produced, Marx is convinced that any present limits in food production could, in principle, be overcome through the appropriate technological measures.[25]

But though Marx does not subscribe to a Malthusian version of *absolute* scarcity, he is committed to a *relative* treatment thereof. This is grounded in a twofold dialectical treatment of creativity: our species has unlimited productive potential, but such creativity itself implies the incessant recreation of expectations and demands at ever new levels. The "infinite" potential of human beings entails that the prospects of overcoming scarcity—of eventually making any given element of the good life as plentiful as might be desired—are without limit. But it also implies that the expansion of our desires is, correspondingly, without limit. Any given good can move from scarcity to abundance, yet such abundance always expands our horizons: it brings other goods into view that are now felt to be scarce. And that means that there will, at any given time, be scarce goods, goods whose production is just now on the horizon of human accomplishment.

What we denote "scarce" are those goods which are in the process of being made more abundant. Of course we wish to realize our creative desires, make them full-fledged realities; and indeed, in time, we can always do so. But scarcity as such—the condition of regarding *some goods or other* as scarce—is itself not some unfortunate blemish that might possibly be removed.

Because each technological solution is at the same time the opening of a technological vista not yet explored, mastery of this new vista constitutes the entire project of an era. Even if we have made some desirable aspect of life abundant, it will take time before the new forms of gratification just now appearing on the horizon can yield, in their turn, to such mastery. As abundance in one area is arduously and slowly achieved, this creates a new horizon of productive accomplishment, hence a new sense of what is scarce. Whatever the point we have reached, there will be aspects of the good life in the process of becoming abundant.

We see that the *limitless* overcoming of scarcity is not the same as the *total* elimination thereof. The idea of a society that has overcome scarcity entirely makes no dialectical sense. Though there is no specific limit that cannot be surpassed, scarcity is not a transient historical phenomenon. To eliminate it in one area is always to generate it in another. Assuming that the species continues its creative odyssey indefinitely,[26] the expansion of needs, and hence the "sublimation of scarcity," is interminable. Whatever level of abundance has so far occurred merely defines a new benchmark relative to which further progress is not only possible, but certainly to be expected.

Hence the problem.

On the one hand, it seems that the logic of incentive schemes makes perfect sense under conditions of scarcity.

On the other, it seems that Marx is committed to the idea that scarcity, inherent in the dialectic of creativity itself, is perennial.

How, then, can Marx escape the conclusion that incentive schemes are inevitable? That is: how can he deny that economic punishment, on his own understanding of this concept, is with us to stay?

4. "Free Labor" as "Damned Serious"

How is Marx to reply? We must seek an answer in his dialectical understanding of what rewarding (or "disalienated") work would involve.

To think as Marx does, we must distinguish between two different senses of "dissatisfaction." Though dissatisfactions attendant to creative work ("free labor") will be a feature of even the most advanced and emancipated society, these need not be alienating in a strictly dialectical sense.

How could frustration be anything *but* "alienating"? I think Marx would say that this very question betrays a failure to see that, dialectically speaking, certain discontents are inherent in human gratification. For Marx clearly does believe that there are benign forms of frustration which are indeed essential to a fulfilled human existence: frustrations we voluntarily seek rather than avoid—work that need not be "shunned like the plague."[27]

Only if it is thus shunned does it deserve the appellation "alienated labor." For in that case it is much more than merely "frustrating." It is more than merely difficult, or perplexing, or tiring—for the most gratifying forms of labor, the kind we would like to do if we only could, are typically difficult, perplexing, and tiring. As Marx himself says:

> [L]abor [cannot] be made merely a joke, or amusement. . . . Really free labor, the composing of music for example, is at the same time damned serious and demands the greatest effort.[28]

Thus Marx thinks that, under communism, "damned serious" labor in one sense continues unabated, while in another sense it can be eliminated.

"Damned serious" work goes on, indeed increases, in the sense that fertile forms of difficulty and frustration—the kind felt by a Beethoven—continue to motivate human activity. There is no question, in Marx's writings, of abolishing the problems inherent in creativity itself.[29]

But alienated labor as such is eliminated: society, having largely overcome technological inadequacy, is finally equipped to make the "damned serious" difficulties and frustrations of creativity the *only* sort that dominate their lives. Joyless, unpleasant labor comes to an end.

From the same perspective, to say that scarcity will always be with us is to admit (or insist) that we will always have problems to solve and hard work to do. The generation of new needs out of the satisfaction of the old—this is inherent in our incessant creative odyssey, in technological-scientific progress itself.

In that sense, economic "development" is everlasting. Since we will always have further creative projects, there will always, obviously, be at least the burdens of creativity itself. Among these "burdens" is the fact of incessant scarcity: that we are never sated.

But Marx could, consistently with this, insist that in another sense development ends. That we are never sated, even when creative, does not mean that we cannot abolish the social order in which only some people are permitted to be creative.

Let us use the term "privation" to refer to such estrangement from creativity. This can indeed be abolished. And so there is another sense—the one Marx thinks relevant to the emancipatory concerns of Historical Materialism—in which economic "development" does reach a climax. We are able to reach the milestone at which the conditions of creative, emancipated labor are at last available to all.

Communism, thus conceived, is not the overcoming of scarcity, or frustration, or pain.

It is the achievement of a form of society that is at last an apt vehicle of fulfilling forms of damned serious, and damned difficult, work and struggle.

Dialectical "strife" remains a fact, but it has come out of its estranged, dehumanized condition: it has become fully aesthetized.

Work, arduous as it is, becomes an artistic enactment.

5. Marx's "Promethean" Commitment

Marx and Engels often write as if we were, in our time, on the verge of achieving technological command so radical that all work might become a "labor of love." In the unqualified language of the *Critique of the Gotha Program*: the communist society of the future is one in which "labor has become not only a means of life but life's prime want. . . ."[30]

This has a utopian ring. How could such a society possibly come about?

Here we approach the inner sanctum of Marxian theory.

Marx's historical approach, I will argue, ultimately depends upon what I will call a "Promethean" premise: the assumption that industrial progress reaches a point of *radical automation* at which it is possible to eliminate all toilsome activity.

It is with reference to that sense of "labor" that Engels flatly proclaims: "the perfecting of machinery is making human labor superfluous."[31] Marx himself is equally blunt:

[A]s heavy industry develops, the creation of real wealth depends less on labor time and on the quantity of labor utilized than on the power of

mechanical agents which are set in motion during labor time. The powerful effectiveness of these agents, in turn, bears no relation to the immediate labor time that their production costs. It depends rather on the general
state of science and on technological progress. . . .[32]

These machines, says Marx, should be viewed as

natural material transformed into organs of the human will to dominate
nature or to realize itself therein.[33]

As soon as society seizes upon the opportunity opened up by this technology, we can

reduce the necessary labor of society to a minimum [so that] all the
members of society can develop their education in the arts, sciences, etc.,
thanks to the free time and means available to all.[34]

Lest one think that such formulations are Marxian effusions made en pas-
sant, to be taken with a grain of salt by mature communists, one should
note that a virtually identical pronouncement occurs in the Program of the
Communist Third International adopted in 1928:

The development of the productive forces of world Communist society
will make it possible to raise the well-being of the whole of humanity and
to reduce to a minimum the time devoted to material production and,
consequently, will enable culture to flourish as never before in history.[35]

Such Promethean radicalism has had a strong appeal to many futuristic
thinkers. That the march of science and technology entails a long-run
diminution of "necessary labor" is an idea that has animated many, and
perhaps most, of the revolutionaries of the past two centuries.

Thus the famed anarchist Kropotkin asserts, "If there is still work which
is really disagreeable in itself, it is only because our scientific men have
never cared to consider the means of rendering it less so." Kropotkin is
convinced that "[t]he progress of modern technics . . . wonderfully sim-
plifies the production of all the necessaries of life. . . ."[36]

The same conviction continues to animate Marxian writers to this day.
André Gorz—inspired by both Marx and the futurologist Alvin Toffler—
has argued that ongoing automation entails a long-run decline in society's
need for labor, so that we face the very real possibility of "liberation from
work," and hence of a radical transformation that would produce a

culture without norms, without hierarchies, without timetables; where
the family no longer consists of mum, dad and the kids but includes all
possible sex and age combinations; where we produce for ourselves, as
members of a family or a co-operative, many of the things which nowa-
days we buy with money. . . .[37]

This futuristic image of emancipation is thoroughly Marxian in spirit. But it is Marx himself who tells the most sophisticated version of the Promethean story of the rise and ultimate fall of "alienated labor." It is this Promethean reading of human history that we must now consider.

Notes

1. Marx, from the Preface to *A Contribution to the Critique of Political Economy* of 1859, in *The Marx-Engels Reader*, ed. Tucker, Robert (New York: 1978), p. 5. This anthology hereafter referred to as "Tucker."
2. Ibid., pp. 5–6.
3. Tucker, pp. 146–200. Though Marx and Engels collaborated in the writing of *The German Ideology*, scholars agree that the writing of Part 1 fell to Marx.
4. Marx, *The German Ideology*, Part 1, Tucker, p. 154.
5. "The transformation, through the division of labor, of personal powers (relationships) into material powers, cannot be dispelled [as the Young Hegelians seem to think] by dismissing the general idea of it from one's mind, but can only be abolished by the individuals again subjecting these material powers to themselves and abolishing the division of labor." Tucker, p. 197, emphasis mine, spelling Americanized.
6. Marx, *The German Ideology*, Part 1, Tucker, p. 191.
7. Marx, *The Poverty of Philosophy* (New York: 1963), p. 144.
8. Marx, *The Grundrisse*, ed. and trans. McLellan, David (New York: 1971), p. 120. Hereafter, "McLellan."
9. Ibid., p. 121.
10. "*das erste Beispiel.*" The translation offered in the Tucker anthology renders "erste" as "first"; but since the priority here has to do with significance more than chronology, "primary" seems a better choice.
11. Marx, *The German Ideology*, Part 1, Tucker, p. 160.
12. I have put the word "only" within scare quotes because it will presently become clear that there is nothing "mere" about the elimination of the coercion of labor itself.
13. Under fairly primitive technological conditions, there is little room for any specialization of skills. Marx hypothesizes a state of "primitive communism" as a pretechnological starting point: an economy, approximated by early hunting/gathering society, that can have little human differentiation beyond that inherent in the biological endowment of the organism: hands, brain, and so forth. Though, in the case of the human animal, this physical endowment is impressive, the functional differentiation among human beings that can develop on such a meager natural basis is so restricted that such a society is, in Marx's words, typified by a kind of "herd consciousness [by which] man is only distinguished from the sheep by the fact that with him consciousness takes the place of instinct . . ." (Tucker, p. 158).
   Only as greater and greater technological sophistication is attained, do we see, correlatively, ever-increasing diversification of the human powers. And as this

process of human differentiation continues, we find the growth of what we call "individuality." Differentiation of productive functions is therefore the key to the movement beyond the herd mentality of primitive communism.

14. Marx, *The German Ideology*, Part 1, Tucker, p. 160.
15. Ibid., p. 160.
16. Marx and Engels, *The Manifesto of the Communist Party*, Tucker, p. 486.
17. Some of the prose of the last few paragraphs, including that of the imagined Marxian soliloquy, is adapted from one of my own articles: see Weiss, D. D., "Marx versus Smith on the Division of Labor," *Monthly Review* (July–August 1976). At the time of that writing, I was (as I am no longer) unequivocally sympathetic with the sentiments of the soliloquy.
18. Marx and Engels criticize the limited "bourgeois" conception of freedom in many contexts. Engels's discussion in Part 1 of *Socialism: Utopian and Scientific* (see esp. Tucker, p. 684) is a locus classicus, as is Marx's "On the Jewish Question" in its virtual entirety (Tucker, pp. 26–52). There are similar passages in the *Grundrisse*, e.g., McLellan, p. 131.
19. I would assume that some communists might wish to put in the following, apparently reasonable proviso: "assuming that you act in good faith."
20. Marx, "Critique of the Gotha Program," Tucker, p. 531.
21. Tucker, p. 156.
22. Marx, *Capital*, Vol. I (New York: 1967), p. 171.
23. Ibid., p. 512.
24. Malthus's emphasis in his celebrated *Essay on the Principle of Population* was on the (alleged) limits in increased food supply relative to population growth. But neo-Malthusians—we find them today in the "zero population growth" movement, for example—have emphasized the (alleged) limits of all productive resources, most notably, perhaps, fossil fuels.
25. The Malthusians of our day worry that fossil fuels are running out; Marxists, far more sanguine, argue that this only signals the need to develop alternative energy sources.
26. Marx does seem to have made this assumption, but those of a "postmodern" stripe do not. Since our argument against Marx works even insofar as we grant the assumption, and since it is worthwhile to ask what progress entails when it *does* occur, there is no harm in granting the assumption for the sake of argument.
27. Marx, "Estranged Labor," Tucker, p. 74.
28. McLellan, p. 124.
29. Nor, incidentally, is there any reason to suppose that social life is such that never is heard a discouraging word. When people are interacting creatively, the best of friends, at the best of moments, can disagree. The point is that there is no need for disagree*ment* to be disagree*able*.
30. Tucker, p. 531. It should of course be remembered that this *Critique* was not written for publication, but for internal circulation among Marx's fellow social-ists. Marx, in a published work, might have toned down this phraseology somewhat.
31. Engels, in *Socialism: Utopian and Scientific*, Tucker, p. 707.
32. McLellan, p. 141. Spelling Americanized.
33. Ibid., p. 143. Spelling Americanized.
34. Ibid., p. 142.
35. From *The Program of the Communist International*, 1928, excerpted in Cohen, Carl, *Communism, Fascism, and Democracy* (New York: 1972), p. 169.

36. Kropotkin, Peter, in *Kropotkin's Revolutionary Pamphlets*, ed. Baldwin, Roger (New York: 1927), pp. 71, 285.

37. Gorz, André, *Paths to Paradise* (London: 1985), p. 81. The phrase "On the Liberation from Work" serves as the subtitle of this book. Readers may also wish to consult Alvin Toffler's *The Third Wave* (London: 1981).

2

The Modern Prometheus:
A Fundamental Contradiction
in Marxian Social Theory

1. Prometheus Bound and Unbound

Prometheus filched from the gods not only the secret of fire, but the recipe for technical skill of every kind. And Marx, as is well known, made the mythic Titan the patron deity of his own revolutionary career.[1] In less mythic terms: the founder of communism believed that the ever-increasing technological prowess of our species makes it possible for us to attain forms of emancipation which, till now, have only been the objects of our most desperate longing.

Till now, such emancipation could only be dreamt—could only be the "fantastic realization of the human being insofar as the human being posses-ses no true reality" and "the sigh of the oppressed creature, the heart of heartless world, and the soul of soulless conditions."[2] This is because the Promethean quest for emancipation requires an entire epoch of privation—of toilsome and degrading "alienated labor"—before we are able to over-come the lingering legacy of our merely "natural" (animal) starting point and achieve real mastery over the world.

Alienation is rooted in the sacrifices that we have had to make if we are finally to attain understanding and control of our environment. We can achieve technological command only if we are willing to pass through a lengthy and arduous period of painful tutelage. Though Prometheus is at last triumphant, he must at first be punished for his audacity. The human species must first labor in the service of emancipation, if the conditions of emancipation are to be brought into existence.

Or in other words: alienation centers on the poignant "contradiction" that obtains whenever technological conditions are still so primitive that, unavoidably, many toil to *create* a world antithetical to their own *creativity*. Alienation encompasses those facets of labor that are contrary to the unim-peded, noncontradictory fulfillment of labor itself, and above all else estrangement from truly "universal," communicative "species existence"—that is, from intelligent life itself.

The product of our hands, which should by its nature (and will in the fullness of time) be the fulfillment of our human needs, instead imposes upon us an inhuman form of life-activity, and so turns out to be our dreaded enemy.[3]

But though alienated labor has been necessary during much of human history, it is not eternally so. Scientific command finally does become possible. The possibility of emancipation is determined by the Promethean potential of human intelligence itself: the ability to "appropriate" nature, to make it our own.

The process begins in the prehistorical past. Arduously, haphazardly, gradually, the species masters the various departments of craft. Specific skills become incorporated into the repertoire of the human body. But this process—the development of skilled labor—implies, in turn, an increasing scientific grasp of the physical movements needed to produce desired results in the various departments of labor.

And this growth in scientific comprehension sets the stage, in its turn, for automation. Our millennia-long labors finally come to full fruition. The hand's command of the tool consummates in the mind's grasp of how to replicate these movements in the automatic routines of machines.

Nature is, at first, merely "external": we do not understand it, hence cannot control it. But it becomes, at last, part of our "internal" repertoire. And once this process is consummated, we need no longer take natural conditions as an unalterable given. Rather we attain the ultimate form of skillful labor: conscious and intentional "mastery" *over* nature.

Marx's Promethean proposal is that we can, at long last, master the techniques that will overcome privation and produce civilization in its fullest flower. Alienated labor can—in the final analysis—be reduced to an incidental factor in human life. Marx calls that final analysis "communism."

Now, finally, mechanical tasks can be programmed to be carried out in a repeatable, reliable manner. Because *we* (at first) embody the mechanisms of production, we learn (at last) how to make literal mechanisms—machines— capable of replacing our own robotlike labor. The products we have produced can now perform tasks we would rather avoid.

An ever-decreasing part of our life bears the imprint of our former, "natural" impotence. Correspondingly, an ever-decreasing proportion of social labor time needs be devoted to unfulfilling human activity. The time needed for unpleasant *human* labor—industrial tedium—shrinks to the vanishing point. As scientific mastery grows, our initial, "natural" (prescientific) condition recedes further and further into the past.

Marx, in his more careful theoretical moments, does qualify this conception somewhat. The idea of *complete* "domination" over nature, and hence of *complete* emancipation from alienated labor, turns out to be, at best, an approximation. In an important passage in the third volume of *Capital*—published posthumously and never as well known as the works printed in his lifetime—Marx does admit that we can never fully overcome our bondage to nature. The most we can hope for is to reach the point at which toil ("necessary labor") will be rationally and cooperatively administered:

> . . . the realm of freedom actually begins only where labor which is determined by necessity and mundane considerations ceases; thus in the very nature of things it lies beyond the sphere of actual material production. . . . Freedom in this field can only consist in socialized man, the associated producers, rationally regulating their interchange with nature . . . and achieving this with the least expenditure of energy. . . . But it nonetheless still remains a realm of necessity. Beyond it begins that development of human energy which is an end in itself, the true realm of freedom, which, however, can blossom forth only with this realm of necessity as its basis. The shortening of the working day is its basic prerequisite.[4]

The qualification may seem a small matter. Marx himself seems to think it is. After all, it is unreasonable to expect social ideals to be attained with Platonic perfection. Why should it not be enough for us to realize them approximately?

And indeed, cautious as Marx sometimes is when it comes to the *total* eradication of alienated labor, he seems convinced that communist society will witness its virtual elimination—its minimization or (as I will say) "marginalization." Such labor will, he seems to suggest, no longer play a significant role in limiting human development.

This can be seen in a passage that probably represents the most circumspect and balanced statement of Marx's view in this regard. In this text, from the *Grundrisse* of 1857–58. Marx is elaborating upon his claim that, under communism, automation will largely replace "direct" human labor:

> As soon as labor in its direct form has [owing to automation] ceased to be the main source of wealth, then labor time ceases, and must cease, to be its standard of measurement. . . . Production based on exchange value [i.e., monetary value in the marketplace] therefore falls apart, and the immediate process of material production finds itself stripped of its impoverished and antagonistic form. Individuals are then in a position to develop freely. It is no longer a question [as it was under capitalism] of reducing the necessary labor time in order to create surplus labor [hence profits], but of *reducing the necessary labor to a minimum.*[5]

Only when we can approximate this Promethean result can we make a creative and gratifying life available to all. This occurs through the gradual development of automated production.

The species breaks its back in the process of building a technology capable of freeing it, in the end, from backbreaking labor. Our Promethean sufferings produce a world in which such sufferings can occupy an ever-diminishing portion of our time. The historical process is completed only when we have machines to do our bidding.

If we are to become masters over the machine, we must first be servants to it. Only because *we* have engaged in alienated work can we find out how *things* work; and only so, can we put such "things"—thoughtless automata—to work in our place.

Alienation, thus understood, is not inherent in "the human condition," but rather is due to the exigencies of industrial development. It must exist wherever we lack immediate means for converting drudgery into machine-routine: *in*human labor into *non*human labor.

While society is still only in the development phase, tedious and repetitive labor falls to human workers. This is a world of economic privation: for, of necessity, the conditions of universal creativity and gratification are temporarily in short supply, and therefore cannot yet be made universally available.

But finally we overcome our servitude to nature: we are able to direct natural processes to our own ends. The conditions of the emancipated life now fall under our control, and indeed can be made available to all.

Work need no longer be coerced. Once upon a time, it was shunned like the plague. Now it has become coterminous with creativity itself: our fulfillment rather than our negation.

Thus sounds the death knell of alienated labor. Prometheus can, at long last, be released from his bondage.

2. The Temporary Necessity of Capitalism

Viewing history from these Promethean heights, Marx is able to offer an account of capitalism's temporary usefulness. If, he reasons, culture is to take the most direct route to emancipation, it must pass through a penultimate, transitional phase in which material privileges are rationed in accordance with the logic of the market.

In such a world, material incentives are a primary means of motivating productive behavior. The elements of a fully rewarding productive life are still in short supply. There is no option about "coercion" itself: there must be a "struggle for existence" whether we like it or not. The only option concerns whether we exploit that struggle rationally: whether we make a virtue of necessity by administering and structuring competition so as to stimulate development. We can do this only by adopting a procedure that apportions the goods of life in rough accord with people's productive contributions.

Especially in the latter stages of society's development toward the fully industrialized stage, a competitive, money-based economy has the peculiar advantage of imposing the rigors of efficiency accounting upon labor. Capitalism *rations* goods in accordance with the austere logic of "wage labor," and in so doing ruthlessly ensures that rational investment continues.[6]

This regime must be in place until capitalism has itself generated wealth sufficient to render the logic of rationing obsolete, and a fully creative life possible for all.

Thus, as long as privation prevails, Marx resembles an orthodox apologist for capitalism. Communism, he believes, presupposes the industrial development wrought by capitalist methods. Until such development nears completion, the market system itself is the most advanced economic system. Capitalism is the natural precursor of communism itself.

We must not read Marx's citation of the accomplishments of the bourgeois epoch—in *The Communist Manifesto* and elsewhere—as merely sardonic.[7] Marx was in earnest about this: he not only praised capitalism in his writings; he allied himself with it in the actual field of struggle. During the revolutions of 1848, for example, when there was in his view no question (especially in his native Germany) that society might take an immediate leap to communism, he sided forthrightly with the progressive bourgeoisie against the far more backward aristocratic elements still in power.

In this vein, Marx takes a "dialectical" position toward the great tradition of "political economy." His treatment of what I will call the "Classical Defense" of capitalism is intentionally and systematically ambivalent.

His response to Adam Smith's formulation of that defense—the "Invisible Hand" doctrine that competition provides the best means of economic allocation—is not that the latter is flatly wrong, but that its truth is limited to the period of economic development. The mistake is in thinking that the conditions which give competitive capitalism its basis are eternal. Marx, equipped with an analysis of the abolition of alienated labor in the advanced industrial context, is convinced that they are temporary (even if protracted).

A "communist" revolution presupposes an advanced technological basis, and this, Marx thinks, can occur only when the fruits of the bourgeois order have already grown ripe. Only then do market methods become obsolete. If Marx permits himself to speak of capitalism with contempt, it is only because he is convinced that, in the world's advanced industrial sector, this ripening of technology is nearing completion. But, until that point is reached, two basic features of capitalism are all but inevitable.

The first is social *classes*. For, as long as society is relatively underdeveloped, human activity clearly must consist mainly in tedious manual work. Correspondingly, there must be a relatively emancipated intelligentsia to manage and direct—to *rule*—the manual workers still necessarily trapped within the conditions of toil.

Only when the need for manual labor has been marginalized by the onward march of industry can classes be superseded. Engels gives this point its classical formulation:

> The separation of society into an exploiting and an exploited class, a ruling and an oppressed class, was the necessary consequence of the deficient and restricted development of production in former times. So long as the total social labor only yields a product which but slightly exceeds that barely necessary for the existence of all; so long, therefore, as labor engages all or almost all the time of the great majority of the members of society—so long, of necessity, this society is divided into classes.[8]

In the second place, Marx assumes, like any orthodox defender of the system, that market *competition* is the single greatest goad to industrial progress, and will prove necessary until an advanced industrial stage is reached. This is what freed us from the severe limitations of the feudal epoch. Despite protectionist resistance, "big industry universalized competition," Marx writes; and in so doing it

> established means of communication and the modern world market. . . . By universal competition it forced all individuals to strain their energy to the utmost. . . . It . . . made all civilized nations and every individual member of them dependent for the satisfaction of their wants on the whole world, thus destroying the former natural exclusiveness of separate nations.[9]

Similar formulations occur elsewhere in his writings. The lengthy paean to capitalism in the *Manifesto*[10] is the most famous, but the more technical discussions in the *Grundrisse*[11] of capitalism's revolutionary accomplishments are of at least equal importance.

Marx's conviction that development occurs most swiftly and rationally under capitalism has been neglected by too many of his admirers, as well as by too many critics. Neophyte socialists are sometimes surprised to discover that Marx himself did not even question the economic inevitability of the imperialist expansion being carried out by the relatively industrialized capitalist sector during his own lifetime. He saw the extension of capitalism, vicious as it might be, as a virtually unavoidable condition of the economic modernization of the globe:

> England, it is true, in causing a social revolution in Hindostan, was actuated only by the vilest interests, and was stupid in her manner of enforcing them. But that is not the question. The question is, can mankind fulfill its destiny without a fundamental revolution in the social state of Asia?[12]

Insofar as the question pertains to the section of history in which underdevelopment is still the rule, Marx's answer to this rhetorical question is unambiguous:

> The bourgeois period of history has to create the material basis of the new world—on the one hand the universal intercourse founded upon the mutual dependency of mankind, and the means of that intercourse; on the other hand the development of the productive powers of man and the transformation of material production into a scientific domination of natural agencies. Bourgeois industry and commerce create these material conditions of a new world in the same way as geological revolutions have created the surface of the earth.[13]

This doctrine has the startling implication that much so-called "Communism"—more properly, *Bolshevism*—of the twentieth century is in many respects contrary to Marx's own treatment of capitalism as an essential phase of human development. Marx died in 1883, more than three decades before the Russian Revolution. Yet his instincts are contrary to Bolshevism by anticipation.

It is a striking fact—always known to scholars, but never given enough attention by them or anyone else—that Marx and Engels explicitly deny that a backwater like Russia could have an indigenous communist revolution in their sense of the term. Anyone who thinks otherwise, says Engels, "only proves that he has still to learn the ABC of socialism."[14] Russia, still mainly agrarian, could have such a revolution only if it occurred in concert with a "revolution . . . in Western Europe, creating for the Russian peasant the preconditions requisite for such a transition. . . ."[15]

In contrast with the Bolshevist line that finally prevailed in 1917, the position taken, decades earlier, by Marx and Engels anticipates the Menshevik line: that, ideology notwithstanding, insofar as technological backwardness continues to be a fact of life in a culture like Russia, there is no real option for it but to pass through a capitalist phase.

The point is not that "state socialist" systems—such as have in fact characterized Eastern-bloc Communism—cannot be brought into existence, but rather that this could not amount to a transition to a communist economy in the proper sense of the term, and might, if prematurely imposed, be economically disastrous.

A real communist revolution would have to be allied with a worldwide upheaval able to seize control of the advanced technology already elaborated in the Western world. Absent such a development, the exploitation of labor cannot be avoided—and things would be better left, for the moment, in the hands of a progressive bourgeoisie.

Marx believes that the society of extraordinary wealth produced by competitive capitalism eventually renders the dog-eat-dog logic of that system obsolete—but that this can come about only after our voyage of scientific-technological discovery has reaped its bounty.

Capitalist austerity is dispensable only after capitalism itself has expanded the infrastructure to the point at which radical automation can become prevalent. Only then can we overcome the strict logic of efficiency accounting and incentives: the requirement that society strive to approximate a correlation between productivity and reward.

Only then can we overcome society's need to hold the goods of life hostage against the limits of a wage. Only then can the benefits of our Promethean journey at last be made available to all, and the tyranny of alienated labor ended:

> When a great social revolution shall have mastered the results of the bourgeois epoch, the market of the world and the modern powers of production, and subjected them to the human control of the most advanced peoples, then only will human progress cease to resemble that hideous pagan idol who would drink nectar only from the skulls of the slain.[16]

3. Automation and the Abolition of Capital

Marx holds that, once Promethean mastery has been attained, long dominant forms of social antagonism lose their rationale. Class division and general contention reach fever pitch in bourgeois society—but Marx asserts: capitalism is "the last antagonistic form of the social process of production."[17]

From a Marxian point of view, social antagonism makes sense when, but only when, the conditions of fully emancipated life-activity are not available to all. If the technological basis for the universalization of the elements of a life free from alienation does not yet exist, the elements of such a lifestyle must be the object of generalized social "envy" and contention. Indeed they must fall to a privileged class.

Thus while society is underdeveloped, alienation prevails, and social

relations necessarily contain the seed of struggle. Sometimes this will take
the form of various tensions festering below the surface. But it is no wonder
that, at other times, these pressures explode in outright violence. The
material basis of such antagonism will, Marx thinks, be eliminated only
when we are able to make the possibility of a creative and a rewarding life
available to all.

Though human antagonism does make sense when socially privileged
positions are in short supply, the automation developed under capitalism
now makes this increasingly pointless.

The productive forces developing in the womb of bourgeois society
create the material conditions for the solution of that antagonism.[18]

Because of capitalism's own ruthless productivity, machines come more
and more to dominate the production process. The point is reached at
which it is possible to reorganize society in such a way that people can share
whatever incidental forms of toil are necessary, without unduly burdening
anyone. The society of privation and rationing can finally be abolished.

But, as we have seen, the logic of capitalism *is* that of privation and
rationing. And that is why capitalism, Moses-like, cannot itself enter the
Promised Land. Capital makes emancipation possible, but emancipation
requires the abolition of capital. A social revolution must do away with
wage labor and competitive "anarchy," putting in their place "the social
regulation of production upon a definite plan, according to the needs of the
community and of each individual."[19] This is communism.

Marxian theory does defend capitalism during the development phase.
But it holds that this phase characterizes only a specific, restricted period of
human history. The period of alienated life-activity reaches its climax in the
rational market system, but the bourgeois system's own ruthless devotion
to increasing automation lays the foundation for a new world order, a
post-development world in which whatever tasks seem noisome and toilsome can be replaced by program-driven automata.

This is the nub of the most characteristically "dialectical" feature of
Marx's view of history. The regime driven by money and classes—
capitalism—is the economically most rational method for the development
of society's productive basis, but this development phase is self-
undermining: capitalism produces out of itself the automated production
which, by and by, renders capitalism itself obsolete.

The point is reached at which the productive potential of human beings
stands to be enhanced rather than diminished by the provision of goods
irrespective of any accounting system by which we keep track of "necessary

labor." As alienated labor becomes obsolete, so does the rationality of ration-ing. Once capitalism has developed technology to an advanced level, efficiency accounting itself becomes a growing menace in the arena of rational social planning. The sophistication of our productive basis is demonstrated by our new-found ability to move beyond the logic of the market.

Technology becomes so advanced that most of the burdens of civilization fall on the shoulders of the machine. Whatever small residuum of alienated life-activity does persist will occupy such a marginal part of human life that it can be administered fairly, in a spirit of social cooperation. The decline of the logic of privation undermines the rationale of social antagonism. The world is free to find more civil methods of mediating whatever disagree-ments may arise.

"Wage labor" loses its rationale. Society is now so wealthy that people now stand to be more productive under conditions of fully voluntary labor—working when and as they please—than they were of old, under the tyranny of economic coercion. The system of envy and conflict leads to its own decline and fall.

Till now, we have been creatures half-immersed in nature. Human social existence has borne the clear earmarks of such a prescientific existence. Since we have not mastered nature scientifically, we have been the play-things of forces outside our control.

Till now, nature and society both have been largely out of our control. If we are to be emancipated from such "primitiveness," our conquest of nature must go hand in hand with the establishment of collective, conscious control over social production. Engels asserts this connection with auda-cious eloquence in a passage that has long served as the locus classicus of the radically Promethean tendency of Marxian thought:

> The whole sphere of the conditions of life which environ man, and which have hitherto ruled man, now comes under the dominion and control of man, who for the first time becomes the real, conscious Lord over Nature, because he has now become master of his own social organiza-tion. . . . Man's own social organization, hitherto confronting him as a necessity imposed by Nature and history, now becomes the result of his own free action. The extraneous objective forces that have hitherto governed history pass under the control of man himself.[20]

4. Marx at Odds with His Own Dialectics of Scarcity

We saw in Chapter 2.1 that Marx's position is not that the drudgery of productive existence can be absolutely eliminated. To some extent, work "remains a realm of necessity"—of toil.

In his more expansive moments, it is true, Marx writes as though we can eventually fully overcome our ignorance of natural processes and have machines do any and all dirty work. But at other times he tones down this extravagant claim—though only slightly. Speaking (as we may assume) more circumspectly, Marx allows that alienation, in the strict sense of unpleasant labor, can never be reduced to absolute zero. There will always be a residuum of such labor that has not been entirely transcended by automation, no matter how far technology progresses.

Marx's disquiet (if it is that) ends there. For he is convinced that alienated labor can gradually be reduced, even so, to marginal significance. Because "communism" will "essentially" or "virtually" eliminate drudgery, it will, in that sense, be the dawn of a form of social existence based upon the "all-round development" of all individuals.

But problems lurk an inch or two beneath the surface of such rhetoric: it is where our own disquiet begins. Marx's vacillation on this point leads us to suspect the presence of a deeper difficulty—a problem with the very idea that alienated labor is a transient phenomenon.

If Marx had looked at matters more closely, he might have begun to wonder if alienated labor, far from being marginalized, is the sort of thing that could be "virtually" abolished at all. He might, that is, have begun to take more seriously the more radically "dialectical" proposition that the overcoming of one form of alienation is the creation of another.

The basis for such a revision can be seen in aspects of Marx's own work that we have already considered. Here we discern a basic contradiction in Marxian social theory.

We saw in Chapter 1.4 that communism's founder is satisfied that scarcity and alienation are separable issues. It is another question whether we ourselves can be similarly satisfied. However much Marx might try to divide the issue between scarcity (which he allows is perennial) and drudgery (which he believes is not) the distinction itself will ultimately not hold up. His belief that alienation might be marginalized is irreparably at odds with the deeper implications of his own dialectical conviction that "scarcity" is a historically sublimated factor.

Marx himself insists that the satisfaction of needs at one level always yields newer, even greater needs. And so he admits that "scarcity" is a historically relative thing. And so it is. But what he does not see is that this does indeed imply that "alienated labor" is likewise historically relative: the "dialectical" treatment of scarcity, endorsed by Marx himself, undermines the idea that it might ever become a marginal aspect of human existence.

The connection between scarcity and the alienation of labor is immediate and intimate; indeed, they come down to quite the same thing. Because the one cannot be marginalized, neither can the other. We must now examine this fundamental inconsistency in Marx's conception.

Even if all people could eventually become creative and hence disalienated by current standards, it does not follow—nor is it true—that they could experience this creativity as nonalienated without qualification: for a new standard or paradigm of creative fulfillment would already have arisen on the foundation of the old.

The reasons are rooted in Marx's own belief that scarcity is a dialectically recurrent feature of social history, inherent in our very creativity. Just because we can never reach a stage at which all the elements determining the fully rewarding "good life" have been made simultaneously abundant, we will always be able to see before us on the horizon the image of a more gratifying form of "life-activity"—*of labor itself.*

We will always be able to envision a future having forms of "freedom" we now lack. As long as we remain creative, we will always feel the lack of conditions that would make our working life even more creative. To convince ourselves of this, we need only consider an example from our own period of history.

Once upon a time, if a memorandum needed some reworking, a secretary faced the time-consuming and boring task of retyping the entire thing. The word-processing revolution, by making revision and reformatting so easy, has done away with much of the tedium that characterized the "alienation" of that earlier phase of secretarial labor.

We reach a stage in productive development at which a certain type of programmable routine has become part of the automatic repertoire of the species. With the achievement of such mastery, a particular type of drudgery is transcended.

But the very advances in computer technology that free secretarial labor from prior forms of tedium, are but one aspect of a revolution that creates even more ambitious technological dreams. The success of the micro-processor means that society's technological benchmark itself has shifted. The advance creates a new baseline of automated routine. And just because it does so, it also carries, on its own shoulders, the promise of a new technology that is in the process of formation.

Let us complete our own example. Computer technology has given us the word processor, and this solves a problem of productive tedium that characterized an earlier time. But the sophistication of computer technology that made such a feat possible now places the possibility of parallel processing—and of office machines that can take voice dictation—on the horizon. The more realistic these new forms of emancipation are, the more sense it makes to complain about the "drudgery" of the present that might be technologically transcended. These are, presumably, the tales that the coming decades will tell.

Or, to vary the example: at the beginning of this century, the word "drudgery" would have described sweatshop labor and the like. If those who ruined their eyes and backs (and shortened their lives) in those drear and dangerous places could futuristically have imagined what it would be like to work in a fast-food restaurant, 1990s style, they would no doubt have regarded the latter—with its air-conditioned, fire-safe environment, eight-hour days, employee insurance plans, and what not—as a veritable paradise.

By today's standards, fast-food workers certainly do not epitomize "emancipated labor." The point, rather, is that the material character of "drudgery" is itself transformed with each step of the historical dialectic.

"Drudgery"—"alienated labor"—is itself a thoroughly historically relative category. It is only relative to the not-yet-fulfilled prospects of emergent emancipation that its antithesis, "alienation," makes any sense. Each phase of technological mastery necessarily opens up technological vistas of the yet-to-be-mastered. Each epoch must have its own version of "alienated labor."

What Promethean writers from Marx through Kropotkin to Gorz fail to see is that the relevant sense of "alienation" is a forward-looking one, in which our discontents are always measured against the promise of the future. What makes a form of activity mere "work," in the sense of an endeavor one would rather have taken over by a machine, is that some better way of life, freed from that complained-about aspect of "alienation," can be realistically conceived and put on the historical agenda.

But, just because this is so, we always experience the quality of our life-activity as lower than it might be. However we lead our productive lives, however we *labor*, there will always be a sense in which we feel *alienated*. The conditions of labor, as of everything else in life, are such that, as long as we work and plan and transform our world, we will—we must—always yearn for an even more gratifying life.

Assuming that the disalienation of labor, as our epoch conceives it, really is achieved, a future society will take this as its point of departure, and will on this basis project its own unfulfilled agenda. And so it, too, will feel itself to be living "in alienation" until *those* goals are achieved. Such achievement always defines a new historical "baseline" relative to which ever new projects, defining ever new forms of alienation, must arise.

We saw in Chapter 1.3 that Marx rejects the Malthusian theme that scarcity is inherent in the limits of the world's resources. We may join Marx in this judgment. Consistently with this anti-Malthusian stance, our suggestion of "inevitable alienation" has nothing to do with the pessimistic view that there are any technological limits to the emancipation of labor. Let us grant: there is no particular form of alienated labor that cannot be transcended.

The alienation of labor, understood in the forward-looking dialectical sense, is rather a consequence of the assumption that our species's journey of technological discovery is ongoing. It is this fact of incessant creativity which implies that there will always be some aspects of creative work which are in the process of formation. Indeed, because such alienation is inherent in the forward-looking character of human creativity itself, it makes no sense to lament the general condition of "alienated labor." It is reasonable for us to complain about any given condition of work; but to escape alienated labor, one would have to flee from the inventive project of the species.

If that project is, as we hope, interminable, then we must indeed *hope* that alienation—the yearning after better conditions of life-activity—is itself without end.

Here we come up against one of the ironies of Marx's own achievement. When it comes to scarcity itself, Marx seems to see the need for a fully "dialectical," forward-looking theory: he sees that the relevant point of comparison is the not-yet-attained future that we are always in the business of projecting. But when it comes to alienated labor as such, he seems to lapse into a curiously backward-looking approach.

If Marx had faced squarely the implications of his own dialectical treatment of scarcity, he would have seen that the wish to overcome "alienated labor"—in the more plausible, forward-looking sense of the term—is to wish to disengage oneself from the ongoing process of discovery of new forms of emancipation.

Marx is right: "alienated labor" is work that we would, for good reason, prefer to be done by machines.

He is right: technological advance can free us from the forms of drudgery now prevailing. This is indeed true at every stage. When we move from simple tools to complex, steam-driven machines, a radical emancipatory leap becomes possible. The same is true when we move from the age of steam to that of microchips and supercomputers. We have, each step of the way, a gradual replacement of unpleasant tasks through technological innovation.

Yet every age will have its own conception of the distinction between drudgery and rewarding labor. The very same technology that abolishes alienated labor in one way, opens it up in another. If we have just eliminated a given aspect of human drudgery—by making unheard-of levels of human existence possible for the first time—there will emerge other problems which it will be the task of the present phase of development, the phase we are just now passing through, to solve.

Our concrete discontents are rooted in our aims for the future—in the never-ending condition of discovery rather than in the alleged pull of our "primitive" past. If Marx had seen this, he would have had to face up to the conclusion that "development," in the strict Marxian sense of the overcoming of alienation, is no mere "phase" of human history, but an ongoing, endless process.

We are always, at one level or another, in a "developmental phase"—are always in the process of overcoming "alienated labor." The character of the real, and (relative to it) the ideal, is constantly shifting. But since it makes no sense to say that we could ever overcome the essential discrepancy *between* reality and ideality, we must rather say that alienation is constantly sublimated but never eliminated: it changes its specific form through the endless development of industry.

Relative to whatever historical baseline has been established, there will always be important "elements of the life of full creativity" which are, in the judgment of that epoch, in short supply. There will always be discontents attendant to our productive life: discontents as "radical" to us, by our own standards, as the discontents of earlier cultures were to them. What Marx does not clearly see is that we are, in a historically relative sense, always "technologically backward," always "impoverished," by comparison to the next phase of technological discovery.

Every age has, if you will, its Promethean task—its own idea of the now-transcendent Zeus who must, in time, be forced to yield to our demands. But each successful overthrow of Zeus sets the stage, creates the need, for a phoenix-like rebirth of Prometheus on a new dialectical level— and hence also for a new Zeus, representing a future emancipation not yet attained. The secrets of the gods are forever being stolen.

5. *Marx contra Marx*

There is much in Marx's visionary idea that really can help unlock doors to an emancipated future. Marx sees that the accomplishments of advanced capitalism are beginning to make possible a form of social existence that is a quantum leap beyond most people's wildest dreams. In raising high his Promethean banner in the impossible pursuit of the overthrow of alienated labor, he has some intuitions about the next stage of society that may prove far from impossible. We will ourselves defend the very radical claim that social classes are—in a sense dear to Marx himself—becoming obsolete.

But we have rejected the Marxian conviction that a close approximation to a life of full creativity can become everyone's birthright. The alienation of labor is rooted in scarcity—and so it, like scarcity, is historically relative and ongoing. And this is no mere quibble. Our disagreement with Marx's treatment of the feasibility of overcoming alienation opens the possibility of a radically different view of the historical destiny of capital.

We saw in Chapter 2.2 that Marx himself believes that, given society's need to impose the logic of rationing and incentives while privation still prevails, capitalism is essential to the project of "development" beyond "alienated labor." Marx is convincing on this score. Utopian schemes seem naive because, in such contexts, they ignore the incentives to productivity availed by competitive capitalism. The austere logic of capital is suited to cultures in which privation obtains, in which a fully creative and fulfilling form of "life activity" cannot be made available to all.

But Marx has failed to convince us that "development"—the overcoming of the scarce conditions of an emancipated life—is itself only a temporary economic problem. He builds his case for socialization on the premise that capitalism creates the technology that can bring alienated labor to an end. Because he thinks that automation-based communism marginalizes such privation, he can envision a world without discrepancies in people's access to the elements of the life of full creativity. For Marx, such differences belong to the developmental phase of human history in which we are still in bondage to nature—the "phase" he thinks is coming to an end.

By contrast, a dialectical understanding of privation has led us to reject the idea that there is a specific "development phase" of history during which the logic of "alienated labor" is gradually eroded. It seems, rather, that "alienated labor" is always sublimated from one level to the next, and hence that social "development" is itself incessant.

To put these points together is indeed to turn Marx's own defense of capitalism against him. If he is right about the need for capital during development, but wrong in viewing development as merely temporary, we must begin to wonder if capitalism does not have an enduring rationale.

The logic of incentives seems particularly inescapable. Since there will always be some elements of disalienated labor in short supply, some form of impoverishment to overcome, society will *always* have good reason to use these elements to motivate the production of an even higher stage of social wealth. If we must presume development, and so also society's ongoing interest in improving productive technique, then the "rationality of rationing"—of establishing some correlation between productivity and reward—can never be entirely beside the point.[21] We begin to suspect that this feature is no temporary expedient, as Marx supposed, but is, in one form or another, a characteristic of social life as such.

Since Marx does not succeed in showing that there could be such a thing as post-privation society, the idea of a world beyond the logic of productive incentives seems a chimera inconsistent with a persevering and plausible dialecticism.

But this, if true, would mean that, by Marx's own standards, the coercion of labor cannot be eliminated. For the enforcement of desirable patterns of productive behavior *is* the coercion of labor—given Marx's own persuasive treatment of this phenomenon. Here we recall[22] that it is Marx himself who, in his exposé of bourgeois ideology, enables us to see that material freedom within a functioning economic system is not a simple matter of allowing everyone to have the same abstract contractual rights. Freedom under capitalist society is necessarily limited by the degree to which "economic punishment" is constantly meted out in order to motivate appropriate patterns of human behavior.

There is only one thing that can permit Marx to conclude that a noncoercive society is possible: his quixotic conviction that development climaxes in the marginalization of the conditions underlying an unfulfilled productive existence. Only then would incentives become superfluous.

But Marx is wrong in thinking that society's "development phase" might ever come to an end. And this lets us put the coup de grâce to his claim that the coercion of labor is a historically transient phenomenon. If toilsome labor is historically relative and hence perennial, so must be the rationale by which we motivate such labor in accordance with the logic of material incentives and, in that sense, impose "punishments" on those we do not deem productive.

6. Privation and Coercion as "Moments of Motion"

Let us take stock. We have supposed that Marx is right about society's need to motivate productivity by means of incentives as long as development proceeds, and right in claiming that a system of incentives is a veiled system of punishment—of coercion.

We have only insisted that we can no longer believe that there is any meaningful sense in which economic development ever *does* come to an end.

We must therefore conclude: economic coercion, subtle as it may be, is itself a permanent feature of economic life, inherent in social existence as such. It is not, as Marx thought it was, a historical and contemporary reality ultimately destined to pass from the world scene.

We have argued that it is always possible for us to raise the absolute standards of life, and so to shift the line between poverty and wealth—

between alienated and emancipated forms of life activity. The types of coercion and unfreedom that afflict one time can give way to much more subtle kinds of enforcement—forms of force which are, in absolute terms, far less onerous than those that went before.

Slavery must be regarded as a great curse to those who are able to push beyond it. The same may be said of the manorial system of the Middle Ages—as well as of the factory system of the nineteenth century, which made such a deep impression on the thought of Marx and Engels.

And if the argument of Part Two of this book turns out to be even faintly sound, our own age has the opportunity to undergo a social transformation that is, by its own standards, every bit as profound and far-reaching. We will always need genuine revolutionaries: people able to see the emancipatory steps possible in their time, and willing to help humankind to take them.

Marx shows that the freedom brought about by capitalism is, if more refined than what preceded it, nonetheless a form of force appropriate to that system's own peculiar logic, to its own more sophisticated level of social organization.

The point is an important one, and ought to be granted without qualification. And Marx is right about another thing as well: our own form of capitalist society may, through hard work and good luck, give way to a new society able to pride itself on forms of force that are even more subtle and less cruel than any before. This would be a revolutionary accomplishment.

The "sublimation" of force is always possible. We can move away from the relative crudity of the past and into the possible refinement of the future.

What does not seem possible is the complete elimination of coercive labor as a generic feature of social life.

The coming society, radically liberatory as it may be, will not only have new and better ideals than ours; it will also have new and better ways of motivating their attainment. But that is precisely why we must expect that there will be incentives and sanctions—forms of force—relevant to that society's own level of development.

Our thinking, in these respects, is broadly Hegelian.

In his "Critique of the Hegelian Dialectic and Philosophy as a Whole," Marx observes that, in the approach taken by Hegel in the *Philosophy of Right*,

> private right, morality, the family, civil society, the state, etc., remain in existence, only they have become *moments* of man—states of his existence and being—which have no validity in isolation, but dissolve and engender one another, etc. They have become *moments of motion*.[23]

Marx's interpretation is right: Hegel does believe that, in one form or another, these generic features are to be found in any social system.

Marx sees that this does not have the static implications one might think it has. For these factors are, in Hegel's hands, *persistent* ways of grasping the essential *dynamism* of social life. For example, out of the unending interaction between civil society (the sphere of privacy, property, and individuality) and the state (the domain of centralized political authority) there are indeed "engendered" altered specific forms of these same generic factors.

For Hegel, the distinction between the private ("civil society") and public ("the state") cannot be eliminated: these are "moments of motion" of social life itself. The incessant interplay of the private and public produces ever new relations between the public and private.

Thus speaks Hegel; but Marx wishes to break entirely with the civil-society-cum-state constellation. Attachment to this constellation is, in Marx's view, an aspect of Hegelian "uncritical positivism":[24] it marks the spot at which Hegel tries to impose his own political conservatism upon social dynamics as such.

Thus, where Hegel is able to see civil society and the state as ever-present if ever-sublimated realities, Marx is led to proclaim that these phenomena are historically local, bourgeois factors: a sphere of private accumulation and "greed" backed by a coercive political authority. Marx holds that these factors are destined to be superseded, in the post-privation world, by a society wealthy enough to organize itself on a noncompetitive, communitarian, and fully voluntary basis.

Marx is right: Hegel is committed to the view that the essential tensions and conflicts underlying civil society and the state are with us to stay. That, to Marx, is one way of summarizing what is wrong with Hegel. But to us, it reveals the need to split the difference between the conservatism of Hegel and the radicalism of Marx.

Marx is right insofar as he calls our attention to the fact that we can, indeed must, always ask what specific steps might be taken to ameliorate the specific conditions under which people interact. And he is right to criticize Hegel for lamely rationalizing some of these conditions. There indeed are some aspects of Hegel's vision of a rational society that we cannot read today without a smile: his attempt, for example, in *The Philosophy of Right*, to "prove" that a rationally ordered society needs to be surmounted by a monarch.[25]

Marx is right to interrogate any such specific Hegelian claim. As a revolutionary, he is right to call for radical changes in the contemporary social landscape. There is not a thing wrong with revolutionism as such.

But there is something very wrong about a revolutionism that takes itself to be the consummating historical act, and builds an impossibly utopian economic conception upon that faulty basis.

We neo-Hegelians have no difficulty distancing ourselves from Hegel's actual conservatism. And yet we insist that there is nothing inherently conservative about his underlying approach. We believe, moreover, that Hegel comes closer to the truth than Marx in thinking that privation, competition, and coercion are, though always displaced to newer and higher levels, recurrent "moments" of social existence, never to be eliminated.

They are indeed "moments of motion," just as Hegel said. By suggesting that these factors might be swept into the dustbin of history, Marx leaves himself open to the charge of having abdicated one of the chief insights of dialectical social theory.

Notes

1. Marx's son-in-law Paul Lafargue tells us that "Marx read Aeschylus in the original Greek text at least once a year." Cited in Mehring, Franz, *Karl Marx: The Story of His Life* (London: 1936), p. 503. Marx was indeed strongly identified in the public imagination with the figure of Prometheus. To cite just one well-known example: the drawing of the young Marx as a Prometheus-in-chains, published shortly after the Prussian censoring of the radical paper *Rheinische Zeitung*, of which Marx had been editor.
2. Marx, "Contribution to the Critique of Hegel's *Philosophy of Right*: Introduction" (1843), in *The Marx-Engels Reader*, ed. Tucker, Robert (New York: 1978), p. 54. Hereafter referred to as "Tucker."
3. A credit is due here to Mary Wollstonecraft Shelley—and not just because I have borrowed the words of my chapter title, "The Modern Prometheus" from the subtitle of her *Frankenstein*. For indeed, this novel, published in 1816, two years before Marx's birth, has "Promethean" resonances somewhat similar to those found a bit later in Marx's work. The fate of Victor Frankenstein can be treated as an elaborate trope on the "alienation" inherent in scientific-technical intelligence: by the product of our genius are we slain. Marx, of course, is convinced that this alienation, though quite real, is historically transitory; Mary Shelley is content to remain systematically ambiguous, or open, on this point.
4. Marx, *Capital*, Vol. III, ed. Engels, Friedrich (New York: 1967), p. 820.
   Marx, in his Hegel-intoxicated youth, used the term "alienated labor" to capture this broad sense of inescapable drudgery, while the allegedly more sober Marx of later years tended to prefer "socially necessary labor." These phrases may be used interchangeably here.
5. McLellan, David, ed., *The Grundrisse of Karl Marx* (New York: 1971), p. 142. Emphasis mine. My interpretation of Marx in this chapter rests on this premise that the *Grundrisse* is the most balanced and comprehensive statement of Marx's view of capitalism as the last—and most rational—stage in the formation of the automated production that finally frees us from toil. This text is available in

English in an unabridged version: trans. Nicolaus, Martin (Middlesex: 1973). But even scholarly readers will rejoice in McLellan's collection of excerpts. Since, in the latter, much of the very technical economic analysis is omitted, the underpinning "Promethean sweep" of the Marxian conception is even closer to the surface. If ever an abridgement served a useful purpose, this is it.

6. This theme is fundamental to Marxian economics, and will be familiar to all readers of *Capital* and the *Grundrisse*. A nice exposition of this and related points can be found in J. E. Elliott's "Marx's *Grundrisse*: Vision of Capitalism's Creative Destruction," *Journal of Post Keynesian Economics*, vol. 1 (2) (Winter 1978–79), pp. 148–69.

7. Shlomo Avineri, in his Introduction to *Karl Marx on Colonialization and Modernization* (Garden City: 1969), remarks that Marx is able, in *The Communist Manifesto*, "to sing, tongue in cheek, the praises of the bourgeoisie" (pp. 2–3). If my understanding of Marx is right, Marx's song is not quite tongue-in-cheek.

8. Engels, *Socialism: Utopian and Scientific*, in Tucker, p. 714. Spelling has been Americanized.

9. Marx, *The German Ideology*, Part I, Tucker, p. 185.

10. Tucker, pp. 475–78.

11. See especially sections 9, 11, and 15 of McLellan.

12. Ibid., p. 94.

13. Ibid., p. 138.

14. Engels, "On Social Relations in Russia," Tucker, p. 666.

15. Ibid., p. 673. Marx and Engels express a similar thought in their Preface to the 1882 Russian Edition of the *Manifesto*: "If the Russian Revolution becomes the signal for a proletarian revolution in the West, so that both complement each other, the present Russian common ownership of land [among the peasants] may serve as the starting point for a communist development" (Tucker, p. 472).

16. Avineri, *Karl Marx on Colonialization and Modernization*, pp. 138–39. Translation slightly revised.

17. Marx, Preface to *A Contribution to the Critique of Political Economy*, Tucker, p. 5.

18. Ibid., p. 5.

19. Engels, *Socialism: Utopian and Scientific*, Tucker, p. 712.

20. Ibid., p. 715.

21. The only way one could escape this conclusion, it seems to me, is by opposing the logic of incentives and rationing on ethical or "Christian" grounds. That is what I meant when I said that this avenue is not open to Marx so long as he stays within the bounds of anything resembling Historical Materialism.

22. See Chapter 1.2.

23. Tucker, p. 119.

24. Ibid., p. 111.

25. Hegel, *The Philosophy of Right*, trans. Knox, T. M. (London: 1952), pp. 179–88.

3

Speculation and Surplus Value: Marx and the Failure of Orthodox Communist Theory

1. Alienation as Expropriation

We have so far rejected Marx's notion that human history is characterized by a development beyond the conditions of drudgery. It may seem that, given the failure of this idea, communist theory is undermined beyond any possible redemption or salvation.

But in reality, most "orthodox" communists will not be terribly impressed. For there is yet another understanding of communism—one underlying the most familiar forms of twentieth-century Marxism—that is also suggested by Marx's own work. From this latter perspective, the discussion thus far may seem to leave Historical Materialism's main defenses unassailed.

For the purposes of the present chapter, we may indeed imagine the communist to concede that Marx may have been wrong in thinking we might ever abolish drudgery. She might grant that this is a historically relative, incessantly sublimated aspect of human life, and that Marx's tendency to believe otherwise is "utopian."

She might therefore concede that any conception of communism that tries to do away with the coercive aspect of the management of labor is likewise utopian. A system of incentives—and the differential rewards (that is, inequalitarianism) such a system implies—may well be an essential aspect of any form of economic organization.

But, our communist might insist, this utopian dimension of Marx's thinking is not enough to prove the failure of the most important element of his revolutionary project. For even if we must jettison the more extreme form of Marxian Prometheanism, there may be other, sounder, defenses of the communist ideal prominent in Marx's own work.

Perhaps "alienated labor" can be eliminated; but, if so, it will be in some other sense of the term. On the alternative Marxian approach that we must now consider, the essence of "alienation" centers upon the exploitation or (more precisely) expropriation that obtains whenever the product of my own hands is allowed to become the property of another.

This sense of "alienation" closely corresponds to the legalistic sense of "alienation" (as "transfer of property"). The idea we must consider, in a nutshell, is that both the relevant meaning of "alienation," and the possibility of its overthrow, are supplied by the "Theory of Surplus Value," the doctrine that forms the argumentative center of Marx's attack, in his economic works, upon the bourgeois order. However "utopian" Marx may be in other respects, the more sober treatment of expropriation we find in *Capital* may be enough to vindicate his claim to having pinpointed the source of social alienation.

The theory to be examined in the present chapter centers upon the (alleged) phenomenon of sheer expropriation: the distinction between (A) those who produce but do not receive the full product of their labor, and (B) those who do not labor but who nonetheless reap the lion's share of the product of those that do. I will call this approach the "Economic Theory" of classes and alienation.

The argument thus far, our communist might suspect, loses much of its power if this apparently less utopian conception of alienation is kept in mind. Communists need not maintain that we might ever marginalize unpleasant labor, or thoroughly eliminate incentive-based coercion of labor—but only that we could eliminate the expropriative relation that constitutes the core of class differences, especially under capitalism. They need not argue that economic development comes to an end, in order to defend the claim that capitalist social organization eventually loses its raison d'être.

Communism itself need not set itself up as the system suited to a world beyond privation and development—but simply as the means of finally putting the ongoing project of development itself on a rational footing. When "the social anarchy of production gives place to a social regulation of production upon a definite plan,"[1] the logic of exploitation and expropriation can finally be undermined, and the state itself can "wither away."

It would be easy to make a travesty of this notion of the "withering away" of the state" by taking it to mean that communist society, as conceived by Marx, utterly lacks a decision procedure for getting the collective business of society done. That would indeed be a silly idea of the future, but it is not what Marxists intend. What "withers away" is rather the need for what Lenin calls a "special apparatus"[2] of political repression:

[U]nder capitalism we have the state in the proper sense of the word, that is, a special machine for the suppression of one class by another . . . [T]he exploiters are unable to suppress the people without a highly complex machine for performing this task . . . [O]nly communism makes the state absolutely unnecessary, for there is *nobody* to be suppressed—"nobody" in the sense of a *class*, of a systematic struggle against a definite section of the population.[3]

Under communism, it is precisely the existence of a nonclass-based, cooperative decision procedure (a "state" in what is to Lenin not the "proper" sense) that makes the "state" in the strict and narrow sense (imposition of class interests by force) a thing of the past.

2. Expropriation as Surplus Value

Marxism actually contains two theories of class. According to one, class differences are a fundamental aspect of the division of labor: the distinction between those trapped in largely unrewarding manual labor, and those free to develop their more properly human, mental functions.

This theory is prominent in the more general, sociological treatments of the trajectory of technology, from *The German Ideology* through the *Grundrisse* to *Socialism: Utopian and Scientific*. We may therefore call it Marx's "Sociological Theory" of class. It was presumed earlier (in Chapter 2.2) in our discussion of Marx's conviction that capitalism is temporarily necessary, and will indeed prove useful to our own argument in Part Two of this study.

Insofar as Marx applies such an analysis to the conditions of modern capitalism, he must conclude that both the proletariat and the bourgeoisie typically have essential work to do. He must conceive the visibly evident "directly productive labor" of the "working class"[4] as complemented by the various sorts of mental labor of the capitalist class. The bourgeoisie's mental work might not constitute "direct" labor, but it would nonetheless be essential to the overall production process, at least during the capitalist phase of history.

The Sociological Theory is not committed to the silly idea that everything the bourgeoisie does is justified. Engels rightly observes that the necessity of the mental-manual division of labor

> does not prevent this division of classes from being carried out by means of violence and robbery, trickery and fraud. It does not prevent the ruling class, once having the upper hand, from consolidating its power at the expense of the working class, from turning its social leadership into an intensified exploitation of the masses.[5]

And of course the point is well taken. Class privileges can be abused—extended and exaggerated far beyond any historical justification. No doubt capitalists have been guilty of myriad forms of such abuse.

Even so, the Sociological Theory is committed to the view that, within proper bounds, the capitalists perform essential functions. Insofar as the system is performing within those limits, there seems nothing exploitative or expropriative about it. The mental labor of the bourgeoisie is labor indeed. And to that extent, as Engels puts it, the "division into classes has a certain historical justification."[6]

Though it is the Sociological approach that is (in my view) ultimately more useful in helping us see the grounds and limits of social class, it is the Economic Theory that predominates in Marx's work—and which will form our focus in this chapter. This approach is rooted in the Theory of Surplus Value—the theoretical heart and soul of Marx's most influential text, *Capital*.[7] Though the theory is there given a quantitative presentation, a qualitative understanding will allow us to grasp the main claim of concern to us here: that what the capitalist does should not count as "labor" at all.[8]

The profound difference between the Sociological and Economic approaches can perhaps be most clearly discerned in a passage from the famous seventh chapter of *Capital*. Marx, taking a yarn manufacturer as his example, rejects, one by one, the capitalist's claims to have made a real contribution to the production process. The imagined capitalist makes one last stand:

> Our [capitalist] friend, up to this time so purse-proud, suddenly assumes the modest demeanor of his own workman, and exclaims: "Have I myself not worked? Have I not performed the labor of superintendence and of overseeing the spinner? And does not this labor, too, create value?" His overlooker and his manager try to hide their smiles. Meanwhile, after a hearty laugh, he re-assumes his usual mien. . . . He leaves this and all such like subterfuges and juggling tricks to the professors of Political Economy, who are paid for it. . . .[9]

Marx accordingly depicts the capitalist as a despicable "Mr. Moneybags" (his own term[10]): a social parasite who apparently can find nothing better to do than to speculate on the stock market, clip coupons, spout ideological claptrap—and leave all the real work to his hired hands.

On the Economic Theory, unlike the Sociological, the capitalist does not count as a worker; rather, as owner of the business, he is the one that hires both manual and mental workers. Mental labor is of course necessary, but it is provided by overseers and managers, and so is just another form of wage labor, even if somewhat better remunerated.

I have been careful to say "the capitalist as such," for it is of course possible for one and the same person to function in the role of both capitalist and manager. In that event he is, strictly speaking, both (a) the employer of workers and (b) one of those workers. Wearing the first hat, he is a capitalist, and he reaps profits. Donning the second, his work counts as labor in the ordinary sense, and he draws a salary, "just like everybody else." Since the capitalist's "wage bill" represents all such payments to labor, it includes payment for the managerial work that he may employ himself to do.

Both mental and manual work are, in the Economic Theory, labor in the strict sense: productive human activity. Only after the bill for such labor has been paid in full, do we get to "profits" as such. Thus, assuming the wage bill has been paid, the remaining profits cannot, by hypothesis, amount to payments for labor.

And indeed there is, in the Economic Theory, no room for the notion of capitalist "labor" per se. The margin between the value *produced* by productive mental and manual workers and the value *received* by those same workers counts as a pure surplus which capitalists are not obliged to pay their workers. Though such "surplus value" is the property of the capitalist to dispose of as he likes, the Economic Theory does not permit us to consider this as remuneration for services rendered.

This is not to say that the capitalist does nothing. He invests; and investment is essential to social development.[11] In any expanding economy, society must, to expand its productive base, make sure not to consume all of what it produces. This means, from a macroeconomic viewpoint, that the total value of society's production must exceed the total paid out to all types of labor in the form of wages and salaries.

The profits reinvested by capitalists are in this sense the key to industrial expansion. Indeed, in a competitive scenario, the capitalist *must* reinvest most profits, at pain of losing his edge in the marketplace. Luxury consumption, though a familiar reality, cannot be the primary trajectory of profits, nor the principal determinant of the behavior of capitalists. That is one of the main reasons why the competitive scenario characteristic of capitalism is, in Marx's view, so useful during the period of development: the omnipresent threat of ruin imposes the austerities of efficiency rationing.

During this entire period, the purchasing power awarded to labor, in the form of wages, will tend to be neither more nor less than that necessary to maintain that labor's effectiveness. Anything less would fail to maintain labor's effectiveness and so be counterproductive. Anything more would amount to nonproductive consumption and so would be irrationally squandered: it would, from the point of view of any capitalist, be better spent in the expansion and improvement of plant and machinery.

The Sociological and Economic accounts can agree that "profit" denotes returns on capital as such. But they veer sharply apart in their accounts of what "capital" *is*.

Applied to modern capitalism in particular, the Sociological Theory bids us consider as the *differentia specifica* of ruling classes (the bourgeoisie presumably included) the fact that they perform essential forms of mental labor—real (if not "directly material") productive work. On this approach, unlike the Economic, such "returns" would have the theoretical status of actual payments for whatever kinds of mental work capitalists do.

On the Economic Theory, by dramatic contrast, "Mr. Moneybags" is a nonworking expropriator who, as it happens, is forced to invest a goodly proportion of his profits if he is to keep his firm afloat, and who therefore half-wittingly contributes to the historical process of capital accumulation.

3. Capitalist Speculation: Non-Science as Non-Work

But why should we regard the Economic Theory as plausible? Even if Marx is right in thinking there is a margin between the value produced and the value reaped by ordinary workers, why should we not conclude that this margin represents (as the Sociological Theory would have it) "just returns" upon the capitalist's peculiar form of labor—payments for the capitalist inventiveness and innovation?

We will have time, later in this chapter, to enunciate our own Hegelian sympathies with those who think that the moment of capital investment *is* a moment of labor. But the first question we must address is this: why does *Marx* reject such a treatment out of hand?

There is no obvious answer to this question. Engels, in his graveside eulogy of Marx, hailed the Economic Theory as one of his collaborator's most important accomplishments:

> Marx . . . discovered the special law of motion governing the present-day capitalist mode of production and the bourgeois society that this mode of production has created. The discovery of surplus value suddenly threw light on the problem, in trying to solve which all previous investigations, of both bourgeois economists and socialist critics, had been groping in the dark.[12]

But though Marx himself devoted thousands of pages to the elaboration of this great "discovery," as well as to the critique of alternative economic doctrines,[13] there is, in my view, only one thing that can ultimately give the Economic Theory whatever plausibility it has: Marx's underlying, tacit commitment to a "scientistic" analysis of "labor." Given this commitment, it is no wonder that he is predisposed to view "speculation" as idle indeed—as *non*labor.

In order to understand Marx's tendency to disparage Mr. Moneybags as a nonworking parasite, we must return once more to a point developed in the previous chapter: that Marx is in all these respects a representative of the Promethean aspirations of the nineteenth-century European intelligentsia.[14] For many of those who lived in that audacious period, a thoroughgoing "conquest of nature" not only made perfect sense, but seemed to be in the offing.

I want to argue that it is this presumed Promethean notion which, in Marx's hands, leads to the overly "scientistic" account of human labor, from which vantage-point capitalist speculation must appear to be merely "idle."

For, as a matter of course, the idea of communism—the Promethean telos of history—sets the Marxian standard of a fulfilled and intelligent mode of existence. It is this standard that must inform the communist's assessment of all precommunist forms of culture.

Now, from this perspective, what the communist retrospectively judges to have been real work is largely (and necessarily) determined by the conviction that an epoch is dawning in which ignorance and privation will no longer be the problems they once were. By such a standard, the human community can claim to have achieved a communally uncontroversial form of productive labor only insofar as such labor has finally come to rest on a firm scientific basis. *Real* labor, retrospectively judged from the "scientific" perspective attained by communism, would be dependable and regularized activity whose contribution to the production process is clear and uncontroversial.

Capitalist speculation, viewed through the same prism, would not count as real labor, even if it is an unavoidable phenomenon during previous stages of development. The unavoidability of speculation would rest, rather, on the fact that, during an age not yet fully scientific, there is necessarily a residue of precommunistic irrationality.

We can, I suggest, make the most sense of the Marxian Theory of Surplus Value when we see that it rests upon Marx's conviction that, until human productive intelligence matures, the best we can have is a society largely based on *prescientific conjecture*. From the perch of "scientific socialism," it appears that capitalist behavior constitutes a kind of "irrationality" which must nonetheless characterize social relations until the conditions for achieving scientific planning—the basis of communism—are in place. Until that basis is laid, there will be a wager-like dimension to social existence.

For in a prescientific age, it will be "anybody's guess" how economic development—and that is to say *investment*—should proceed. The natural conclusion: a period of development, just because it is somewhat immature and unscientific, is best served if speculation by this capitalist is allowed to vie with speculation by that one—let the chips fall where they may. We have to put up with such irrationality for the time being, simply because we have not yet reached a fully scientific stage of culture at which we can finally do without the kind of investment "bets" capitalists make.

It is only in this very restricted sense, I am suggesting, that Marx considers capitalist speculation and competition as "necessary." That is why it should not count as real "labor."

We must be careful to distinguish two senses of "necessity." To Marx, capitalist speculation turns out to be "necessary" in the sense of being a historically unavoidable token of cultural backwardness. But it is not "necessary" in the sense of representing any enduringly significant phase of human activity.

4. Science and the Appropriation Problem

Those who have such an account of labor will also have, as a natural correlate, this idea of communism: a form of society in which the wager-like dimension has ultimately been eliminated. When, at last, communism becomes possible, investment decisions can be handled rationally, socialistically. No longer need they be, as they are now under competitive capitalism, the outcome of a discoordinate hodgepodge of decisions made by individual capitalists acting independently of one another.

Once communism is achieved, there is in principle no room for mere speculation in the realm of industrial development. The rational procedures of fully mature society can now supplant all the competitive guesswork of developing society.

Only then can the expropriators be expropriated. As long as society is prescientific, it must be presocialistic: a sizeable portion of the social product, representing *investment*, must be funneled into the pockets of those that live by speculation. Only when rational procedures replace prerational shots in the dark, will such parasitic exploitation end.

Science itself is, as Marx never tires of insisting, the very basis of communism.

This far-reaching trust in what we call "scientific method" underlies the communist's equally strong conviction that, when scientific administration does finally become possible, a publicly administered process is the best vehicle for investment decision-making. Then and then only, the communist believes, can there be a political solution to the *appropriation problem*: the question of how we ought to *use* the material, productive resources of society in order to *develop* those very resources.

The communist need not believe that, when it comes to concrete social planning, there will under communism be one and only one scientifically plausible answer to each aspect of the appropriation problem. She can, in a fully scientific spirit, believe that typically there will be a healthy diversity of opinion regarding the best trajectory of social investment.

What defines her as a communist is her conviction that there can be a publicly recognizable—that is, political—decision procedure by which to resolve this healthy plurality of opinions into an actual, determinate decision or result. The communist must believe that, within tolerable limits, we can describe the kind of testing procedure hypotheses must pass if they are to prove themselves.

This means in practice that any proposal must be subjected to the fair-testing procedures as defined within the community of science. To believe in scientific method is to think that the progress of science and technology is best assured if administered by properly credentialed, publicly identifiable experts in their fields.

Thus, although there might be a plurality of competing hypotheses regarding this or that issue of appropriation, the communist believes that there would be no difficulty in principle in defining publicly acceptable conditions under which adequate scientific results are most likely to emerge. The experts, on the basis of recognized procedures, will determine which ideas are worthy of research and development at all; and which, having gone through preliminary testing, show promise—and so on. Lenin succinctly sums up this technocratic ideal:

> Socialism . . . is inconceivable without planned state organization, which keeps tens of millions of people to the strictest observance of a unified standard in production and distribution.[15]

In Hegelian terms: the Marxian thinks that in the rational course of history the growth of science gradually erodes the power of "civil society" in the name of the political collectivity. Though something akin to civil society—a domain of legitimate personal differences with respect to policy issues—might exist under communism, this would not be "civil society" in the robust economic sense: a domain of private discretion over the appropriation and investment of the social product.

The champion of capitalism insists upon just such a domain. He need not take issue with the importance of centralized authority in the maintenance and furtherance of the economy. Smart capitalists recognize, as much as do socialists, that economic well-being depends on a pervasive role for political administration that far exceeds the minimalist "umpire" function conceded by laissez-faire theorists of old: that the state, guarantor of ever more impressive "human rights," may in their name legitimately set conditions and limits on what may be done in the name of private appropriation.

But capitalism's proponents maintain that, however inclusive the "socialized" domain may become, a main function of state power must be to foster a significant preserve outside the political process as such: a "private sector" within whose four walls social investment is largely determined. Granted, the modern state may intervene in economic affairs; but this must always be to promote private economic initiative, not undermine it.

5. Hegel and the Vindication of Speculative Labor

There will be an important isomorphism between the argument of the present chapter and that of the last. Underlying our argument, in both cases, is the neo-Hegelian conviction that Marx does not fully grasp the radical implications of a resolute dialecticism as applied to questions of an economic nature.

In Chapter 2, our Hegelian instincts led us to conclude that alienative aspects of social life are forever "sublimated." Though there is no limit to how far our horizons may be pushed, there will always be a horizon looming before us.

I propose that, in the present chapter, we reason on a parallel basis to a parallel conclusion. We neo-Hegelians ought to reject the very idea of "positive science" capable of taking over where "speculation" leaves off. Marx is mistaken in principle in thinking that life in a "prescientific" age is a merely temporary condition, destined to be surpassed by an epoch of "scientific planning." This notion is not only an abdication of a properly dialectical understanding of "science," but, in obscuring the very logic of "capital," it also wreaks great mischief in the realm of economic analysis.

The issue before us cuts to the philosophical bedrock of economic theory. It can, in my view, be properly addressed only if we return, once again, to the Hegelian background of the tradition to which Marxism itself belongs.

Our critique of Marx will focus on the fact that he has what we might term a "thin" or "ontic"[16] defense of capitalism. For him, the world's need for the "speculative" behavior of capitalists is limited to a specific (if lengthy) historical period: it is not essential to human creativity as such.

Capitalist speculation has, in Marx's view, been historically necessary, but not because "speculation" is an ineluctable aspect of "work" in the deepest sense: inherent in human intelligence. Rather Marx sees the need for entrepreneurial activity as a passing phenomenon in world history, a token of underdevelopment, to be dispensed with as soon as production can be put on a fully scientific footing under communism. Though, during the bourgeois epoch, it is rational for society to orient its economy explicitly around the speculative activity of capitalists, once society has successfully traversed this developmental phase and realized the aims of scientific social-ism, production need no longer be mediated by the competitive market: it can be tailored directly to people's material talents and needs.

Our own neo-Hegelian sense of social dialectics will, by contrast, lead us to a defense of capitalist behavior which might be termed "robust" or (more precisely) "ontological." Speculation regarding the future course of tech-nology should be treated as not merely local to this or that time or place, but inherent in the very character of human intelligent/creative processes as such.

Marx's Sociological Theory might have led him toward an unambiguous appreciation of the ontological character of entrepreneurial behavior—had it not been for the fact that the assumptions underlying the Economic Theory exercised so strong an influence in the opposite direction.

In dissociating ourselves from the Economic Theory, we will have to repudiate Marx's contemptuous attitude toward the apparently idle capital-ist speculator, "Mr. Moneybags." Even in the context of development, Marx does not see the full significance of entrepreneurial activity per se.

To accomplish this, and so to refute Marx most decisively, we must vindicate economic "speculation" as real "labor."

We must, to that end, turn once again to Hegel himself. It is Hegel who gave us what remains to this day the most trenchant defense of speculative activity as such. His treatment of the distinction between "Reason" and "Understanding" provides the basis for the critique of the excesses of Marxian scientism.[17]

Students are often puzzled by the fact that Hegel seems fond of labeling his own work "speculative philosophy." The rubric makes it seem as though the writer of the world's most ponderous *Logic* considers his work to rest on something less sturdy than Reason. The truth is the reverse: Hegel is convinced that speculation is central to any robust conception of Reason (that is, logic) itself.

In our own time, there is still a tendency to think of "speculation" in derogatory terms: as "mere guesswork." This itself is a legacy of the scientism that infected Marx's own work. Marx, who made important contributions to a dialectical view of human history, did not fully absorb

Hegel's point about the "speculative" character of the human mental powers. Those of us who have been misled by Marx's approach to this subject
must learn some Hegelian lessons all over again.[18]

In Hegel's dialectical metaphysics, "Reason" (*Vernunft*) is the consummating moment of "Spirit" (*Geist*[19]), and must be rigorously distinguished
from "Understanding" (*Verstand*).[20]
For our purposes, the important point is that Spirit ultimately comes to
an appreciation of its own incessantly self-transcendent dynamism. Hegel's
philosophy rests on a "paradoxical" Absolute: the express denial that there
are any "absolutes" in the *usual* sense of the term—that is, determinate and
specific forms of being (that is, "entities," as the Heideggerians put it)
immune to historical revision.[21]

A thumbnail summary of the judgment embodied in Hegelian "Absolute
Knowledge" would be this: absolutely nothing can escape the dialectical
process of change. In Hegel's hands, this amounts to an "absolute" in the
sense that development itself, the incessantly revolutionary character of
Being, emerges as the one eternal reality obtaining "infinitely" and
"universally"—that is, to all things at all times.
Everything is born to die. There is no entity, no particular, no system, no
idea—there is, in short, nothing determinate at all—that can ever avoid the
reaper's scythe. The only "thing" that escapes (and hence can claim "absolute" status) is not a *thing* at all, but rather the ubiquity of that very reaper.
To put the point in theological terms: the circumstance that all gods must in
time be slain itself emerges as the only divine principle, the inescapable,
eternal reality—"God."
The dialectical Absolute is generated, by a kind of self-reflective reversal
of field, from this circumstance that there can be no eternal essences. That
circumstance itself must be, as Heraclitus long ago suggested, the Eternal
Essence: the Logos of a world in which all determinate essences must have
their rise and fall in ceaseless self-reformative flux.[22] Hegel's own *Logic*
must accordingly be read as the detailed articulation of the Logos of this
essentially counteressential universe. Of Hegel's various rubrics for such a
counteressential grasping, one of the most prominent is "Reason."[23]

By contrast, Understanding is, in Hegelian parlance, the realm of theory
in the strict and narrow sense. Though any such form of Understanding
will tend to set itself up as a self-consistent "sphere of knowledge," it is
always conceived in response to a specific phase of Spirit's relation to its
"reality," and valid only within those bounds. It is therefore typical of

Understanding to fall into error insofar as it takes itself to be valid without qualification.

Marxists have had a tendency to apply this insight to one particular purpose: showing *both* that the classical political economy of Smith and Ricardo is a splendid scientific achievement, directly relevant to an important phase of human reality, *and* that this classical theory loses relevance and breaks down when the bounds of that phase have been traversed. Thus we should not be surprised to find Engels, once again, giving us one of the most trenchant summations of the necessary limits of such theorization:

> [J]ustifiable and necessary as it is in a number of domains whose extent varies according to the nature of the particular object of investigation, [it] sooner or later reaches a limit, beyond which it becomes one-sided, restricted, abstract, lost in insoluble contradictions. In the contemplation of individual things, it forgets the connection between them; in the contemplation of their existence, it forgets the beginning and end of that existence; of their repose, it forgets their motion. . . .[24]

Viewed with reference to any historical subject matter, Understanding, "respectable fellow that he is,"[25] is good at revealing the "state of the art" in this realm or that. But, from a historical perspective, the fact remains: each state of the art has only limited relevance to reality, and is destined to be superseded by a new such state.

In this sense, for example, Euclidean geometry gives us a self-consistent form of Understanding valid to a wonderfully inclusive degree: it works for all spatial planes experienced prior to the twentieth century. But even though Euclid was once "the state of the art," he is no longer so: his system has, in the context of general relativity, especially as applied to problems of celestial magnitude, been superseded by non-Euclidean treatments of plane space.

Such examples put us in a position to see why "speculation" has such an important role in the Hegelian system. Reason, for Hegel, is always *speculative* Reason.

That means: the nature of Spirit (qua Reason) is such that it is always calling its own "state of the art" (qua Understanding) into question. No matter where Spirit is, it is oriented toward self-transcendence.

This is hardly to say that there is "nothing scientific" about historical progress. It is rather to say that there is nothing *narrowly* "scientific" about it. From the point of view of any adequate philosophy of Spirit, there can be no segregation of "science" from "speculation." This is so however narrowly or broadly we use the word "science."

One might use "science" in a narrow sense—in the sense of "specific theory." Science in that sense always is an aspect of human endeavor. Every age has its "normal science"—its already codified Understanding of how things work. It goes without saying that there always will be—and always has been—a scientific dimension to human intelligence in that sense. But, in that same sense, there must always be a place for something else as well: a trans-scientific moment of "speculation" on the cutting edge of development. Every age's codified Understanding of the world is in process of being undermined by Speculative Reason, a process that (so long as progress itself continues) must produce a new Understanding in the next generation.

But sometimes we use "science" in a broader sense. When, in that vein, we speak of a Darwin or Einstein as a great scientist, we are at least partly appealing to that broader sense, in which such a thinker is a paradigm-smashing iconoclast who had the speculative genius "to see beyond the science of his time." To be a great scientist in this sense, one must be able to challenge established science in the first sense. This latter sense of "science" is quite defensible because, since the "speculative moment" is already essentially *included* in the meaning of the term, it gives us a more full-bodied sense of what science as a dynamic historical reality is all about. So that, here again, though in a different terminology, we must conclude that "speculation" is essential to Spirit.

In a word: real scientific *Verstand* is always in a context of discovery, the domain of *Vernunft*. The reverse is equally true: for in reality, of course, Einstein could not have been the epoch-making speculative genius that he was (in that sense an exemplar of "Reason") if he had not been thoroughly immersed in state-of-the-art physical science (and in that sense a representative of "Understanding").

These two moments of Spirit are never in practice segregated, but rather inextricably intertwined. It follows that the contrast between a prescientific age in which speculation was unavoidable, and an era of fully scientific production, is itself a chimera: speculation (Reason) and "normal science" (Understanding) are two ineluctable moments of Spirit. Nothing can ever dissever either dancer from the dance.[26]

There is a *social* aspect of this that must not be missed. A normal science can be constituted only after it has emerged triumphant from its speculative, hence controversial, beginnings. To say that an idea is *still* speculative is to say that differences of opinion about it make sense, at least for the time being. Insofar as we are, with respect to this or that problem, still in a speculative phase, any idea we might propose must in principle compete with alternative conjectures and hypotheses which likewise have legitimacy.

I say "compete"—for it becomes clear that *speculation* and *competition* are, necessarily, perennial bedfellows. It follows that if, in order not to vitiate industrial progress, it is important for us to retain, in the design of our social system, an important place for speculation, the same must be said of competition.

The impossibility of disentangling speculation from understanding points to the conclusion that, in exemplary instances of scientific and technological progress, it is a mistake to conceive "mental labor" as separable from "wagering" that this or that hypothesis will be borne out.

But if my attempted reconstruction of Marxian reasoning has been on the right track, that is just what the treatment of capitalist behavior provided by Marx's Economic Theory does: it wrongly segregates the "regularized" aspect of labor from the "speculative," consigning the latter to the category of *non*labor. We must now consider some implications of this misconception.

6. *Postmodernism and the Problem of Political Economy*

We have repudiated the idea that economic "speculation" is some merely temporary aspect of social existence. The speculative moment is relevant not merely to an allegedly prescientific epoch, but to any period at all, no matter how far advanced.

In order to put the coup de grâce to the Marxian fetish of scientific management, we must, on the basis of the foregoing considerations, now directly discredit the Marxian notion that "research and development" might be viewed a proper function of centralized public authority rather than of private enterprise.

We can perhaps make this point most persuasive to the contemporary reader by considering how the Hegelian treatment of the limits of *Verstand* has been ramified and extended—indeed radicalized—in our own time by thinkers in the "postmodern" idiom. A thoroughly political approach to the appropriation problem will seem plausible only to those willing to subscribe to the—now largely discredited—idea that the day is approaching when a rational society will steer the course of technological development in accordance with publicly acceptable, uncontroversial scientific methods.

Is there no difficulty in setting up public agencies that can, in a spirit of impartiality and fairness, fund various research projects according to their scientific promise?

Might we administer and fund science and technology in a way so methodologically regularized as to fall within the bailiwick of thoroughly objective scientific experts?

This is just what we neo-Hegelians can no longer believe.

The naïveté of such a notion of disinterested technological administration has indeed become a central theme of Hegel's intellectual grandchildren. Postmodernism—itself largely a revival of the Hegelian dialectical critique of Understanding—looks upon the rival "modernism" as still mired in the notion that there is a universally applicable, unbiased "scientific method" capable of settling theoretical differences.

If postmodernism could be defined around one tendency above all, I think it would be this: systematic skepticism that there could ever be some universally acceptable procedure by which humankind, at long last methodologically unified, might with full confidence blaze a scientific-technological trail into the future.

To believe in such trailblazing is to assume that scientific progress is itself subject to methodological normalization. The proponent of "scientific method" must, I repeat, believe some version of this tale; but it is just this tale that writers in the postmodern tradition descended from Hegel have, I think, effectively discredited.

In the realm of science and technology, the postmodernist case "against method"[27] is built, to a significant degree, upon Thomas Kuhn's classic study of the significance of deep, "paradigm-level" differences in the history of science.[28]

A celebrated example, discussed by Kuhn and developed by Paul Feyerabend, is the clash between Galileo (representing the Copernican worldview) and Cardinal Bellarmine (representing the church-backed Ptolemaic view).[29] The Kuhnian point here is that there are no mutually acceptable criteria, applicable at the time of the controversy, capable of deciding between the rival theories. Each theorist is blinded by his own paradigm-level commitments to the merits of the opposing theory: each—naive empiricisms notwithstanding—sees what he is predisposed to see.

There is no way of mediating disputes that are as deep as disputes actually do get. There is no neutral method. Each paradigm is impressed with its own standards of evaluation: there is no Archimedean point from which to weigh them, no noncircular grounds on which their comparative merits can be decided.

Philosophers in search of a method want something that *grounds* theories of the workaday sort, some metatheory that can tell us which is sound and which is not. But, as Richard Rorty puts it, one cannot "escape the vocabulary and practices of one's own time and find something ahistorical and necessary to cling to."[30]

This is not to say that one must utterly reject the concept of scientific method. Kuhn does not go that far; nor does the even more radical Feyerabend, who appears to admit that, after the dust settled, an after-the-fact adjudication between Copernicus and Galileo was of course possible. With the benefit of hindsight, we can see that the heliocentric model far surpasses the geocentric in explanatory elegance and power.

The point, says Feyerabend, is that such adjudication *"cannot be given at the time of the quarrel."*[31] The problem is that if we are going through a time of ferment, it is by hypothesis too early to tell which complex viewpoint adheres more closely to sound "method." The special poignancy of Kuhnian paradigm-level differences stems from the fact that Galileo's theory was, while the controversy raged, as yet so underdeveloped that no scientific canons, applied then, could decide the case.

The lack of methodological standards at the time in question is all that is necessary in order to undo the notion that there might be a "method" applicable to the process of scientific discovery itself.

There may of course be reliable and normalized procedures in industrial research and development. But these are nothing more than ways of methodically extending research programs that we have creatively and nonmethodically established in the first place. Only after a breakthrough has already been made can we codify it, axiomatize it, and make it the standard stuff of textbooks.

The error is in thinking that such normalization could ever be the whole story. This is precisely the mistake made by those who think that it is a good idea to put the fate of technological progress in the hands of a state-run bureaucracy. This is the matter to which we must now turn.

7. *The Call of the Wild*

We can now see why the idea of "disinterested administration of scientific and technological research" can no longer impress those who have inherited the Hegelian distinction between Reason and Understanding and have applied it with full seriousness. Those who uncritically cling to the notion of "socialistic" planning have not yet appreciated the radical implications of this distinction with respect to the arena of industrial innovation in particular.

There can be no regularization or normalization of the "procedures" of technological advance. It is a mistake to think that there are any such "procedures" at all.

This is not to say that we could not in fact decide to impose some sense of "scientific method" on technological research. It is only to say that *if* we took such a step, it would be the canonization, not of pure scientific neutrality, but of a *particular* research program of one kind or another. The apparently noble goal of scientifically administered industrial innovation would in that event take on a totalitarian aspect.

We have been following out the Hegelian suggestion that there is a speculative moment of Spirit that incessantly defies the possibility of regularization—that cannot ever be flatly scientized. Marx says that "[w]here speculation ends—in real life—there real, positive science begins. . . . Empty talk about consciousness ceases, and real knowledge has to take its place. . . ."[32] By contrast, those of us who have Hegelian instincts will, when it comes to questions of cultural innovation, find little attraction in this idea of the supersession of "speculation" by "positive science."

Any good Marxist believes that, in a technologically advanced context, the most rational vehicle of industrial development will be some form of central social planning. But in order to make this idea seem compelling, she must argue that industrial development itself might become a department of Understanding—an arena of thought and action amenable to methods and procedures which are themselves monochromatically "scientific," hence not, on any important level, essentially vexed or controversial.

The communist believes in method. Confidence that there are public criteria of "expertise" grounds the conclusion that the appropriation problem can be given a political solution: society under the aegis of an enlightened technocracy. Though there is a range of reasonable scientific debate, we know how to give research programs an objective assessment: we can describe and define the kind of muster such proposals must pass if they are to prove themselves. It may not be clear ab initio which proposals will in the end measure up. But we do, in principle, possess the proper yardstick.

We postmodernists view things differently. For us seventh-generation descendants of Hegel, the idea of a methodological guide with which we may blaze trails into the future has become as close to meaningless as an idea can get. The future is not merely unknown: it *isn't* in any sense at all, until we get around to making it. And only after we have made it are we able to issue retrospective judgments as to which of our ancestors' futuristic ideas have turned out to be good ones.

This necessarily prompts a different attitude toward "authority" itself. For us there is no longer an authoritative means of getting off whatever ground we stand on: bootstrapping is all. Breakthroughs would not be breakthroughs if they did not come from out of left field: Edison has a weird idea and sinks $40,000 of his own good money (a small fortune in those days) into the project, for which seven-eighths of the world thinks he's crazy.

Here is where our own comfortable retrospective judgment itself misleads. It makes us forget that Edison *was* a lunatic—which is why we owe so much to him.

For many of us, this postmodern reorientation has important implications for social theory. It may, in particular, imply the need for a reassessment of social forms that Marx pronounced obsolescent. Writing in this postmodern vein, Richard Rorty, for example, sees

> the sort of cultural pluralism which rejects metaphors of centrality and depth as chiming with democratic politics—with the spirit of tolerance which has made constitutional democracies possible. . . .[33]

Though Rorty's own focus is on political institutions, he does not hesitate to label his own view "postmodernist bourgeois liberalism."[34] His repeated use of the term "bourgeois" will indeed seem provocative to those postmodernists who retain a mistrust of capitalism as such: it seems clear that, in Rorty's view, the economic institutions of the marketplace, in one form or another, are among those that "chime with" the philosophical decentering wrought by postmodernism.

At stake here is the direction of what Rorty calls the "Cultural Left." Rorty is locking horns with some writers in the postmodern vein (for example, Michel Foucault and Paul de Man) who reject the traditions of bourgeois democracy "as 'complicit' with the 'discourses of power' which are the invisible regulators of life in the bourgeois democracies."[35] Rorty himself believes that the mantle of honorable leftism sits most comfortably on the shoulders of American pragmatists like John Dewey, for whom bourgeois institutions (with all their defects, and need for constant reform) remain our best defense against the totalitarian nightmare.

Such pragmatism might provide the best framework for those contemporary radicals who wish, in Rorty's words, "to recapture the drive and direction which the left of the 1930s thought that it had gotten from Marxism."[36] Our own reflections in this chapter are indeed in this same Deweyan-Rortian spirit. For us, one important upshot of the collapse of "method" ought to be a renewed—that is, counter-Marxian—respect for the "bourgeois" domain of "civil society."

Marx treats this as a sphere of avarice that we ought to supersede. He does not see it, as Hegel does, as a realm of economic "particularity" that must, in the interests of social progress, counterbalance the "universality" of the collectivity.

The state does represent the "universal." But the universal is what it is, and nothing more: what has come to be agreed upon by the public at large—and realized in social institutions at large. It is, in a word, the conventional.

The conventional is not the stupid: social life would be inconceivable without it. But social life would be inconceivable if there were not also a domain of the nonconventional: both are "moments of motion" essential to any economy as such.

The problematic of social existence can never be reduced to the problem of statecraft. This is especially clear in the economic realm—the domain of the appropriation problem.

It took an Edison to guess that it would be possible, conventional wisdom to the contrary, to find or make something that would glow white if an electric current were run through it, yet not instantly melt of its own heat. It took the Wrights, just a little later, to defy the same conventional wisdom, and show that an engine-driven craft would not instantly fall to the ground of its own weight.

One should grant that, by the standards of the time, the incandescent filament and the powered plane did not make much sense. In a Feyerabendian spirit, one should say: there was no way, at the time in question, to tell the difference between such ideas, which in retrospect are revered as masterstrokes of genius, and countless other notions that appear now just as they appeared then: as sheer lunacy.

"Method" is nothing less, but also nothing more, than the conventional as it is realized at a given time and place. To see this is to stop thinking that the operation of an economy could be conventionalized: reduced to a thoroughly regularized, normalized, bureaucratized social decision procedure.

It matters not how sensitive and well-intentioned a public panel of experts might be. Once one takes to heart what Hegel taught and Marx forgot, one sees that it is, in principle, a big mistake to leave investment in our society's material advancement in the hands of any state-appointed committee.

8. Speculation as Mental Labor

Marx wishes to give his argument a "scientific" cast, distinguishing it from forms of "utopian socialism" which fail to ground their proposals in a rigorous analysis of what the evolving technological infrastructure permits.

And yet there are basic aspects of Marx's own "science" of history that seem irredeemably "utopian" themselves. Foremost among these is his notion of a world in which all labor is emancipated, and in which the reign of speculative profits on the part of "Mr. Moneybags" has been put behind us.

For us postmodern inheritors of the Hegelian tradition, there can, by contrast, be no unbiased methodology that might be installed by a social revolution. This is as true of Marxism itself as it is of any pretender, actual or possible, to the role of "scientific objectivity."

For us, every revolutionary program, no matter how democratic and emancipatory it may be, should be thought of as a way of "understanding" things in the Hegelian sense. Which is to say: each such program has its own prejudice, its own agenda. Every social project excludes or suppresses what is other or alien to the particular interests which, perforce, it represents. In privileging its own emancipatory aspirations, it turns a deaf ear to other voices.[37]

There is no purely "objective" or "scientific" perch from which to observe the sweep of historical development; no model of emancipation that might establish stable control over a theoretical or practical "center." Social thought and practice must explicitly adopt the resolve to de-center and displace models and metaphors that pretend to full adequacy. We must adopt a de-absolutized view of revolution for which there is no ultimately privileged mode of theoretical intervention, and in which each determinate theoretical construct—each controlling metaphor—is itself immersed in an indeterminately wide field of "alterity": a range of alternative terms of analysis, any of which might serve as the occasion for a meaningful self-critique leading to a new avenue of theoretical and practical intervention.

For us, the "deconstruction" of "totalistic" revolutionary discourses becomes a never-ending need. Revolution itself becomes permanent revolution.

I argued in Chapter 2 that the specific contents of the economic factors of "drudgery" and "coercion" are historically relative: always dialectically "sublimated," never eliminated. On that accounting, it makes no sense to say that "economic development" is only a "phase" that might ever be "successfully traversed." To us, this seems to spell the need for efficiency "rationing" in the form of economic incentives.

Our further explorations of the dialectical underpinnings of Marxism have now led us to see every historical stage of "science" or "technology" as but a particular phase of Understanding. From this viewpoint, every methodological "state of the art," no matter how puffed with pride it may get, sets the stage for its own speculative-competitive immolation in an interminable process that essentially defies political normalization.

Thus, not only do we (as per Chapter 2) need incentives; we need room for private appropriation as well. Our neo-Hegelian reflections have led us to the point of suspecting that market relations are defensible in at least this robust, twofold sense.

For us, the essential wildness of Edisonian speculation—its utter untameability—itself emerges as an aspect par excellence of Spirit: as (if you will) a moment of mental labor.

And capital investment appears a moment par excellence of speculation: an essential aspect of human industrial creativity.

This means that profits can no longer be treated as margins of expropriation pure and simple: as constituting social parasitism. The "circulation of capital" is now seen to be an essential "moment" of economic behavior, wherein those who successfully engage in speculative investment are awarded with the wherewithal to engage in further speculation in the next round of social investment. Thus does industrial innovation proceed.

In the previous chapter, we attacked one basic component of Marxian communism: the idea that economic incentives are limited to a particular phase of history.

But we observed at the outset of the present chapter that the communist could admit this (and therefore concede the need for market methods in some minimal sense), and yet go on to argue that capitalist appropriation of "surplus value" might nonetheless come to an end.

But this rearguard defense of communism is, as we now see, itself quite dubious. Profits, in the normal course of events, now appear instead as legitimate "payments" for a form of activity just as essential to the production process as those recognized by Marx and Engels.[38] Not only material incentives, but also capitalization as such, have emerged as necessary moments of economic activity.

I said that profits are legitimate "in the normal course of events." For I do not mean to suggest that everything that parades as essential "speculation" really is so. At least *some* of what capitalists do *is* "parasitic." (This is hardly shocking: no doubt some of the things done by any broad group of people are exploitative.) In the real world, there is much mere "coupon clipping"; and at least *some* of what capitalists say in their own defense is the ideological claptrap Marxists think it is. In that case: so much the worse for capitalism as it actually exists.

One can admit all this and still insist that, even when all cases of parasitism have been subtracted, there is a considerable remainder: a speculative-competitive component of human endeavor that society must fund in order to further industrial development itself.

We began this chapter with the observation that the orthodox Marxism of the twentieth century rests upon a premise that is *apparently* less utopian than the "Promethean" assumption, examined in the previous chapter, that technological progress is capable of bringing us to the point at which unpleasant labor could be marginalized.

But we now can see that this is a somewhat deceptive appearance. For our reflections have led us to the conclusion that the idea of overcoming entrepreneurial labor is covertly Promethean in its own right: it rests on the presumption that humankind is verging upon an epoch in which all will have come to agree upon an uncontroversial, fully "scientific" methodology.

At bottom, *both* ideas—the marginalization of unpleasant labor and the attainment of an unvexed methodology—are broadly Promethean: they depend upon the nineteenth-century notion that we are about to emerge from the prerational mists into the fully scientific clear light of day.

In the context of the present chapter, the failure of Prometheanism means that the entrepreneurial moment of human existence is with us to stay. The communist "ideal" of the elimination of this factor misconceives the nature of human intelligence in a fundamental way.

This is not to say that such an "ideal" could never be realized. To varying degrees (though always only approximately), it has been. The attempt to undermine the entrepreneurial moment of social existence, in the name of "scientific" central planning, has been a salient fact of the twentieth century, definitive of what we know as "Communism."

The implication of our Hegelian reflections is not that central planning is impossible, but that such a development would be dysfunctional and hence could be realized only if enforced by tyrannical means. It is an "impossible ideal" in the sense that it could never become a stable, permanent feature of the world economic picture. It is in this respect that proponents of the Classical Defense of capitalism are correct in regarding "scientific socialism" as a god that failed.

Recalcitrant Marxists might find this result a bit more palatable once they note that it does not have some of the counterrevolutionary implications it might at first appear to have.

For in arguing that the "capitalist" moment of "speculation" is an inescapable moment of scientific and technological experience, we do not mean to imply that such "speculation" must continue to be carried out within the confines of the class system as we know it today. It is, for all we have said so far, even possible to imagine that we could realize the "speculative moment" without "classes" at all.

"Speculation" should indeed be treated as a "moment" of "mental labor"—but this does not mean that some people will perform this function, while others do not. It remains an open question whether, in the future, all people might—in various ways, and to varying degrees—spend some of their hours in productive speculation. If this were to happen, it would mean that, to some extent or other, all people would at least some of the time wear the hat of the "capitalist."

The latter scenario would indeed be quite meaningful in a context in which the mental powers of all people were radically cultivated by an advanced education. It will have fundamental relevance to the approach I will take in Part Two of this study, in which I do try to salvage one very "deep" Marxian idea that I believe is of enduring significance: that of the classless society.

9. The End of the Matter?

Is Marxism "refuted"? Here one must own up to the limitations of argument itself: that I cannot persuade you with arguments unless I am able to appeal to some premise you yourself happen to accept. There are no "knock-down" arguments which can settle the issue between those with radically different worldviews. As Rorty says:

> The idea that moral and political controversies should always be "brought back to first principles" is reasonable if it means merely that we should seek common ground in the hope of attaining agreement. But it is misleading if it is taken as the claim that there is a natural order of premises from which moral and political conclusions are to be inferred. . . .[39]

The most successful kinds of persuasion must always have the following Socratic form: I succeed in showing you that some idea you are fond of is inconsistent with another idea that you would be even more loath to abandon.

I must, in this vein, admit that the "neo-Hegelian" arguments of Part One of this study will not move those who, operating entirely outside the Hegelian framework, can go on blithely believing that there *is* a final stage of substantive "method" which fully "rational" or "scientific" planning can invoke: a decision procedure that enables us to program the conditions under which scientific and technological innovation will occur, and measure the relative merits of competing theories and hypotheses.

I have no decisive arguments against a "Communism" of that sort—none that will dissuade those who reject Hegelianism root and branch. My "argument" against Marx will (at best) seem compelling only to those who have these deep Hegelian commitments.

There is a point at which argument runs out: at which debate degenerates into a sterile exercise in onus-shifting and self-congratulation. When that juncture is reached, one can only invoke the oft-heard Marxian adage: history itself will be the judge.

I have provided the only kind of "argument" that the Marxian might find compelling: one that shows that some of the fruits of Historical Materialism are at variance with its roots. Here is where a certain ad hominem turn is not only permissible, but unavoidable.

It is a familiar fact that Marx regards his own theory as a critical extension of the dialecticism bequeathed by Hegel. This inherited Hegelianism is a powerful engine indeed: it enables Marx to open some remarkable prospects—including that of a classless society, a proposal that will pre-occupy us in Part Two of this study.

But, if I am right, not everything that Marx does in "going beyond Hegel" amounts to a salutary radicalization. In some crucial respects, Marx abdicates some of the principal insights of the master dialectician concerning the untameability of industrial innovation. This, above all, lies at the basis of Marx's failure to perceive the continued need for private appropriation within a sphere of "civil society."

Notes

1. Engels, *Socialism: Utopian and Scientific* in *The Marx-Engels Reader*, ed. Tucker, Robert (New York: 1978), p. 712. Hereafter referred to as "Tucker." This passage was already cited in Chapter 2.3. Similarly, Engels says: "Socialized production upon a predetermined plan henceforth becomes possible." Tucker, p. 717.
2. Lenin, V. I., *The State and Revolution*, in *Selected Works* (one-volume edition) (New York: 1971), p. 328.
3. Ibid., pp. 328–29.
4. The qualificatory quotation marks are essential to my meaning here. On the Sociological Theory, the proletariat is not, strictly speaking, the only "working" class. Interestingly, the very phrase "working class" carries a bias in favor of the Economic Theory, to be considered in a moment.
5. Tucker, p. 714.
6. Ibid., p. 714.
7. Marx always regarded the Theory of Surplus Value as his chief economic discovery. It is the theoretical centerpiece of the entire argument in *Capital*, Vol. I, ed. Engels, Friedrich (New York: 1967), especially Parts II–IV.
8. Many have found fault with Marx's Theory of Surplus Value in its quantitative interpretation. Thus understood, the theory says: under equilibrium conditions, the hours' worth of labor power that goes into the product, minus the hours' worth of labor power required to maintain workers at the historically prevalent subsistence, *equals* the hours' worth of surplus value available to capitalist expropriation.

Even in Marx's time, critics were unimpressed by such quantitative claims, and some, indeed, by the entire Labor Theory of Value—inherited by Marx from Smith and Ricardo—which underlies them. But though this controversy has long been one of the standard issues at the foundations of Marxian economic theory, it need not occupy us here. For our purposes, it is not necessary, and indeed it would be misleading, to hold Marx to the theory in a strict quantitative sense at all. As the tenor of the foregoing discussion clearly indicates, the gist of Marx's theory may be given a *qualitative* rather than a quantitative interpretation.

Thus construed, the Theory of Surplus Value holds that, to some degree or other, and by some measure or other, unproductive members of society—capitalists—are able to sustain themselves only by appropriating the product of those who *are* productive. Marx's general approach to capitalist exploitation would remain sound if the latter claim were true. And that is why I have been careful to keep the discussion on a qualitative level in this section.

It is also clear that, if Marx is to be refuted, we must show that it is not even true that capitalists are unproductive in this general qualitative sense. We will accept this challenge later in this chapter.

9. Marx, *Capital*, Volume I, p. 193.
10. Ibid., pp. 166, 176.
11. There are two ways in which profits may be disposed: either for the capitalist's own personal consumption or for reinvestment in the business itself.

In the first case, the capitalist consumes this margin of profit out of the luxury goods sector. To that extent, he is not a worker, but rather a social parasite in a strict sense: he lives off the fruits of the labors of others.

In the second case, the capitalist lays his profits out for the purchase of further means of production. To that extent, he is again not a worker, but rather a pure investor.

On this score, capitalist bookkeepers and tax auditors seem to be in agreement. The surpluses received by capitalists as such are not payments for services rendered. Even in the accountant's sense of the term, entrepreneurs do no work.
12. Tucker, p. 681.
13. Besides *Capital*, Volume I, and *The Grundrisse*, frequently mentioned in these pages, we should mention the fifteen hundred pages or so of Marx's *Theories of Surplus Value*, trans. Burns, Emile (Moscow: 1963). This work (in itself occupying three volumes) was posthumously edited from Marx's manuscripts, principally by Engels and Kautsky, and published—not altogether plausibly—as "Volume IV" of *Capital*.
14. I should perhaps add "male" to this characterization. Such a qualification in terms of gender would not be a vague nod in the direction of what is today called "political correctness." I have in previous notes mentioned the connection between Marx's Promethean conception and that of Mary Wollstonecraft Shelley in *Frankenstein*; but the big difference between them is that Victor Frankenstein's Promethean quest is, in Shelley's hands, a systematically ambiguous matter: rather than being a flatly "scientific" matter of assured prediction and control, Victor Frankenstein is unable to foresee his fate—because he is hardly in control.

I join others who suspect that it is no mere coincidence that this vexed turn in Promethean writing is taken by a female author, though exploration of this point would obviously take me beyond the bounds of this study.
15. Lenin, V. I., *Selected Works*, p. 443.

16. Readers of Heidegger will recognize the "ontic" as the domain of what happens to exist, as contrasted with the "ontological," that which is inherent in intelligent human existence ("Dasein") as such. My argument will be that Marx erred in not seeing that the "speculation" at the roots of "capital" is indeed ontological in this sense.

17. "Scientism"—Marx's included—has of course been subjected, in our own time, to a far-reaching attack by "postmodern" thinkers of various stripes; but most of these, and certainly the best of these, belong to the Hegelian tradition. In Chapter 6.4 we will consider the relation of the present work to "postmodern," "feminist," and "new age" critiques of commodification.

18. The reader is right to sense that I include myself in this critical judgment. In that respect, this study marks a significant step in my own scholarly itinerary. As I said in the Preface, I have been forced to reconsider much of what, as a "critical Marxist," I took for granted in the 1970s. Because my own understanding of such notions as "alienated labor" and "capitalist speculation" has suffered such a sea change, I would be wrong to classify myself as a Marxist any longer, even in some qualified sense—this, despite the fact that this study is dedicated to the defense of one central Marxian claim: that social classes are in an important sense obsolescent.

19. As Hegel scholars never tire of telling us, neither translation is fully adequate. In English, "spirit" has some religious overtones that tend to be too ethereal, while "mind" narrows the focus to the psyche of the individual, neglecting the cultural collectivity and the world of material culture. Though *Geist* has both sorts of resonance, I must resist the temptation to clutter the page with Germanisms. My friend and colleague Dennis Schmidt, whose German is infinitely better than mine, prefers "Spirit"; I accordingly use this word, capitalized, as the Hegelian term of art intended to capture the above twofold meaning.

20. A locus classicus of this basis Hegelian distinction is Chapter 6 of the Encyclopedia version of the *Logic*: trans. Wallace (Oxford: 1975), pp. 113–22.

    There are, strictly speaking, three moments at work here: (1) "*Understanding*, [which] sticks to fixity of characters and their distinctness from one another . . ." (ibid., p. 113, emphasis Hegel's); (2) "the Dialectical stage [in which] these finite characterizations . . . pass into their opposites [i.e., fall into contradiction]" (ibid., p. 115); and (3) "[t]he Speculative stage, or state of Positive Reason, [which] apprehends the unity of terms . . . in their opposition [i.e., resolves the former contradictions by attaining a higher level of Understanding]" (ibid., p. 119). In keeping with the simpler mode of exposition familiar to readers of Hegel commentaries, we may treat the crucial role of the transitional, "Dialectical" moment as clear enough not to require independent reference.

21. It is true that Hegel believes that Spirit ultimately achieves a transparent grasp of the eternally valid Logic of dialectical creativity. And it is also true that this involves Hegel in difficulties from the postmodern (i.e., broadly Heideggerian) perspective. But despite such difficulties, it is clear that Hegel never supposes the process of dialectical development itself will ever come to an end.

    The conception of the Absolute as an achievable level of being, of consciousness, has of course always been the biggest obstacle in the way of its full appreciation, not to mention acceptance. I do agree with those postmodern readers who maintain that, in this respect, Hegel never fully freed himself from the "logocentrism" that it seems the predominant purpose of his own philosophy to surpass. We may, in this vein, applaud Jacques Derrida's essay, "From Restricted to General Economy: A Hegelianism without Reserve," in *Writing and Difference*, trans. Bass, Alan (Chicago: 1978), pp. 251–77.

I also agree that it is just this difficulty that opens the door to simplistic "end of history" readings of Hegel, such as we found earlier in the essay by Francis Fukuyama. See Section 2 of the Introduction.

22. Consistently with this treatment, and as our remarks in the previous note imply, we must avoid treating this grasping as "just one theory among others." Strictly speaking, it is not a specific theory about the world at all, but rather a kind of metatheory *about* the defeasibility of all specific theories. Paradoxical though it may sound, and vulnerable as it may be to the deconstructive insights of Derrida et al., Hegel does not regard the way in which such a metatheory grasps the defeasibility of specific ideas as a specific idea, itself defeasible. Rather it is *the* "Idea."

23. Readers accustomed to belittling talk of "absolutes" must watch their step. Hegel's conception of the Absolute is hard to avoid, especially by those who issue the universal judgment that "all things shall pass." For that very universal judgment *is* (in very abbreviated form) the Hegelian Absolute. The very denial that there are any absolutes seems to terminate in a contradiction, since this denial is tantamount to the idea that absolutely—notice the word!—nothing is immune to change, revision. Hegel in effect bids us to ask: how could one achieve such confidence that admits of no exceptions, unless one had grasped the incessancy of change as itself a changeless, necessary, absolute truth? This truth, systematically formulated, is precisely what Hegel attempts to supply in his logic. The Hegelian Absolute in this sense seems necessitated by a kind of reductio ad absurdum of any attempt to deny that there are any absolutes.

Though Hegel is (on the one side) vulnerable to the charge of having exempted his own "logic" from the ongoing dialectic, those deconstructionists who (on the other extreme) wish to do away with "the Absolute" entirely may face equally insuperable difficulties. It seems to me that it is the unavoidable self-referential paradoxicality of the dialectical absolute that is at issue here: an issue that will not go away.

24. Engels, *Socialism: Utopian and Scientific*, Tucker, p. 696. Engels's usual term for Hegelian *Verstand* is "the metaphysical mode of thought."

25. Ibid., p. 696.

26. I must beg the reader's forgiveness for this barbarous fusion of phrases from Poe ("Annabel Lee") and Yeats ("Among School Children").

27. Feyerabend, Paul, *Against Method* (London: 1975).

28. Kuhn, Thomas, *The Structure of Scientific Revolutions* (Chicago: 1962).

29. The absence of a neutral method in the case between Ptolemy and Copernicus has been a major focus of discussion at least since the appearance of Kuhn's book (ibid., esp. chap. 7). It became the centerpiece of Paul Feyerabend's more radical casting of the Kuhnian point in *Against Method*. I am not of course suggesting that Kuhn himself was self-consciously influenced by Hegel. I would go further, and suggest that many soi-disant postmodernists underplay, and sometimes fail altogether to grasp, their own Hegelian roots.

30. Rorty, Richard, "Pragmatism, Relativism, Irrationalism," in *Consequences of Pragmatism* (Minneapolis: 1982), p. 165.

There are, Rorty says, "no constraints on inquiry save conversational ones— no wholesale constraints derived from the nature of the objects, or of the mind, or of language, but only those retail constraints provided by the remarks of our fellow-inquirers" (ibid., p. 165). It is all right to be methodologically inclined.

"Getting . . . a synoptic view," Rorty says, "often does require us to change radically our views on particular subjects" (ibid., p. 168). But that is hardly enough to vindicate something so glorious as what the philosophers have called "scientific method." Rather, the "holistic process of readjustment is just muddling through on a large scale" (ibid., p. 168).

This entire postmodern tendency may indeed be defined around the idea that, contra "foundationalism," there is no way of settling truth-claims independent of the play of biased languages. The antifoundationalist maintains that (a) empiricist "representationalism" is wrong in thinking that there is a neutrally describable and accessible extralinguistic reality against which the adequacy of languages can be checked; while (b) rationalist "transcendentalism" is wrong in thinking that there is a logical essence to language use able to tell us which linguistic practices are logical and which are not. If foundationalism does fail, as we assume here it does, then there is no way that I, as a party to a dispute, can appeal to a "neutral method" in order to "ground" the claim that I'm right and you're wrong. The door swings open to the broadly "Nietzschean" view that there's no way to compare the adequacy of competing formulations at all.

31. Feyerabend, *Against Method*, p. 207. Emphasis Feyerabend's.
32. Marx and Engels, *The German Ideology*, Part I, Tucker, p. 155.
33. Rorty, Richard, "De Man and the American Cultural Left," in *Objectivity, Relativism and Truth* (*Philosophical Papers*, Vol. 1) (Cambridge, Eng.: 1991), pp. 197–202.

"Chiming with" is no loose metaphor: Rorty explicitly disowns any attempt to transform pragmatic remarks favorable to "bourgeois democracy" into a knockdown defense—a "proof"—of such principles. That is what he means when he says that "[no] argumentative roads lead from this kind of philosophy to any particular brand of politics" (ibid., p. 132). Rorty is willing to "argue" for bourgeois democracy, as long as we understand that it is not an "argument" in the transcendental style but merely a statement of what seems to "chime with" a Deweyan mistrust of sociopolitical absolutes.

I should add that although in this chapter I too "argue" for bourgeois institutions, the spirit of the argument is, like Rorty's, Deweyan rather than transcendental. I see no way of "proving" the need for bourgeois institutions to the satisfaction of anyone who finds my underlying pragmatic biases uncongenial.

34. This is indeed the title of a short essay by Rorty, in *Objectivity, Relativism and Truth* (*Philosophical Papers*, Vol. 1) (Cambridge, Eng.: 1991), pp. 197–202.
35. Rorty, Richard, "De Man and the American Cultural Left," in *Essays on Heidegger and Others* (*Philosophical Papers*, Vol. 2) (Cambridge, Eng.: 1991) p. 133.
36. Ibid., p. 133.
37. Charles Taylor attributes this discovery to Nietzsche, and joins us in saying that it "has brought some important insights: no construal is quite innocent, something is always suppressed; and what is more, some interlocutors are always advantaged relative to others. . . ." "Overcoming Epistemology," in *After Philosophy: End or Transformation?*, ed. Baynes, Kenneth, Bohman, James, and McCarthy, Thomas (Cambridge, Mass.: 1987), p. 484.
38. This is what we will say, insofar as we are willing to have any discussions at all within the Marxian bounds of the Theory of Value.
39. Rorty, "The Priority of Democracy to Philosophy," *Philosophical Papers*, Vol. 1, p. 190.

PART TWO:
The Prospect of
Classless Capitalism

4

The Ideal of the Classless Society: The Challenge of Formative Parity

1. What Can Be Salvaged?

A specter is haunting the modern world—the specter of a classless form of capitalism.

Though the world will have a continuing need for market methods, some of the central ideals of the Marxian tradition are not only meaningful, but defensible on the basis of Marx's own approach to social evolution.

Historical Materialism is a quite general methodological approach that focuses our attention on some crucial linkages between human emancipation and technological progress. While it is not the only useful historical methodology, it has in some respects been one of the most fruitful.

Marx was the greatest elaborator of this methodology. And even if some of his own conclusions are theoretically erroneous, it does not follow that the methods and aims of Marxism are bankrupt through and through.

Even if, as seems the case, Marx's economic argument is fundamentally flawed, important aspects of "Marxism" may continue to be quite useful, especially when reconceptualized in a market context. Marx may have been right in thinking that technological progress makes it possible to supplant the forms of social strife that have dominated our entire epoch with more pacified forms of social existence.

In particular, it remains an open question whether the type of social antagonism specific to our own age—and in opposition to which socialists have largely based their program—might indeed be obsolescent. Even if we cannot accept the strictly Marxian defense of the possibility of a classless society, the goal Marx seeks might be otherwise interpreted and defended.

Even when detached from the impossible ideal of the transcendence of alienated labor and the market, the overcoming of classes is an ambitious enough objective in its own right. It may even make good sense, once suitably framed.

2. The Sublimation of Commodification and Class

The argument against Marx in Part One was an application of the "neo-Hegelian" conviction that whatever solutions and insights can be attained along a given path of inquiry will produce further problems and puzzles of their own. Ignorance and privation are not conditions pertaining to a specific age of underdevelopment which, by and by, might come to an end. They are dialectically recurrent, incessantly sublimated features of the process of discovery itself.

But this does not mean that there is *no* sense in which we can say that "alienation" is overcome. Here we must steer a middle course between two extremes. Resisting, on the one side, the temptation to say that alienation per se is ever overcome, we must equally avoid, on the other, the notion that any specific form of alienation need be with us to stay.

The perenniality of alienation does not imply that there is no such thing as progress. Indeed, my defense of market methods does not show that there is no important role for "socialization" in human history. Rather it signals the need to rethink what "progress" and "socialization" are. We should stop conceiving human history (as Marx seems to have) as a process which approaches a condition of zero alienation as asymptote, and begin thinking of it as a process whereby *each* era overcomes *its* most vexing forms of unfreedom.

The fulfillment of one era's idea of progress transfigures human existence and thus engenders a new horizon of emancipation, and hence a new sense of alienation. It is therefore still possible for us to conceive history as a step-by-step process of emancipation. The profound changes wrought by the development of an economy make possible (and sometimes all but inevitable) basic shifts in human values. These changes can, in turn, react back upon the logic of economic organization itself.

For us, this historical process raises important questions concerning social stratification. An implication of our argument in Chapter 2 is that competition within a given epoch's "domain of scarcity" results in a shift in the line between the scarce and the plentiful. We must now observe that this typically implies a shift in society's conception of what may or may not be subject to the vagaries of the market.

We can always look back on a prior epoch and see in it a "struggle" over goods that were, then, necessarily in short supply. Such struggle is only the flip side of technological development: there must be a period of vying for scarce goods, if we are to pass through the technological development that will render them so plentiful that they can be enjoyed by all.

This has profound implications regarding the rationality of successive forms of social stratification. At each historical step, a relatively disen-franchised group, toiling under rigors from which the privileged are ex-empt, finally succeeds in overcoming this discrepancy. Those who have been deprived gain access to privileges formerly restricted. What once was "particular" now becomes "universal."

At one stage of history, a struggle had to occur if the right to the "life-activity" of a free laborer was to replace the lesser standards of slave or serf. Further struggle had to occur if we were to establish universal rights to the basics of literacy and general education. Later yet, even more ambitious projects begin to appear on the horizon.

When elements of the good life make their first appearance, they are typically available only to part of the population. Only gradually does their production yield to technical mastery and become part of the standard repertoire of the species.

Consider the trajectory of development of any good. At its first appear-ance, it will hardly even be recognized as a good—and indeed may be "known" to be so only as a kind of vague ideality in the mind of some visionary. For at first it is only an idea; it lacks material existence. Only by and by does it acquire a kind of half existence as it is being worked up, developed. As the concept matures, opinions will differ radically as to whether the basic conception is feasible or desirable. Even insofar as there is agreement that it is, there will be disagreement as to how to realize the idea in detail.

It is, necessarily, a long march from such vague and humble beginnings to the stage at which the good in question is recognized, throughout society at large, as being the sort of thing anyone might wish to experience or have. It can indeed become so only when its provision has become a matter of technological "second nature"[1] to the species.

This fact underlies the very meaning of "scarcity" and "plenty" as these concepts are commonly used. "Scarcity" pertains to the time when the threshold has not yet been reached at which virtually universal distribution of a given good has become economically feasible, while "plenty" pertains to the time when it has.

Goods that are now "scarce" will, as our productive mastery improves, become abundant enough to allow universal access. While at one time a given style of emancipated life will belong to the privileged, at a later time a certain threshold is passed: the social costs of producing that good will drop to the point at which the economy as a whole is better served by including it in the society's "basic standard of living"—as part of the *social minimum*.

Forms of social privilege must exist insofar as the universal guarantee of a certain level of well-being is not yet economically feasible. Here is where we find a given society's version of the discrepancy between the "rich" and the "poor." This is roughly the distinction between those who possess an enviable amount of scarce goods, and those largely or entirely restricted to the social minimum.

Though the line between scarcity and plenty is incessantly displaced, there is no reason to suppose that the increasing inclusiveness of the minimum—the process of increasing "rights"—has any inherent limits. The incessant upgrading of the social minimum constantly transforms the very nature of social stratification. The character of "privilege" is itself constantly modified: in each epoch we universalize rights that were, earlier on, restricted to a privileged few.

What is beyond the reach of a king at one moment is, at another, standard fare for the humblest souls. Of course, what is beyond the king's reach is what has not yet even been invented. And this platitude reinforces the point we have been making: goods do not appear all at once, but rather make their first appearance only inchoately, taking experimental, restricted, very expensive form, only gradually becoming normalized—subject to understood and standardized productive techniques—and so more and more widely available.

Only in the final analysis is universalization a practical possibility. But when it does become possible, it allows us to change our very conception of what ought to be subject to market forces. The provision of goods that once were available strictly on a pay-as-you-can commodity basis can now be insulated from the question of wealth or income.

This is a familiar fact of historical experience. To cite an example that will prove central to our own argument: there was a time when your ability to command an education was essentially dependent on whether your family could afford to purchase it; but when a certain stage was reached in the history of our own culture, such schooling came to be guaranteed, whether or not you could have paid for it out of your own resources.

The same phenomenon pertains, in our time, to health care, to legal representation, and to many other goods. Such goods are in that sense no longer permitted to be directly subject to the vagaries of the market, to the calculus of "commodification."

How far might this process go? Might it eventually undermine the essence of "social class"?

3. Marx and the Significance of Birth Privileges

It is here that we can make use of one of Marx's most important insights about what it would mean to abolish social classes.

Marx believes that in society as it has been organized up until now, human beings have been subject to the vagaries of good or bad fortune. Sometimes things have turned out well, other times not so well, but always our social destiny has been largely a matter of luck. But finally, Marx maintains, a radical break is possible: for the first time, we *can* abolish "chance" in the sphere of social existence.[2]

Marx does not mean that social life can be made mechanically predictable, but rather that we can master our fate so as to make sure that the accidents of chance no longer determine one's position in society. From now on, nobody need accept social "fate"—the condition of being lucky (or unlucky) enough to find oneself born into this or that set of social advantages (or disadvantages). Henceforth, we can guarantee people, universally, social treatment that is responsive to, and commensurate with, their talents and needs.

Till now, people's chances of success and happiness have been largely dependent upon a social "given" over which they never had any choice. This simple fact is the source of so much resentment and conflict. I do not resent the fact that you have chosen to devote your life to one thing while I concentrate on another; there seems nothing objectionable about such a voluntary difference between us. But it is indeed a thorn in my side that you were—owing to blind luck rather than choices voluntarily made—dealt, as we say, a better hand in life.

Marx is unambiguous: classes in this sense must be overthrown. No longer can we tolerate what pertained to society's immaturity, when individuals were "abandoned to chance" and social arrangements were "agreements . . . within which the individuals were free to enjoy the freaks of fortune."[3] With a pen dripping sarcasm, he writes: "This right to the undisturbed enjoyment, within certain conditions, of fortuity and chance has up till now been considered personal freedom."[4]

Marx believes that it is precisely this tyranny of "fortuity and chance" that we must eliminate. All people must be given the benefit of "all-round" development and education in a way that is no longer determined by the vicissitudes of the market. Only then will we achieve the first truly voluntary society.

This explains the prominent place Marx and Engels give to *birth privileges*. We can eliminate the most bothersome aspect of the tyranny of change only if we abolish the social condition in which the prospects of children vary with the "accidental" conditions in which, for better or worse, they happen to be brought up. That is why, prominent in the list of demands of the *Communist Manifesto*, Marx and Engels call for immediate "abolition of all right of inheritance" and "free education for all children in public schools."[5]

It is essential that we "replace home education by social"[6] so that "the care and education of the children becomes a public matter."[7]

The fortuity of birth privilege is certainly not all that Marx and Engels mean by social class, but it is one of the central aspects of that phenomenon—one that will become our own chief preoccupation.

4. Formative Parity and the Abolition of Classes

Any society containing a healthy measure of capitalist speculation will necessarily have some distinctions of wealth. If one concedes that market methods are necessary, one forgoes the expectation of eliminating the profits enjoyed by the capitalist. Investment-driven "privileges" are an indispensable aspect of capitalist social organization.

I use "privilege" here in a somewhat strict (or technical) sense: as describing the circumstance in which a person, by acting in accordance with the rules of society, happens to reap a greater share of some kind of social benefit than others do. In light of the argument of Part One, I will assume that, in a market society, many forms of privilege—defining forms of social stratification—are well-earned and, under all circumstances we can now foresee, eminently defensible.

What is interesting about this is that the notion of "birth privilege," introduced in the previous section, is in principle detachable from the idea of privilege as such. For even if privilege-based social stratification is with us to stay, the form of stratification heretofore most prominent—that of social class in the strict and narrow sense—may indeed be obsolete: a "classless society" may at long last be feasible.

Class is not the same thing as privilege. It makes good economic sense to think of abolishing the first of these, but not the second. Class is a special case of privilege—a prominent case indeed, but not the only.

The difference between class society and classless society is not that the former has privileges and the latter does not. It is that a class society confers basic "formative" privileges as a luck-of-the-draw matter of "birth privilege," while a classless society guarantees—in a strictly "socialized" way—that these benefits will be conferred with sole regard to aptitude, intelligence, and trainability.

This suggests the formula: paradigmatic "class distinctions" exist not when the different privileges people enjoy are determined by the choices or contributions they have made, but only when determined by conditions falling outside the range of their consent or voluntary control. The paradigm of such nonconsensual determination is: determination by formative circumstances—that is, by the conditions into which one happens to be born.[8]

Partisans of the classless society can regard certain inequalities as perfectly acceptable, indeed desirable: departures from equality which, far from compromising the ideal of classlessness, would seem to realize it even more perfectly.[9]

That is because the idea of a rational and efficient economy is best understood as "Formative Parity": the investment of social wealth in the "formation" of children in accordance with the productive use to which that investment can be put. The degree of such productive use is mainly determined by the talents of those children. This would imply formative inequalities insofar as there is unequal talent, but such inequalities would not be—insofar as they are real[10]—redolent of social class.

Since aptitude is important when it comes to optimal use of formative benefits, we should, from an economic point of view, regard the abolition of classes a matter of *parity* rather than *equality* of benefit.

In the pages that follow, we will therefore explore the implications of treating Formative Parity as the core of the notion of a classless society.

We will consider such a society to be founded upon a socially mandated proportionality between a person's talent and the amount of social resources invested in her during her minority years. By contrast, classes will be said to exist insofar as there is some significant deviation from parity social investment.[11]

Class advantages, on this reckoning, exist only insofar as some children come of age with levels of relative social advantage which are out of proportion with their ability. This distinction seems in keeping with a good many of our everyday intuitions. We normally consider a society to be class-divided insofar as distributions of initial advantages *depart* from the pattern that would be justified by ability alone.[12] Social classes exist because the daughters and sons of the rich have access to greater formative resources than their equally (or more) talented poor cousins.

If you and I have been given parity treatment, with respect to the social "inputs" with which to cultivate and develop our capacities, all the way up to the point at which we are conceded to be adults, then we will not say there is any difference in "class" between us. This will remain the case no matter what happens later as the result of our adult performance: despite whatever privileges may be won by you but not by me. It will be so even if you end up a woman of wealth and honor by the standards of our society, while I die in obscurity, having lived out most of my adult days at the social minimum—that is, in our society's version of poverty.[13]

Proponents of Formative Parity stand opposed to all forms of disparity in the upbringing of children, no matter what the source of, or the motivation behind, such disparity. Many different kinds of violation of this ideal are possible.

Thus violations can occur through the impersonal and "blind" operation of the market: this would define "economic classes" in a fairly strict and narrow sense. But infringements of Formative Parity can also take the form of the familiar forms of discrimination on grounds of race or gender or life-style, insofar as these do differentially affect the formative resources available to children.

The elimination of any particular non-talent-based form of discrimination should be regarded as the solution to a component aspect of Formative Parity: the achievement of parity in a given respect. If gender-based discrimination were abolished, then in that respect parity would be achieved, though Formative Parity might still be violated in other respects.

The ideal of the classless society, as we will understand it here, means the absence of disparities in any of these senses. To ask whether it could be achieved is to ask if all particular forms of formative disparity could be overcome. Thus Formative Parity names a quite comprehensive ideal having a wide, and in principle indefinite, range of instances and aspects. It is a multidimensional objective.

The class issue, on this understanding, will turn on whether it is economically defensible for there to be disparities in the social resources by which people are formed into adults. We will present the following challenge: that the point in human history has been reached at which it will prove economically efficient for us to work toward eliminating social classes.

On what grounds could we suggest so radical a proposal? The answer to this question has, I believe, two basic components, both of which underlie Marx's own reasoning.

The first is that the classless society embodies an irresistible economic ideal.

The second is that, for reasons of economic underdevelopment, such irresistibility can come to the fore only rather late in human history.

To the extent that we find this twofold theoretical model compelling, we will feel confident that the classless society, radical as this conception is, is a supportable proposal.

We must consider these points in turn.

5. *Formative Parity as Inescapable Prima Facie Ideal*

The idea of Formative Parity does indeed summarize an inescapable productive ideal. Interestingly enough, it really does not make sense to wonder if the abolition of classes is, abstractly considered, something worth striving for. It will turn out that the only justification of classes is a merely temporary one: that eliminating classes is sometimes impracticable in fact.

Formative Parity is at least a prima facie ideal: a goal we ought to seek insofar as circumstances permit—insofar, that is, as this ideal does not run afoul of other social needs of equal or greater importance.

It is an inescapable ideal: for it is indeed but a special form of the quite general maxim that resources should be exploited in accordance with their productive potential.

This is because, even under the most ideal circumstances, there is typically a *diminishing marginal utility of investment*. Thus suppose that Josh and Helene are equally worthy recipients of some investable good: each can make as much use of each meaningful increment of it as the other one can. It might be thought that, given this de facto equality, it follows that a parity (in this case, equalitarian) distribution will be the most productive use of that good. But this follows only if we adopt the further factual hypothesis that, in the case of each potential recipient, every new increment is of somewhat less productive significance than the preceding increment.

To see this, suppose that Josh and Helene have just eaten a minimally adequate dinner, and the issue is that of apportioning two apples for dessert. Suppose further that Josh has already been given the first of those apples, and that this will enhance his vitality, hence also his productivity. Now no doubt we would also admit that giving the second one to him as well, instead of to Helene, will increase Josh's vitality and productivity even more, and therefore will, to that extent, augment the productivity of society as a whole. And yet we feel certain that giving that second apple to Helene will yield even greater increase in the actual vitality, hence aggregate productivity, of these individuals taken together.

On the assumption that the two have been given minimally adequate portions, we do not merely think that parity division of new increments of food will be "fair" (or "compassionate"). We are convinced that it will actually be more socially productive.

If such an assumption could not be made, if each new increment of food were, in the case of each individual, at least as productively significant as the prior increment—then the argument for parity distribution could not be based on considerations of overall productivity.

For in that case each new increment of food would be as well spent on (say) Josh alone as it would be if proportionally divided: giving more and more food to Josh, to the neglect of Helene, would by that hypothesis yield an increase in social productivity at least as impressive as would result from a parity distribution.

Our judgment against disparities of investment in human beings is in this sense "overdetermined." It rests not only on compassion, but on more hard-boiled considerations: on the nontrivial, factual hypothesis that something very much like declining marginal utility actually does obtain. Fortunately for our argument, such a hypothesis is highly plausible, and we may join the economists in assuming it here.

This principle of parity investment is quite general. It applies to all resources: to fields of rye as well as to children.

Thus suppose that our farm's lower field is potentially just as fertile as the upper field: it will yield the same amount of product relative to the same investment. And suppose that there is no shortage of input factors—fertilizer, seed, and so forth. In that event, plowing all those input factors into a single field would overtax the latter as compared to the alternative strategy of investing the same amount of seed, fertilizer, etc., in both fields.

The concept of Formative Parity, construed as a principle of economic productivity, is merely the consequence of applying the logic of parity, rooted in the phenomenon of diminishing marginal utility of investment, in the area of human resources in particular. A classless society would be one that (as it were) invests in the "fertilizing"—the nurture and development—of its children in a way that is in strict accordance with their potential.

Any society that did *not* approximate proportionality between (1) the productive potential of human resources and (2) the actual investment in those human resources, would to that degree not be using those resources with full efficiency. That is why, all other things being equal, social classes are counterproductive in the economic sense.

6. The Logic of Thresholds

But all other things are *not* always equal. Though, as a prima facie ideal, Formative Parity is indeed truistic, it is no truism that, in this or that actual circumstance, the ideal ought to be adhered to. This is because parity—hence efficiency itself—is not always possible. For, until a certain critical *threshold* of productivity is achievable, the prima facie rationality of parity treatment of resources may nonetheless sometimes be overridden.

Thus, in the example of our equally fertile fields, what if we have only enough fertilizer to cover one field effectively? That means: if we were to try to spread the fertilizer over both fields, the amount allotted per unit area would make only a negligible improvement in the fertility of the land. In a case like this, the prima facie good sense of developing both fields would be overridden by the fact that the factors of development would, in that event, fall below the threshold level of fertility for either.

In such special circumstances, we would be right in drawing two conclusions. The first allows for a violation of parity: that, as things stand now, circumstances can dictate the arbitrary choice of one field or the other. The second conclusion would testify to the continued and potential relevance of parity as an ideal: that we would look forward to (and work toward) the time when these "unfortunate" circumstances might change—when the fruits of the fertility of both fields could equally be enjoyed.

In human affairs, the same twofold logic applies.

On the one hand, the failure to realize the efficiencies inherent in parity can sometimes be defended. It may even be true, as Marx believed, that the threshold at which parity is a possible social practice arrives fairly late in history.

On the other hand, and as Marx also believed, social classes inherently involve an aspect of inefficiency—economically viewed, irrationality—in investment policy, one that we should wish to get beyond as soon as we can.

This logic of thresholds is quite general. Thus suppose that there is a certain quantum of food and a certain number of people to feed. How should the food be distributed? The hard-boiled economist must say: we ought to favor one distributive scheme over another if and only if it is the most productive pattern of investment. Parity treatment of the population is the apparent implication: in order to maintain the most productive population, the food should be distributed in proportion to the actual nourishment, hence the real vitality, it will engender. If Elena needs half again as much caloric value as Joseph in order to maintain a minimally acceptable level of health, then—we want to say—the food ought actually to be distributed in just such a proportion between them, and so on for all the others.

But, though parity is indeed such a prima facie ideal or presumption, in this instance too a parity distribution should be imposed only if a certain minimum threshold of effective investment has been surpassed. The familiar "lifeboat" scenarios from the ethics textbooks are but an extreme example of how this logic works. Thus if there is enough food for ten people to survive, but twenty people in the lifeboat, the apparently "fair" procedure of dividing the food in proportion to individual caloric need would result in a quantum of food for each that was well below the threshold of individual survival. Everyone would die. Straitened as lifeboat scenarios are—and unfortunate as *any* outcome would of course be—it seems better to devise some procedure whereby the greatest possible number emerged from the boat alive. Here as well, parity distribution makes sense if but only if, as a result of such proportional allocation, each person is at or above the minimum threshold of daily nourishment. That might mean that of two equally healthy and deserving people, one might be enabled to survive, the other not.[14]

A distributive scheme makes sense only if it puts a minimally meaningful quantum of that good in as many hands as possible. Only when, given the nature of the good in question, and the nature and size of the group that might make use of it, such a threshold has been surpassed, does it make sense to insist upon parity distribution.

This threshold logic clearly applies to the question of social classes. The abolition of class is often thought a visionary, merely fanciful ideal. But since (as we have seen) the "abolition of classes" is but an instance of the economic imperative that we use our resources maximally, it is rather the existence of classes that needs to be justified. We now see that such a justification can consist only in the fact that we have not yet reached a certain threshold—in plain language, cannot yet afford such a step.

Here, too, even insofar as we cannot yet afford it, we would be right to regard parity a reasonable ideal: we would pronounce "unfortunate" any scenario in which it could not be achieved. Such unfortunate circumstances do sometimes obtain, and parity should, in those unhappy cases, be violated. But once a society based on Formative Parity—a "classless society"—becomes possible, it would seem to be the most sensible, hard-boiled, economic choice.

The idea that classes should be abolished can accordingly be pushed aside altogether, only if one can show that what we may call the "Parity Threshold" simply cannot be reached by any society, no matter how wealthy.

7. Explaining Social Classes: Marx on the Mental-Manual Division of Labor

Marxian theory, for all its illogic about the obsolescence of the market, does contain a compelling account of the technological threshold that must be surpassed if classes are to be eliminated. In particular, it allows us to see why it is not possible to eliminate classes so long as the elementary facts of social efficiency dictate that we begin training our children, from early life, to the different stations that they must occupy in society's overall metabolism—that is, to their places in the division of labor.

Our rejection, in Chapter 3, of Marx's "Economic" approach to classes gives aid and comfort to an alternative, "Sociological Theory" of class, which counts the activity of the ruling class as a genuine form of labor. We noted at that juncture that this alternative approach, though quite different from the Economic Theory, is also present in Marx's work.

It is now time to see that the Sociological approach also affords us the best perspective from which to appreciate the grounds and limits of the phenomenon of social classes, and thus also to evaluate the prospects of a classless society.

The principal contention of the Sociological Theory is that, until industry is so far advanced that we can make certain elements of the good life widely available, selective investment in mental labor is the best scenario we can afford. Social wealth is not yet sufficient to free all from strictly manual work. Mental labor must, in the meantime, be the preserve of a privileged few. Here Marx and Engels reason like hard-boiled economists: it is sensible to think about overcoming privilege only when we reach a threshold at which the macroeconomic payoff from taking such a step exceeds that of keeping privileges in place.

On the one hand: under conditions of underdevelopment, any attempt to distribute goods evenly would spread their benefits so thin as to nullify their productive potential. On the other: even if a privileged existence cannot yet be provided to *all*, it would also be counterproductive if social privileges did not fall to at least *some*. Lacking such privileges, society would be bereft of the mental labor on which overall productivity depends.

Since, during the period in which society is largely dependent on manual labor, there can be no question of training all people to highly intelligent functions, these functions must fall to a specific group—an intelligentsia. The historical division of society into classes is therefore no optional matter. Engels sums up the point:

> Side by side with the great majority, exclusively bond slaves to [manual] labor, arises a class freed from directly productive labor, which looks after the general affairs of society: the direction of labor, state business, law, science, art, etc. It is, therefore, the law of division of labor that lies at the basis of the division into classes.[15]

Historical Materialists must accordingly admit that "division into classes has a certain historical justification."[16]

This approach depends upon the assumption—a plausible one, I think—that there is a difference in the wealth associated with these two broad social positions. The reason why mental labor is the characteristic of "upper" classes is that these are the skills requiring the greatest investment in order to be produced and reproduced. This is so despite the fact that most manual tasks also require a considerable level of proficiency.

Mental work is literate and highly refined, and so it requires many hours' worth of social investment—in the form, largely, of what we call education—if it is to be produced. It is this relative costliness of producing the literacy skills at the heart of mental labor that lies at the heart of differential social privilege—that is, of classes. More social hours of labor must be invested in the formation and preservation of mental expertise than is typically required for the production of most forms of skilled manual labor, skilled as the latter may be.

The literacy skills at the heart of mental labor require, in any society, a weighty investment; and society, for much of human history, simply could not afford to extend this nexus of skills to more than a small minority of the population. This implies a differential investment in human labor. If society is to service the needs of all in the most efficient possible way, it must invest a certain dollars' worth of social labor in Arthur, a manual worker, but an even greater amount in Kathleen, a mental worker, in order to have effective use of both sorts of skill.

Under conditions of relative social poverty, then, it makes economic sense for there to be a mental-manual "division of labor" in Marx's sense of the term: people must, from early life, be trained to one sort of function or the other. The need for such a vocational separation is most acute when the productive infrastructure is largely geared to the various labor-intensive manual trades and handicrafts. In those circumstances, a great number of children must be directed into such jobs, if society is to get its business done at all.[17]

This division is effective only if begun rather early. During the heyday of social classes, differential social investment is premajoritarian: training must begin long before adulthood is reached. During the greater portion of human history to now, it has been necessary to have some method of "tracking" our young people from a rather tender age: developing in some of them the literacy skills at the basis of mental labor, and in others the physical manipulations definitive of manual skill.

8. Is the Parity Threshold within Reach?

Let us assume that Marxian theory is right: classes could not be abolished . for much of history. Even so, given the prima facie rationality of parity allocations, one suspects that we can continue to sidestep the demands of Formative Parity only if we endorse the quasi-Malthusian idea that the

Parity Threshold will forever remain beyond reach. One would have to argue that we will be too poor, at least for the foreseeable future, to invest in our children in an fully rational way. Like Marx, we are dubious about such Malthusian claims.

Our optimism about the elimination of classes is rooted in the discussion of the previous section, in which the social costs of producing literate, mental skills emerged as the central problem. Since, till quite recently, such skills could be made available only to some, the transcendence of class—the attainment of the Parity Threshold—was a fortiori out of the question.

But the other side of that same theoretical coin is the following conviction: that the conditions conducive to the overcoming of illiteracy are, when developed to their fullest, those which can help us overcome the problem of class.

The universalization of literacy skills is rooted in specific developments in productive technique. Broadly speaking, as the "hardware" of human production advances, two factors become increasingly compelling.

First, an increasingly complex technology increasingly requires laborers to acquire skills that were, in an earlier epoch, restricted to a privileged few. An eighteenth-century farmer did not need to know how to read charts and manuals. A twentieth-century farmer does.

Second, the increasingly capital-intensive character of production makes it possible for society to forgo unskilled child labor in a way that earlier, labor-intensive society could not have dreamt possible.

This suggests that we draw closer and closer to a threshold at which, despite the impressive costs of producing a universally educated work force, the net productivity yielded by such a policy begins to exceed the net productivity of the alternative arrangement in which only some are thus trained.

Our conjecture comes down to this: the overcoming of classes is already on the way to becoming a reality. Its roots are in the movement, initiated several centuries ago in the technologically more advanced sectors of the world, toward the production of a universally literate work force.

It is certainly true that, in its first manifestations, the achievement of universal "literacy" is not the same as the abolition of class. "Minimal literacy," as we may call it, can be achieved while the class system as such is still in place: it is a component of the answer but not the whole answer— necessary but not sufficient for the overcoming of class.

Necessary: for we have followed Marx's Sociological Theory in viewing literacy skills as the core and basis of mental labor. Insofar as access to these cannot be universalized, the overcoming of class is out of the question.

But not sufficient: for the achievement of minimal literacy does not by itself collapse the formative discrepancies between the well-born and the ill-born to the merely incidental level.

The connection between minimal literacy and the overcoming of classes is this: Formative Parity is the result of pushing the revolution in literacy to its furthest extreme.

The hypothesis is this: the development of the productive infrastructure implies that Formative Parity can be more and more closely approximated. This is because advancing technology implies the declining significance of a premajoritarian division of labor between the most skilled ("mental") tasks of an intelligentsia, and the least skilled ("manual") functions. There is less and less rationale for departure from parity allotment of formative benefits.

Minimal literacy itself could become a universal right after, but only after, the means of producing it had come to be within society's technical grasp. Such means probably did not exist, even in the most advanced nations, only a couple of centuries ago.

No doubt some prescient souls could, back then, have guessed that universalizing minimal literacy would, in some world of the future, prove extraordinarily useful. But such a "universal right," as we now regard it, could become institutionalized in fact only when, not so long ago, society became able to bear not only the direct expenses of education for each child, but also very significant "opportunity costs" in the form of the loss of youthful manual labor.

Though universal minimal literacy makes eminent sense as an ideal, much of human history has been spent beneath the threshold at which it could be realized. To those with any historical sense, it comes as no surprise that "mandatory education" began to be bruited about only in relatively recent history. Now, however, it is entirely taken for granted as a "human right." A limited step in the direction of Formative Parity has been taken.

But though minimal literacy is now regarded as such a right, things are quite otherwise when it comes to Formative Parity in the full sense. In Marx's own view, it is only very late in history that we cross the techno-logical threshold at which we can begin to dismantle classes altogether. There will, till then, and despite the attainment of minimal literacy, con-tinue to be class distinctions: a division between those engaged in robustly literate, mental forms of work and those confined for life to minimally literate, essentially manual functions.

Until that ambitious threshold is reached, protests against the class sys-tem are economically irrational, if not outright impossible. No doubt this is why Marx is hostile to moralizing forms of socialism which preach that the problem is that we have been unwilling to *share* society's burdens and benefits in a spirit of fairness. Marx thus expresses "disgust with sentimental socialistic day dreams," and with "mutton-headed, sentimental, utopian, socialism"[18]—for these doctrines are not grounded in the emancipatory power of the history of industry. Engels elaborates:

> [Socialism] could become possible, could become a historical necessity, only when the actual conditions for its realization were there. Like every other social advance, it becomes practicable, not by men understanding that the existence of classes is in contradiction to justice, equality, etc., not by the mere willingness to abolish these classes, but by virtue of certain new economic conditions.[19]

Marx's antimoralizing tendency, rooted in this logic of thresholds, consists in a rejection of all parity schemes in a context of economic underdevelopment. Below a certain threshold of social wealth, any attempts to dismantle classes will be premature and will necessarily backfire—despite all noble intentions to the contrary.

For most of history we have toiled beneath this threshold; and, insofar, the formative disparities associated with class have enhanced the human powers and thus have had a favorable effect on social production. This differential investment in people, from childhood on, is the foundation of class. It has been a necessary aspect of the social division of labor, at least to now. While human industry is still labor-intensive rather than automated, any attempt to overthrow the mental-manual dichotomy in the name of some visionary ideal of social equality would be merely foolhardy.

The point may be illustrated by events in China a few decades ago. During the Great Cultural Revolution of the 1960s, under Mao and the Red Guard, the Chinese attempted a quantum jump to the classless society. This attempt seemed to fly in the face of orthodox Marxian theory, which held that such a transition could be made only when China's technological basis was far more developed. In the face of that objection, the Maoist line was that passively waiting for these advanced conditions to evolve would foster a Soviet-style, privileged bureaucracy that would hold on indefinitely, if given half a chance: thus would class society be perpetuated.

History seems to have been kinder to the orthodox Marxian view. The Cultural Revolution was in reality an economic debacle. And this result apparently confirms the view that the attempt to eradicate class privileges in an industrially underdeveloped context can only wreak havoc. However noble the intentions of the Chinese, a slowdown or even a reversal of China's economic development was the virtually inevitable upshot of this premature attempt at social leveling.

The Chinese had only two real options. They could either allow the development of the special powers—and hence the class privileges—that make for an intelligentsia, or restrict human development to those powers that can be made available to all. The latter strategy appeals to our equalitarian sentiments, but in fact it led China into a quagmire. (This type of misconceived revolutionism was one aspect of the tragedy of Cambodia under the Khmer Rouge.) Only the first of these approaches could succeed in bringing China into the modern world. A society bereft of an intelligentsia must lack an essential condition of economic and cultural development.

Labor-intensive agrarian economies continue to exist in our own time. And such societies simply cannot—at least on their own—afford the luxury of giving all their children training commensurate with talent. The productive needs of such capital-poor cultures are such that it is feasible to educate only some people to the most highly skilled positions. To a considerable extent, those who come of age in such a privileged intelligentsia must thank their lucky stars: they cannot but notice that many people of at least equal ability languish with their talents largely underdeveloped.

While a society is (like agrarian China) largely preindustrial, there seems to be no alternative to the perpetuation of classes: any attempt to universalize educational rights will result in a marked drop-off in social productivity. But it is far less clear that society can continue to make this excuse indefinitely. The difference between agrarian societies and our own industrial culture prompts the conjecture: the threshold of the abolition of class is something that could be crossed in—but only in—the very recent history of the industrialized sectors of the world.[20]

Economic rationality dictates that investment be correlated with talent when but only when society is wealthy enough to give this rational distribution pattern its functional basis. Only when net (that is, benefits-minus-costs) social productivity is enhanced by the universalization of advanced mental skills does an impressive level of education come to be regarded as the "birthright" of all. It is small wonder, once these social costs are reckoned, that only recently has the elimination of social classes appeared a reasonable goal.

Is it a reasonable goal? Does it make sense to say that we could have *comprehensive* Formative Parity?

Consider again the case of minimal literacy. If, toward the end of the eighteenth century, in the first days of the Industrial Revolution, some pessimist were to assert that not even this more modest goal could ever be universally achieved, the partisan of minimal literacy could have said two things in reply.

First: universal minimal literacy would make for a far more productive society as soon as society could meet the considerable expenses of supporting such an educational venture.

And second: the projectable or expectable productive development of Western society would no doubt be such that, in time, society would in actual fact become wealthy enough to bear just such costs.

This would not have satisfied skeptics—and, concerning even minimal literacy, there were skeptics aplenty. On what basis could the partisan of minimal literacy have "proved" that society would, soon enough, be able to bear the enormous costs of what was then such a radical educational proposal? But even though the skeptic's position was "conventional wisdom," the projection of universal minimal literacy as a reasonable social ideal has long since been vindicated.

Those who believe in the inevitability of classes must explain why we cannot yet afford to develop human beings commensurately with their talents. Universal minimal literacy was once beyond the world's wildest dreams. Even today, some people are illiterate. But are we not far beyond the point at which shortsighted souls could defend illiteracy itself as socially "necessary" or "inevitable"? And might not those who think the overthrow of classes "impossible" be similarly myopic?

We must examine the claim that the radical fulfillment of the revolution in literacy—the achievement of comprehensive Formative Parity—is indeed a prospect for our time: that the particularly objectionable form of privilege that we call social "classes" is obsolescent. The achievement of a classless society, radical as such a goal is, may not merely be a utopian dream, but may be facilitated, even functionally required, by material circumstances that are already coming into existence.

Notes

1. This Aristotelian concept is equivalent to the Hegelian moment of "immediacy." For Hegel, as well as Marx, universalization or socialization is achieved when a given skill has become part of our automatic—"immediate"—repertoire.
2. Marx and Engels, *The German Ideology* (1845–46), in *The Marx-Engels Reader*, ed. Tucker, Robert (New York: 1978), p. 198. Hereafter referred to as "Tucker."
3. Ibid., p. 198.
4. Ibid., p. 198.
5. Tucker, p. 490.
6. Marx and Engels, *Manifesto of the Communist Party*, Tucker, p. 487.

7. Engels, Friedrich, *The Origin of the Family, Private Property, and the State*, excerpt reprinted in Tucker, p. 746. In fairness to Engels, it should be noted that he believes that "marriage based on sex love is by its very nature monogamy" (ibid., p. 750). But apparently he does not think that such monogamy will, under communism, entail privatistic upbringing of children.

8. This distinction between "privilege" and "class" is significantly, but imperfectly, in accord with common sense. Though conventional wisdom does recognize, if roughly, the importance of the distinction between earned privileges and the luck of the draw, ordinary language, vague and ambiguous as it is, sometimes obscures this distinction.

   But departure from everyday nonchalant usage is, in any event, no blemish on the face of our argument. Even if workaday concepts are of limited help here, we are right to invent a technical terminology in order to highlight the difference between privileges earned in adult life and those that fall into our lap as children. Whether natural or artificial, the distinction itself is of great importance to our argument here.

9. I do not mean to suggest that a strictly equalitarian (as opposed to parity-based) society would have classes, but only that strict equality is not necessary for classlessness, and indeed would, given its departure from parity, not be the economically most efficient interpretation thereof.

10. I am quite aware that some such *alleged* differences are quite imaginary; and this fact spells unavoidable difficulties when we come to the matter of applying Formative Parity "in the real world." This problem will be addressed in Chapter 6.2.

11. Since the issue of class turns on such socially conditioned good or ill fortune, natural differences in good fortune—handicaps, natural aptitudes, etc.—are not, strictly speaking, class distinctions. If one child has serious birth defects while another does not, then, while this difference in "birth advantage" is not the result of any responsible act on the part of either of them, it is not, even so, a distinction of class. *Social* class is *social* category.

    This verdict would be reversed, of course, if we discovered that the birth defects were themselves the result of relative monetary disadvantage, such as the inability of one's parents to afford good prenatal care.

12. The humorist Tom Lehrer has captured this point in his caustic remark that the armed forces have eliminated "discrimination" in all respects—even regarding intelligence and ability. The conviction that such "discrimination" is precisely what ought to be retained is what underlies our stress of parity rather than equality of treatment.

13. Conversely, the initial advantages definitive of class may exist even if there is no absolute fixity to one's social position. The class into which one was born does not fully determine one's life prospects. This means that I could be advantaged with respect to class in comparison with you, and yet you might equal (or even surpass) me by dint of hard work or superior talent when we came to be adults. Our respective children could accordingly be born into different class circumstances than we ourselves were.

    A class society can, in a word, have much downward as well as upward mobility. If I overcome the disadvantages into which I was born, that does not alter one whit the fact that these were disadvantages. Nor does it argue against the claim that modern society may have very good reasons for abolishing birth advantages—the phenomenon of social class—altogether.

14. We can understand, in this context, why some moralistic souls are too quick to condemn the infanticide sometimes practiced by cultures much poorer than our own. Such moralists fail to see that any attempt to invest social resources in all who are born would, in certain primitive settings, spell the (perhaps fatal) weakening of society as a whole—slow but sure deterioration. In such extreme circumstances, the imposition of parity distribution would result in universal starvation.

15. Engels, *Socialism: Utopian and Scientific*, Tucker, p. 714. Spelling has been Americanized.

16. Ibid., p. 714.

17. We recall that, in the Marxian sense, a division of labor is no mere difference in functions. If I engage in manual labor in the morning and mental labor in the afternoon, while you follow a reverse rotation, these two functions are differentiated; but a *division* of labor, in Marx's sense, occurs only when rotation is not practicable because there exists a productive requirement that I be trained to one sort of task as my occupation, and you to another.

    Though for the purposes of Chapter 1 we distinguished between the division and the coercion of labor, in the context of the present discussion there will be no confusion if we follow Marx in considering the distinction between classes to be a "division" in the specific sense that children are "channeled" into their respective roles from early life.

18. Marx, Letter to P. V. Annenkov of 28 December 1846, in Marx-Engels *Selected Works*, Vol. II (Moscow: 1962), p. 451.

19. Engels, *Socialism: Utopian and Scientific*, Tucker, p. 714.

20. Habermas does not believe that the Marxian theory of class, based on the mental-manual division of labor, will work. In "Toward a Reconstruction of Historical Materialism," he dismisses that theory within the bounds of a single paragraph. This is remarkably short shrift for such an important component of Marxian social theory—especially in an article of this title, on this subject. All that Habermas says is that the Marxian theory

    [d]espite its suggestive power, . . . is not coherent. Social division of labor means functional specification within the vocational system; but vocational groups differentiated by knowledge and skill need not develop opposing interests that result in differential access to the means of production. There is no argument why functions of domination had to emerge from the contrast of interests rooted in vocational specialization. There was a social division of labor within the politically ruling class (the priesthood, military, and bureaucracy) as well as within the working population (e.g., between farmers and craftsmen). (Seidman, Steven, ed., *Jürgen Habermas on Society and Politics* [Boston: 1989], p. 135)

    Habermas is of course right in noting that the social division of labor has a "horizontal" dimension. But there is a vertical dimension too, one that does follow from vocational specialization of a particular sort. All that needs to be done in order to provide a minimal description and explanation of classes is to maintain that classes are relations in which both authority-wealth and subservience-poverty constellations do exist.

    In order to show *that*, we need to argue, schematically, (1) that all societies have had—at least for some stretch of their history—to pass through a phase which, benign as it might be, involved a pattern of command-giving from those higher in the social order to those lower down; and (2) that the maintenance of those higher in that order requires, under conditions of optimal social functioning, a larger share of the social wealth than the maintenance of those lower down. And both claims seem plausible.

5

The Coming of the Classless Society: Two Revolutions in the History of Education

1. The Question of Means

Does a mandate of Formative Parity make economic sense? Is it a reasonable and achievable goal?

We can answer these questions only if we can specify the social practices by which the ideal might be realized. It is one thing to suggest, as we do, that there ought to be, consistently with the market, parity distribution of formative wealth. It is quite another, to turn our attention to the nuts-and-bolts problems of institutional design.[1]

From a philosophical perspective, the questions governing our inquiry must be: What are the main contemporary obstacles that make the achievement of Formative Parity systematically difficult to attain? What kinds of revision of current educational methods would bring us within reach of this goal?

For Formative Parity is indeed, first and foremost, an educational conception. The hypothesis that an essentially equalitarian society is becoming a practical possibility rests on the assumption that this is not just some rosy idea, but makes hard-boiled economic sense.

We have strategically embraced Marx's methodological assumption that the degree of advancement of social relations must correspond to a culture's level of technological development. The movement to newer, more progressive social forms is inherently expensive; and though these newer forms are themselves, when practicable, more productive than the old, they become feasible only when our basic technology—our productive hardware—is capable of generating a definite level of material wealth.

That they do eventually become feasible—this is the aspect of Marxian "optimism" that will be retained here. Two aspects of this Marxian viewpoint will prove particularly decisive.

First: formative disparities have been rooted in the mental-manual division of labor—a division which, in economic terms, has made eminent sense at least until quite recently.

Second: the productive significance of such disparities declines insofar as technological development proceeds, eventually reaching a point at which the benefits of the all-round formative development of all our children begin to outweigh the efficiencies, formerly significant, of the mental-manual division of labor. Classes, therewith, become obsolete.

This suggests the hypothesis that a continued increase of productivity implies a continued shrinkage in the usefulness of formative disparities, perhaps to the virtual vanishing point: that is, as development proceeds, there are fewer and fewer such disparities beneath the threshold of affordability.

The trajectory of modern history seems characterized by a series of thresholds, defining a "possibility curve" that moves ever upward from compulsory literacy toward—increasingly in our own time—the real possibility of universal postsecondary education.

So conceived, half the historical project of abolishing classes has already been accomplished. Or so I will argue.

But I will also argue that a crucial second step will be necessary if the project is to be consummated. And, consistently with our rejection of Marx's notion that the world of the future is a world without the market, that second step necessitates a radical departure from Marx's radically communal vision of the upbringing of our children.

In stark contrast, the achievement of a classless society will require mandated Formative Parity in a framework which, even so, gives wide scope to the private provision of education. The upshot is a surprising "synthesis" of the goals of "capitalism" and "socialism."

2. Money as the Measure

The achievement of parity itself would seem to have two possible facets. In the first place, a society may choose to regard as nonoptional certain qualifications deemed essential to being a citizen in good standing at all. Insofar as we do insist upon the importance of such "canonical" goods—basic literacy and arithmetical skills, for example—we will, in a classless society, insist that all schools provide them on a parity basis, that is, in proportion to need or talent.

But, secondly, the ideal of classlessness goes beyond the question of access to canonical goods. For indeed, insofar as a culture has become pluralistic, diversity will be regarded as a primary value, and that means there will be legitimate differences in formative strategies themselves: parents will have very different ideas about what is best for their children. Some parents may believe that a child will be ill equipped for life unless taught some manual trade. Others may stress travel. Others, music. Still others may believe that a child ought to be brought up with extensive Christian instruction. And so on.

In this second sort of context, canonical goods will no longer be the main focus of interest. Attention will turn, rather, to the distribution of noncanonical goods—goods about whose formative value reasonable people may differ.

For reasons that will become important later in this chapter, I want to define the *quantitative* dimension of Formative Parity so as to leave open the possibility that people might, *qualitatively*, choose very different courses of learning.

But this poses a problem. Parity is inherently a comparative concept. If we say that Andy and Jane should be given parity treatment, we mean that if they are (for example) equally talented, they are to be given equal access to formative goods.

But it may seem as if noncanonical goods are incommensurable. How can we say that so much Christian education is equivalent to so much instruction in the industrial arts?

But of course we can make this claim—in a market society. Even in the case of noncanonical goods, parity can be defined, for it is consistent with diversity of concrete formative conceptions. Equally talented children are entitled to *equal* but not necessarily *identical* upbringing. Even if families have radically different views about childrearing, we can nonetheless be roughly assured that their equally talented children will be equally advantaged with respect to formative goods.

Such a claim can be made only if there is some *quantitative* standard that can plausibly and feasibly be imposed in the context of *qualitative* difference. There is of course such a standard. We call it money.

Money is the measure of abstract wealth. A quantum of money gives me command over so much of the social product—the choice being mine as to what sorts of actual labor I will command.

This abstractness of money is the key to its power. Money can be used to buy any commodity at all. Hence in an economy based on money—a market society—it will be a truism that money is a reasonable measure of benefit.

Marx himself, though critical of the idea that the money system is with us to stay, would have been the first to insist that, while dominant, it is the principal measure of one's position in society.

Nonetheless, money does not enter into Marx's idea of the classless society, for communism is the system which allegedly dispenses with money altogether as measure of wealth and means of exchange.

But we have rejected Marx's claim that the form of society built upon market relations is just a historically transient phase. Money *is* with us to stay, and is therefore an enduring standard of the degree to which social classes exist, or have been attenuated.

In our view, therefore, if Jane and Andy are equally talented and intelligent (though perhaps in different ways), the requirement of Formative Parity is fulfilled if and only if they receive monetarily equal shares of formative resources for the duration of their minority years.

3. Public Schools and the Abolition of Classes

In a public system of education devoted to Formative Parity, money would serve as the measure in a quite direct way: tax dollars would go directly into the funding of schools in which all children are treated commensurately with talent. And education would be treated as a social mandate in the most straightforward sense of "mandate": a requirement serviced by public institutions.

Those who advocate public education as a means of lessening class distinctions can concede that our society still falls significantly short of actual parity. But they can point out that parity education has indeed been the underlying ideal of the "common school revolution" of the past century and a half—the birth of a modern system of education that is, by law, both "compulsory" (mandatory at least for ages 6–16) and "free" (financed through taxation).

Those who believe that the public system has the best prospects of realizing ever higher levels of such parity can indeed cite a good deal of history in their support. Indeed, a cursory review of the main historical steps in the evolution of this system is enough to convince us that the abolition of class is a task that is already half done.

There is a European mystique that the modern world begins with the Bastille. Arguably, it begins in the plain and functional schoolhouses of New England. The revolution in public education in the nineteenth century, so essential to the formation of modern democratic society, was already foreshadowed in measures taken by the Calvinist Puritans of the Massachusetts Bay Colony two centuries earlier. In successive laws of increasing strength, passed in 1642 and 1647, the legislature of the colony sought to make literacy mandatory.[2]

But this revolution could be consummated only when, in the full flush of Jacksonian democracy, successive state legislatures, especially in the North, established the principles of universal tax-supported ("free") education. This was the historical moment when American society committed itself to a basic economic premise: that whenever society can bear the costs of moving closer to parity investment in human beings, it makes good sense to take that step.

Horace Mann, the preeminent leader of this "common school" movement, was quite explicit in his defense of the idea that "the expediency" of universally available "free schools" can be "advocated on grounds of political economy." Mann believed that the productive benefits to society of a generally educated population would more than compensate for the quite considerable social costs of such education. He repeatedly claimed that tax dollars spent in making grammar schools universally accessible would be more than offset by the productivity of the graduates themselves. Writing in 1846, he asserted:

> An educated people is always a more industrious and productive people. Knowledge and abundance sustain to each other the relation of cause and effect. Intelligence is a primary ingredient in the wealth of nations.[3]

It was this conviction about the economic expediency of a universally educated work force, more than anything else, that fueled the common school movement. And the idea of education as a sound economic investment has been a continuous tradition in the United States since Mann's time. That human beings are our most important productive "capital" has, in our own day, been given a technical and scholarly defense by economists of education.[4]

The century and a half since the consolidation of the common school revolution has seen the extension of the logic of formative rights in manifold ways. The system came to be driven by the "ladder" conception governing education from grade school virtually all the way through college, according to which education must be "meritocratic" every step of the way.[5] In the modern form of this system, a student who successfully completes a course of study at a given level is guaranteed access to ever higher levels in the system, all the way through the four years of college—that is, to about age twenty-two:

> [T]he next rung of each educational institution would be available without restrictions or handicaps except the limitations in the desire and ability of the student to continue. [This American] conception of a

universal, free, public, compulsory and, largely, co-educational school system contrasted with a restrictive European system where there were still separate schools for the upper classes.[6]

Though some degree of correlation still exists between the accidents of one's birth and the extent of one's formative opportunities, it seems undeniable that the latter correlation has, all in all, become weaker and weaker as the system itself has become more and more productive.

Once upon a time, a newborn's life prospects were almost entirely determined by family background. Her chances of acquiring basic skills commensurate with talent largely depended upon her parents' wealth and level of cultivation. Today, while the gains in formative rights brought about by the revolution in public education still fall significantly short of comprehensive parity, we do seem to have taken a big step in the right direction. The system, if imperfectly meritocratic, is much closer to that ideal than its educational predecessors.[7] Though far from dead, the class system would seem to be entering its dotage.

Extrapolating from this tendency into what seems a reasonable and feasible future, one is tempted to conclude that parity-based education is an increasingly irresistible imperative of modern society. It seems there is a tendency for formative disparities to approach, asymptotically, a point of marginal or incidental significance.

Champions of public education have, with some justice, long viewed the successes of public education as the harbinger—if not the full achievement—of a classless society. They argue that more and more ambitious thresholds of educational parity have been attained insofar as economic development has continued. As one historian of education remarks, the United States, by mandating free and universal education,

> abolished its class system in theory (although not completely in practice) [and] launched a system of education, by design at least, to make available equality of opportunity. One could go as far as his talents would take him. This opportunity was to be provided through free education made available to all and even a compulsory attendance law to see to it that everyone could take advantage of it. This educational system was to be extended eventually from the lowest levels on through the university.[8]

It will of course be objected: abolishing classes "in theory" is not the same as getting rid of them in fact. Despite the admitted gains of the public system, we still seem far short of the ultimate goal. What remains to be done?

4. Should Education Remain Public?

For indeed, those who think that public education is the best way of attacking social classes will have to admit that large and daunting gaps remain. Despite all the investment that has been made in public education at all levels in modern times, that system has not undermined class distinctions to the degree its staunchest advocates have expected, or hoped, it would.[9]

The studies of Christopher Jencks and others have shown that public education is, as yet, far from a true meritocracy.[10] The role of education in reducing the advantages and disadvantages of family background, though significant, is not yet as decisive as educators would like it to be.[11]

When it comes to investments in "human capital" in the interests of social parity, the facts themselves seem to show (in the words of one historian of education) that "diminishing returns set in very quickly. . . ."[12]

Parity in "educational" rights, from birth to full maturity, can be achieved only if society mandates that all children will have access to comparable formative opportunities. And, because of marked differences in family wealth over which society has exerted no redistributive control, there continue to be wide discrepancies in formative benefits received by children.

Perhaps most significant of these concern the crucial first five years of life, in which the advantages of inherited familial wealth continue to determine so many of children's life prospects. Thus any attempt to mandate Formative Parity will have to be ambitious enough to ensure that children receive comparable formative opportunities on the so-called preschool level. I say "so-called," because one of the consequences of comprehensive Formative Parity would be an increased consciousness of the fact that the educational process should not be conceived as starting at age five or six, by which time the "class" effects of differential wealth have already had an irreversible effect on children's prospects.

One may well wonder if our public schools, good as they may be, can possibly overcome the fateful depth of the "tracking" imposed by such unaltered initial conditions.

But for some people, skepticism runs even deeper than that. Some wonder if the public system is not an organizational dinosaur no longer fitted for the education of our children at all. Here we encounter two types or levels of skepticism.

In the first place, free-market advocates have long argued that since public education does not employ the market mechanism, it cannot avail itself of the efficiencies of competition, and so must readily fall prey to bureaucracy, defensively protecting underproductive methods and people. Only in a competitive environment—where schools sink or swim depending on where consumers choose to spend their dollars—will the business of education, like any other business, provide the best product at the least cost.

In the second place—but as a consequence of the first point—free-market advocates argue that a public system will not even be the best way of attacking the problem of class. If we insist that all children be given a minimum guaranteed level of education, this can be handled on the "demand side," by means of state-issued monetary stipends or "vouchers"— with the proviso that these students be able to spend these stipends where they and their families choose, among an array of schools available (as far as the "supply side" is concerned) on the open market.

Since, as we saw in Chapter 5.2, money is the measure of benefit, parity education of our children could, in principle, be achieved through either public or private education—as long as stipends are commensurate with ability. Free-market advocates are simply claiming that, if public education is not as efficient as private education in providing its product to the people, then it will not be as effective in attacking social classes, either.

A voucher approach has been favored not only by conservatives like Milton Friedman, but, more lately, by some liberals as well. Chubb and Moe, researchers for the left-of-center Brookings Institution, have defended a model that coincides with Friedman's in all but details.[13]

Education is, from the economic perspective, a vital activity, on which the productivity of a culture largely turns. And the most fundamental question in the contemporary economics of education is whether or not, in a society committed to market methods, our school system should be left in its present socialized state.

Public education is a practice so deeply ingrained in our culture that we rarely reflect that it *is* socialistic at its core. Though a market in education does exist, public education is of course privileged because it is tax-supported. Those who wish to purchase an education for their children on the open market must in effect pay double tuition: once, in the form of school taxes,[14] and again, in the form of private school tuition. This would be, to say the least, an extreme burden for most families. For the great majority, public—socialized—education is the only effective option.

Could private provision of education bring us closer to the end of social class? Proponents of a private approach have generally been regarded as "conservatives,"[15] but this may be one more instance in which the old, conventional lines of distinction between "right" and "left" are wearing thin.

Thus Milton and Rose Friedman's book *Free to Choose* has typically (and rightly) been considered an exercise in archetypal economic conservatism. The authors would not top anybody's list of suspected enemies of the class system. And yet one of the Friedmans' main complaints against public education is that it exacerbates rather than ameliorates class distinctions. The lessening of such differences would, they think, be a chief virtue of a voucher system: "Vouchers would improve the quality of the schooling available to the rich hardly at all; to the middle class, moderately; to the lower income class, enormously."[16] Because the public school system has had only limited success in this regard, it is time to seek an institutional alternative:

> The tragedy, and irony, is that a system dedicated to enabling all children to acquire a common language and the values of U.S. citizenship, to giving all children equal educational opportunity, should in practice exacerbate the stratification of society and provide highly unequal educational opportunity. . . . The parents in the suburbs are getting far more value for their tax dollars than the parents in the inner cities.[17]

The Friedmans point to the "armed camp" atmosphere of these inner-city schools as emblematic of the problems public education has failed to solve:

> . . . Parents complain about the declining quality of the schooling their children receive. Many are even more disturbed about the dangers to their children's physical well-being. . . . Increasing numbers of teachers are fearful about their physical safety, even in the classroom. . . .[18]

Are we to jettison public education as economically irrational in the market context? And what are the implications of this entire question with reference to the possibility of moving toward a "classless society"?

A highly vexed issue, to be sure. In the middle of the last century, when the public school system was ascendant, opposition to it—precisely because it is a socialist conception—ran very high: it was second only to the slavery question as America's most hotly contested issue. And today, once again, the battle lines are being more and more clearly drawn. The fight looms large—and ugly.

On the one side, implacably opposed to anything smacking of free enterprise in education, we have the majority of the educators themselves, backed by the rather awesome power of the teachers unions.

On the other side are the conservatives, who argue that opposition to the market is just what one should expect from an entrenched and bureaucratized professional caste fighting tooth and claw to preserve government-protected sinecures.

The two positions, apparently based on radically differing paradigms of education, seem to have little to say to one another.

This suggests—to the dialectically minded—that what is needed is a perspective that can do justice to the legitimate claims and concerns of both parties. If such a perspective cannot be attained, we face a great danger that matters will reach a stultifying impasse.

Lacking comprehensive vision, we could end up wasting billions in tax dollars and, worst of all, squandering myriad opportunities for the development of our children.

In Part One we ourselves turned the Marxian attempt to transcend market methods against itself. One might accordingly expect that we would accept major aspects of the conservative critique of education: that our defense of the market ought (mutatis mutandis) to induce us to support a system of free enterprise—and free familial choice—here as well.

It will turn out that there is a great deal of truth in this. But we must, nonetheless, grasp this truth "*dialectically*"—which is also to say: historically.

On the one hand, only from a dialectical perspective will we see that public schools were all but inevitable during the first great phase of our educational revolution.

On the other hand, only from that same perspective will we be able to see that, in our own age, market-mediated provision of education is increasingly warranted—and indeed may be the precondition of the final overcoming of society built on social classes.

The equalitarian ideals of the public school movement are not misconceived. Our system of public education has been radically emancipatory, just as its partisans have supposed. Any improvement upon it must remain consistent with the underlying aims of that revolution.

Nonetheless, those very aims, though themselves entirely defensible, can be realized only if our institutions undergo a qualitative transformation.

5. The Rationality of Public Education as a Historically Relative Question

For a century and a half, our culture has given a privileged role to socialized means of education. And whatever may be the case in our own day, it is difficult to see how, given nineteenth-century material conditions, there was any feasible alternative. The public school revolution can justly claim to have been, in the conditions in which it arose, the only feasible first step in the direction of undermining social classes and forming a vastly more productive work force. (Even some free-market conservatives seem willing to concede that public schools were all but inevitable in the recent past.)[19]

That is why one should not be too quick to insinuate that educators' defenses of public education have ignoble motives. Such educators are to be pardoned if they are suspicious of any attempts to undermine the system that has proved to be the most progressive to date. Public education, the first wave of our culture's assault upon classes, was a virtual economic necessity in the period in which it was introduced, and at least until recent times.

To appreciate this virtual inevitability of public education, we must keep in mind that, however wrong Marx was about the obsolescence of capitalism in general, there certainly are circumstances in which socialization in the strict sense—"public ownership"—does make sense. Economic efficiency can sometimes dictate the need for a single, unified system. Even the most conservative proponents of market methods recognize that government ownership is appropriate under some very special conditions.

Such conditions are, in the modern world, the exception rather than the rule; and, in their absence, there must be at least a strong presumption in favor of private enterprise. Contra Marx, strict socialization cannot be justified in general terms, but requires special arguments adapted to specific circumstances. But such circumstances do sometimes exist.

In particular: public ownership makes sense insofar as conditions within the system make it very difficult, or impossible, for a plurality of providers of the same sort of good to exist side by side. If such conditions do exist, we will not be able to secure the benefits of competition.

Often this depends on the literally physical, "hardware" aspect of the good or service in question. Thus, given the technology of modern communications, especially in the epoch of satellite dishes and such, there is no reason why we cannot have several long-distance phone companies competing side by side. Things were different when the communications infrastructure required the running of wires from end to end. In that context, it was, arguably, prohibitively costly, from a social point of view, to maintain a plurality of communications companies.

There are, today, no such obvious constraints in the case of refrigerator production, medical provision, or even—as witness the modern boom in express mail services—the delivery of letters and parcels. There are such constraints in the case of our main transportation conduits—our roads, bridges, subway systems, and the like.[20]

And there have been, at least till quite recently, such constraints in the case of education. For, given our resolve to produce a universally educated populace with minimum standards of literacy, any attempt to provide a plurality of choices to each "consumer" would have confronted very significant diseconomies of scale: a fact which puts severe limitations on the possibility of competition in this sphere.

This is but another instance of the "threshold" phenomenon. Competition, with all its virtues, can be stably incorporated into an economic system only if we have passed the point at which having a plurality of providers of the service in question has become scale-efficient. Given the relatively immature infrastructure and dispersed population of America in the nineteenth century, such a threshold had not yet been reached, and we simply could not yet avail ourselves of these advantages. There are times, before such a threshold is reached, when a community or neighborhood cannot afford to have more than one school within hailing distance of each child.

To see this, suppose our imaginary community began with a single school. The question is: why should it not have more than that one school, and therefore reap the benefits of competition? The answer is that the citizens would find that, until that school reached a fairly impressive size, each new education dollar would be more effectively spent on expanding and improving *it*: given the need to stretch each monetary investment to its utmost, any attempt to provide multiple options would involve a reduplication of services which would, in turn, impose unacceptable costs.

In principle, this holds of any good or service. Though, in "typical" instances, it is economically efficient for there to be competition among clothing stores, these competitive efficiencies are beyond the reach of, say, a small and isolated frontier town. We may consider this phenomenon in three phases.

(1) In the most extreme cases, maintaining more than one clothing shop would scarcely be possible: for there to be two, there would have to be a much greater volume of trade, enough to provide at least maintenance-level income to the two shopkeepers. This phenomenon is *quantum-like*: the minimum unit cost of maintaining a given enterprise in a given industry will be some relatively large dollar figure. As a consequence, our town will be able to afford more than one entrant into the field only if, consistently

with the budgets of the townsfolk, the volume of trade in that industry is enough to approximate whole-number multiples of that minimum cost.

For example: if the minimum cost for operating Ida's Clothing Store is $10,000, any marginal volume of trade in excess of $10,000, but still well below $20,000, will not be enough to keep a second shopkeeper in business. Unless the average family is willing to increase its average clothing budget, the opening of Sam's Drygoods Emporium, when the town's volume of trade is (say) still only $16,000, would produce subsubsistence income to—hence subpar performance by—both Ida and Sam, and the eventual bankruptcy of at least one of them.

(2) In some intermediate cases, bankruptcy may not be at issue, but the quantum-like aspect of the efficiencies of scale may nonetheless be felt. While, strictly speaking, two stores might both *minimally* function in an environment of $20,000 volume of trade, *peak* efficiency for such a store might not be reached until the $35,000 point is reached. In excess of $20,000, while duplication of services is an option for the town, it may seem less desirable than expanding Ida's, whose more efficient operation might be expected to be passed on in the form of a lower clothing bill for the entire community. If that were so, the upshot of maintaining both Sam's and Ida's would be that the townsfolk would have to spend a higher percentage of their own income on clothing than is, abstractly, necessary.

I say "abstractly" because, insofar as we do enter this more "optional" intermediate area, the *efficiencies of scale*—though they still exert pressure for nonduplication—now have to contend with countervailing pressures exerted by the *efficiencies of competition*. Exclusive focus on scale efficiencies neglects the fact—which becomes increasingly significant insofar as more than one market entrant is possible—that Ida enjoys the benefits of a local monopoly. As her volume increases, she can (knowing that local demand for clothes is relatively inelastic) continue to price goods as before, so that the decreased unit costs provided by increased scale-efficiency are reflected in profits that go straight into her own pocket, and do not benefit the community one whit.

In this intermediate area, the town will experience pressures of both kinds. Maintaining a plurality of enterprises will not be of peak efficiency in terms of scale, a fact which, in itself, will tend to drive prices up, but the efficiencies of competition will exert countervailing pressures, driving prices down. Whether the town will be better or worse off if Sam enters the field depends on the precise net result of this trade-off.

(3) Finally we reach the point at which there is no question but that the town can afford to maintain more than one provider. The principal reason

for this would be an increase in the population of the area: without raising any family's clothing budget, the town can generate a volume of trade capable of supporting several clothing establishments each of which is able to operate at a level approximating peak scale efficiency.

Since, in this event, the pressures on the side of scale-efficiency no longer come into play, those on the side of competition can become our sole focus. There are no longer any good arguments for maintaining Ida's monopoly: it is an unambiguous fact that the town will benefit if Sam opens up his emporium.

Should we have a competitive market in education? It is clear that there can be no *general* answer.

On the one hand, it seems to me implausible in the extreme that, given the realities of small-town life in the mid-nineteenth century, most communities had any price-effective option but to realize the virtues of "consolidation." Under such conditions, "common schools" are a virtually irresistible choice: the economies of scale seem to outweigh any potential economies of having multiple providers in mutual competition. The "Threshold of Competition," as we may call it, was not yet reached.

It is not precisely right to say that competition did not make a certain abstract sense, even back then: monopoly per se, insulated from competition, always has at least a *tendency* to drive prices up. It is not as if our great-grandparents could not appreciate what an argument for competitive education would look like. The point, rather, is that, for them, the appeal of such a scenario could remain only abstract: it could manifest itself only as a dream that might someday be realized by their descendants. In their time, the benefits of competition were, in this area, inconsequential by comparison with the overwhelming benefits of consolidation.

Thus, for much of our history, it has been economically unfeasible for there to be more than one "common school" for each community or neighborhood. Given population densities and the existing state of transport, insofar as children are within easy reach of some central location, consolidation of services at that place allows us to avoid an economically unacceptable duplication of resources. In those circumstances, if the children of a local community can reach one school about as easily as they can reach two, communities will find it cheaper to choose the first option.

Under such conditions, when monopoly is virtually dictated by the efficiencies of scale, every community will have some strong motivation to try to avoid the negative aspects thereof. And indeed this is possible—by means of *moral* and *political* pressures and processes.

Consider our "intermediate" scenario (2) above. Suppose the town recognizes that maintaining Ida's, as the sole clothing store, is in principle a scale-efficient strategy. This means that if Ida does not pass on some of the benefits of her increased scale-efficiency in the form of lower prices to the community, she will, under the rather close-knit social circumstances presumed, be perceived as an exploitative presence. She will hear grumblings that some townsfolk would prefer to give Sam a chance—in her place. Such moral pressures can be quite strong: if she wishes to be a viable enterprise, she will have to keep her profits "reasonable"—or else move to the big city.

Alternatively, in the case of some essential services, a community may wish to move beyond such informal, moral controls on monopolistic abuse and establish direct political control over the de facto monopoly in question. This has long been the chief argument behind government-run monopolies: since avoiding monopoly is, for the time being, out of the question, the best we can do is make sure that the abuses thereof are minimized; and the best way to do this is to administer them within the public sector.

Historically, this argument had preeminent strength in the case of education. Pressures for *common* education amounted to irresistible pressures for *public* education. These arguments remain effective until monopoly itself is no longer a virtual economic necessity.

One argument of this book has been that, contra Marx, there must be a presumption in favor of market methods. But we now see that this presumption can be effective only when the economy of a region has become so developed that it can afford to move beyond consolidation.

With respect to some given good or service, a society that had not yet reached this state would still be in an immature stage of capital development. It would not yet have reached the threshold at which the full advantages of economic competition—the core of capitalist rationality—could be enjoyed.

6. Transition to the Question of Privatization

We are therefore led to endorse one Marxian axiom, but to invert another.

The axiom we endorse: basic changes in the material conditions of production eventually accumulate to the point at which a qualitative transformation of social institutions becomes possible and desirable. According to a "dialectical" view of things, institutions which are the emancipatory forces at one stage of infrastructural development become fetters at a later stage.

The axiom we invert: the idea that, in all the main branches of human industry, the virtues of consolidation follow upon those of competition. Marx did believe that the "anarchy" of the competitive marketplace is superseded by community ownership; but we suggest that, at least in many typical instances, unity and consolidation are superseded by plurality and competition.

The privatization of education may be the next logical step in the evolution of our formative institutions. Reasons for suspecting that this is so are implicit in the historical approach to public education just presented. The threshold of competition may indeed be surpassed in an age of urbanization and high-tech telecommunications and transport.

These world-shrinking factors spell a marked lessening in the effective distances separating people from services they might wish to seek, a dramatic increase in the number of services that can fall within striking distance of each family. Correspondingly, they entail an increasing volume of sales potentially available to each enterprise.

Thus, whereas once it made sense for a community or a neighborhood to exploit the efficiencies of consolidation rather than those of competition, today most children live—or could live—within effective traveling distance of a multiplicity of schools, each one of which is large enough to be scale-efficient. In principle, this should mean that, at long last, the desiderata of scale-efficiency and competitiveness can both be satisfied. In that case, we might have what our great-grandparents could not: an effective market in education.

What has all this to do with class? Even if it be granted that a competitive market in education would be economically more efficient, why should we suppose that such a development is a step in the direction of Formative Parity?

Given our own anticlass commitments, a transition to privatistic provision of education would be of central interest to us only if we had become convinced that, because of fundamental developments in the social infrastructure, such a changeover was in the service of the same revolutionary goals advanced by the public school movement at an earlier stage of the game.

That is just what I want to argue. Though the public schools were necessary in the first phase of our culture's assault upon social classes, a movement toward privatization is necessary if that revolution is to enter a second vital—and perhaps consummating—stage.

Marxians assume that competition generates and maintains class distinctions. By contrast, I will defend the proposition that a competitive market in education would bring us nearer to the goal of the classless society than our public school system can get us.

We saw (in Chapter 5.4) that the Friedmans do believe that a lessening of class distinctions would be a virtue of the voucher system. But though they do, to that extent, appeal to our equalitarian sentiments, their ultimate commitment is not to any form of mandated parity, nor to any very close approximation of a classless society.

It is noteworthy that, although their name is associated with the strongly redistributive "voucher" system, the Friedmans do not personally favor the vouchers—except as a faute de mieux concession to contemporary political realities. Strictly speaking, guaranteeing each student a certain level of educational spending power, by means of a government-administered scheme of taxation and redistribution, would (in their view) be one more instance of "the sickness of an overgoverned society."[21] In the best of all economic scenarios, matters would be left to the operation of the market itself:

> We regard the voucher plan as a partial solution because it affects neither the financing of schooling nor the compulsory education laws. We favor going much farther. Offhand, it would appear that the wealthier a society and the more evenly distributed is income within it, the less reason there is for government to finance schooling. The parents bear most of the cost in any event, and the cost for equal quality is undoubtedly higher when they bear the cost indirectly through taxes than when they pay for schooling directly—unless schooling is very different from other government activities.[22]

From the Friedmans' perspective, the virtue of a voucher system is that it goes half the distance to free-market methods. Ideally, they believe, the open market itself ought to be put in a privileged place—whether on the side of supply, or on that of demand. Since mandating specific levels of educational funding violates open-market priorities on the demand side, such mandates should, under ideal conditions, be dispensed with. Since a voucher system is such a mandate, the Friedmans recommend it only as a first step in the right direction.

This has some striking implications. True, the Friedmans believe that a free-market economy—sans vouchers—would, as a natural result, "soften" class distinctions. But though they are convinced (for instance) that in a free-market society "most" people will in fact be literate,[23] they do not advocate making literacy a social guarantee, nor education itself compulsory.[24]

The Friedmans regard the free market as itself the chief desideratum. Any attenuation of class distinctions is, from their perspective, a welcome side benefit. But it is in no event to be construed as a social mandate.

I will argue in Chapter 5.9 that a mandated stipend or voucher system is, contra the Friedmans, not merely a second-best, compromise gesture, but an economically essential moment of the overthrow of classes, and hence of the rational use of human resources under the market system itself.

But the first point to occupy us here is pro-Friedman. We who argue for the overthrow of classes can adapt the argument of free-market advocates to our own purposes. The arguments in favor of private provision of education contain a truth we radicals must learn.

Almost two centuries of radicalism have been built around the notion that *parity* schooling must be common, public, *socialized* schooling. Today we must entertain the possibility of a dialectical shift. It is just possible that, without a move to privatization, an essential component of the classless society would necessarily be left largely unfulfilled.

7. Public Education and the Bias of the Canon

We now come to the heart of the argument. I will, in this section, argue in defense of two claims: (1) that only the private system gives families the effective ability to choose from a spectrum of schools; and (2) that only if this condition is present, can we fulfill that most radical of dreams: the creation of a classless society in the most robust sense of the term.

Taken together, these two contentions point to this conclusion: classes can be overcome only in an environment in which there is radical diversity and freedom of choice of educational options—where a pedagogical core or canon is not imposed as a mandate, though it may continue to exist as a quite legitimate matter of choice.

This diversity, though often labeled "individualism," is not strictly a matter of individual behavior. Rather it involves the freedom of the most elementary social units—families—to define the manner of their existence, and the terms and conditions in which those born into them will be brought up.

What we must now argue is that a strictly socialized system of education, in necessarily curtailing the freedom of families to decide for themselves what course of instruction is best for their children, necessarily bereaves our educational life of essential diversity, and thus throws a roadblock in the way of the overcoming of class itself. In a truly classless society, parents will need far wider latitude in determining the style and substance of the formation of their children than they have at present.

We saw in Chapter 5.2 that, in a pluralistic market society, Formative Parity is a quantitative concept. If Eric and Marie are equally talented, they will be given, during their minority years, formative benefits of equal monetary value.

We noted then that, abstractly considered, this demand could be fulfilled by either the public or the private sector, so long as monetary investments in children's education remained proportional to talent.

This is correct. But what must now be added is that such *quantitative* parity cannot be optimally achieved unless the fulfillment of some *qualitative* "boundary" or "initial" conditions is presumed. And once this qualitative proviso is taken into account, it turns out that there is an important sense in which a private system can more adequately provide parity benefits to a diverse population. We must look at this point more closely.

Real parity would, of course, have to be measured in actual purchasing power; but we must beware a shallow understanding of this. It does not mean merely "equal dollars for equal talent." Formative Parity concerns the comparative command—power—minors have over formative resources. If we were to discover that, despite equal dollar stipends, Eric was able to find what he desired in the marketplace, while Marie was not, it would be a cruel fallacy to conclude that she and he had equal market power.

The dollars concerned must be effective means of exchange, and that means there must be a spectrum of meaningful options wide enough to give each of the various consumers a meaningful choice. People must be able to purchase real *goods*: commodities actually reflecting their cultural and personal commitments.

Dollars are a good index of your power—but only if they can bring you what you reasonably desire. If, despite equal dollar allocations, the market services the reasonable desires of Eric's family, but not of Marie's, the appearance of parity purchasing power is refuted. Full parity does not, insofar, really exist.

Such discrimination is indeed a covert but powerful reality in the case of public schools. These are not merely public, in the sense of "open to all," for this very openness has further implications. By virtue of the fact that schools are public, they have a particular, determinate character. Some parents may, quite legitimately, find that this sort of school is exactly what they are looking for. Others, just as legitimately, may not.

The determinate character of public schools is rooted in the very commodity they have, historically, been asked to provide: an education, both basic and well-rounded, suited to a population of great cultural and subcultural diversity. Our public schools must serve, without appearance of prejudice, Italian and Jew, Black Muslim and white Protestant, boy and girl.

Public schools could not have provided this service if they had not been able to define their existence around an apparently *neutral canon*—a "core" of essential doctrine deemed valid for any citizen of our general culture, whatever the specific culture from which she derives.

Because we ourselves are products of a system dominated by public schools, we often assume that the education they provide is the only one possible. We do not think of the canon as a qualitatively "determinate" social choice, to which there may, in some circumstances, be alternatives. If we think of it as a canon at all, we are apt to regard it as the heart of a "standard" education.

That, indeed, is what it is. Its middle-of-the-road standardness is indeed its distinguishing mark, even its point of honor. To consider only high school: the standard quadrivial departmentalization into mathematics, English, social studies, and science (with foreign language optional); each of these fields with its definite sequential character—as in math, from elementary algebra (ninth year) through plane geometry (tenth), thence into intermediate algebra and trigonometry (eleventh), with advanced algebra and solid geometry elective in twelfth grade. Minor variations in this pattern occur from state to state; the body of doctrine is remarkably constant.

In many respects, core schools provide—at least in principle—an admirable curriculum for a majority of our people. They will probably continue to do so into the indefinite future. What is not clear is why such a curriculum should be regarded as the only legitimate choice. There is nothing wrong with our culture's version of a solid, general education. Problems arise when certain other valid cultural options do not effectively exist.

This reflects a lesson that postmodern criticism has taught us: that the social act of defining any apparently "neutral" canon is in reality a determinate and tendentious political act. Far from being neutral, it privileges certain specific attitudes and values. These are the "melting pot" values of a cosmopolitan or "universal" sort: a common language over the old tongue; "objective" scientific method over "superstitious folk belief."

By its nature, public education must demote various forms of cultural "insularity" and particularism, and put generalist, assimilationist priorities in their stead.

Two types of demotion deserve special notice here.

The first is cultural or ethnic. Though what one does at home remains legally and morally one's own business, in school one must master trans-ethnic, culture-neutral skills. These skills emerge as "essential." Specific ethnic abilities—the speaking of Italian or Yiddish, for example—are deemed "optional."

Given the commitment in time and effort that an education involves, it is no wonder that students must give pride of place to the canonic skills, over against "optional," culturally specific talents. And so the latter must have a long-run tendency to atrophy. Many of the old languages and folkways begin to die out.

It is true that one can, in our system, resolve to keep more closely to one's own folkways, and can express that resolve in one's choice of schools. Irish families can send their kids to parish schools; Jewish families can send theirs to yeshiva. But since such families would be subject to the unacceptable "double tuition" already noted in Chapter 5.4, a culturally specific education is not on most people's effective menu of choices.

The second type of demotion has to do with particular talent. Our canonical system is biased against those who would choose, if they could, to give unusually strong emphasis to the development of one or two very specific abilities.

If Josh is a talented oboist, his best option today is to attend a good suburban school which, on an elective basis, provides good music teachers and a good orchestra program. This is a quite valid approach. But what if Josh's family wished to send him to a school where math and social studies took a backseat to music studies? Such an option does not effectively exist.

Perhaps you would not wish to send your child to such a school. Perhaps you would find it too "narrow." And you might also not wish to send your child to a school in which students received a steady dose of Christian doctrine. You would in that event favor a generalist direction for your children. And that is what public schools provide: a culture's definition of "general" education. It is an entirely legitimate choice.

But it is difficult to produce reasons why our culture's notion of a general education is the *only* valid path. The bias in favor of generality is no worse than any other bias, and may have a good many arguments in its favor. It may even be the best option for most people. But it is hard to see how this bias can claim universal or absolute validity. Specialization, too, has its virtues—and its arguments.

Thus even if, in a public system, students are equally funded, the "equality" in question may be a misleading appearance conditioned by a deceptive abstraction. When we penetrate beneath the abstraction, we see that the parity is to some extent bogus: the semblance of transcending classes does not wholly fit the facts.

For since the system strongly privileges a single type of commodity—the specific product public education offers us—it discriminates, in effect, against those who would, if they had any real option, choose a different path for their children. Even if, abstractly, equal talent gets equal dollars' worth of support, the system discriminates against those whose talents might just as validly incline them to choose the path of particularity and specialization.

We must now consider the implications of this point.

8. *The Market as Essential to the Attenuation of Class*

A system of private provision, as we understand it, would be one in which there would be very wide latitude in the schools families could choose for their children. No longer would each and every one of these schools be charged with the task of defining a neutral canon that is supposed to pertain to all. A school could, to the contrary, define itself as broadly or narrowly, in this or that way, as its officers and staff chose.

Each school would concentrate, instead, on providing a particular kind of education—religious or secular, general or musical—to a particular clientele.

There is scant reason to fear that, given an open market in these regards, we will witness a landslide in the direction of ethnic particularism and professional narrowness. Cosmopolitanism and assimilationism are landmark triumphs of our culture, from which there is no going back. One cannot become a successful business person, or lawyer, or teacher—or, indeed, car mechanic—if one does not become at least minimally conversant in *all* the areas of our standard curriculum, our canon.

That is why, at *any* good school, this canon will tend to be strong. The very fact that an area is canonical means that it serves as essential preparation for a wide range of careers and life-styles in our culture. If we assume, as we must, that parents are deeply concerned about the future success of their children, we must conclude that few would be so foolhardy as to send their children to schools that did not provide at least good and basic training in all canonical areas.

Perhaps the canon would not, at the school of music attended by Josh, play quite the central role it does elsewhere. But this school would lack appeal to most potential consumers, hence would not survive in the marketplace, if it did not devote several hours a day to math, English, social studies, and science.

It nonetheless does make a big difference whether or not (or to what degree) embracing the canon is an optional matter. A change to a private, choice-driven economy of education would enhance the educational options available. Realistically, we would see a twofold phenomenon: (A) a great variety of idiosyncratic modes of human being, orbiting around (B) a nucleus of core skills universally recognized as absolutely essential to success in our cosmopolitan culture.

Thus, without any threat to the canon, we could allow schools to manifest much wider and subtler differences in coloration. One could send one's child to a school of performing arts, or to a school of technology, or to a

Christian school, or to a yeshiva, or to a Black Muslim school, or to a school of fashion design, or indeed to a general canon school of arts and sciences.

We all can find some school on such a list to disapprove of. White secular humanists, including most of our university folk, might not think much of Black Muslim schools, but Muslims have no difficulty returning the favor. Controversy on the level of life-style is indeed intrinsic in a diversified culture: it happens on all levels of social being.

And it has a clear economic dimension. There are ever so many products I buy, expressing my choice of life-style, and hence also the formative life-style of my offspring, of which people from different backgrounds will disapprove. We should not deny this; we should insist upon it.

But those of us who are committed to a market economy must likewise insist that social rationality ultimately depends on each responsible person's retention of the right to obtain what she, by her own lights, deems best for herself and her children.

I, as a Black Muslim, may not think much of your choice of a thoroughly secular school for your daughter; but I will, if committed to the ground-rules of the market society, defend your right to choose it.

There are those who would object that giving such freedom of choice, such power, to parents will result in ill-informed pedagogical decisions. Teaching professionals typically maintain that these matters are better left to experts—namely, themselves. Albert Shanker, president of the American Federation of Teachers and opponent of voucher schemes, has recently made the caustic remark, "If your goal is merely to recruit students, you can do that by offering a trip to Disneyland or with a good football team."[25]

Years earlier, the Friedmans had fully anticipated this vision of consumers led by the nose by market hype. Their reply:

> Social reformers, and educational reformers in particular, often self-righteously take for granted that parents, especially those who are poor and have little education themselves, have little interest in their children's education and no competence to choose for them. That is a gratuitous insult. . . . U.S. history has amply demonstrated that, given the opportunity, [such parents] have often been willing to sacrifice a great deal, and have done so wisely, for their children's welfare.[26]

Indeed, when it comes to the inner-city schools over which so many of these battles are actually being fought, one cannot but wonder if the "gratuitous insult" does not border on a kind of unconscious racism.

Here we see why privatization may hold the key to a qualitative leap in the war against class. It would, to adapt the Friedmans' phrase, be a gratuitous insult to say that the plight of inner-city schools is rooted in anything more or less than disaffection—or alienation—on the part of the children themselves concerning what the schools are offering them.

Let us at least state our own bias forthrightly: there is no child that will not flourish in an educational environment that engages her intelligence on whatever level such intelligence—by the historical accident of birth and upbringing—happens to be.

And therefore: if we are to conquer educational disaffection, we need schools that pay specific respect to the specific forms of human being that actually exist.

The forms of human being are variegated and fluid, and so we also need an economic environment in which schools can pass into and out of existence depending on the extent to which they address themselves to one or another specific form of such being.

The Classical Defense of capitalism maintains that no economic system can insure such an automatic homeostasis of demand and provision as well as a well-adjusted market system. We have agreed with this fundamental claim, with the proviso that the conditions must first evolve in which competition can occur without producing marked diseconomies of scale. We have acknowledged that such conditions did not always exist, and that this fact explains why we have been dependent for so long on public education.

But now such conditions do exist: a fact which makes a movement in the direction of private provision eminently rational.

No one can guess what Jews and Muslims will be like five hundred years from now. No one can know if there will be people calling themselves Jews and Muslims.

But we do know that there are children in these categories today, who no doubt would do best with teachers that are both attentive to the canon and culturally en rapport with them. Such rapport can often only be the result of a specific commonality of cultural life and value. Without such commonality, the level of communication—hence the level of real teaching—often remains comparatively superficial.

We who were brought up with public school values are often mistrustful of the idea that a school should be in "spiritual rapport" with its students. This is an understandable attitude, given the fact that our schools had, of necessity, to define themselves around a neutral, secular canon. In that context, separation of church and state manifests itself in keeping schools clear of ethnic and religious favoritism.

These attitudes themselves can, however, undergo a shift if a changeover to private provision occurs. In that event, separation of church and state would manifest itself in the freedom guaranteed to all citizens of all backgrounds to attend, and indeed to create, schools of their own choosing.

The biggest challenge faced by educators today is that of making the learning process *interesting*—not in the shallow sense that teachers rightly mistrust, in which we pander to the transient whims of schoolchildren, but rather in the deep and proper sense, in which we engage the specific and varied forms of intelligence that these children bring into the classroom.

In an increasingly diversified culture such as our own, this goal is increasingly hard to meet. Some of us have begun to suspect that it will best be met by allowing people to organize and patronize schools which—though they provide the canonic skills all children need—are at the same time directly responsive to where our children are (as we say) "coming from." We have also begun to suspect that privatization, backed by a guarantee of Formative Parity, is the most promising means of achieving this.

Some older folks will intervene at this juncture: "*We* were just as ethnic as *they* are; and *we* had to go to melting-pot schools; what's different about *them*?"

We have here the barely veiled suggestion that the problems of inner-city schools are due to some malady or perversity of today's racial or ethnic minorities. We need waste no time on such covert racism. There really *is* something about "them" that is "different," but it is neither sickness nor perversity. Rather it is something about the waters in which modern cityfolk must swim.

What's different, I suggest, is that privatization of education was not, for the reasons given in Chapter 5.5, a live option during the childhood of these older folks in the way it is now. Back then, public school was the only choice; there could be no issue of anything better, relative to which one might experience the present system as wanting.

These considerations reflect a main theme of Part One of this study: that "alienation" itself is a historically evolving thing. The disaffections of a given age will always be relative to the prospects of emancipation forming the horizon of that age. These horizontal prospects must be felt to be real possibilities, if one is to bemoan their absence in anything more than a fanciful way.

The old folks learned what they had to learn in schools that were in many cases as good as schools could be in their time. These schools—however indifferent and callous they sometimes were in their treatment of our grandparents—could hardly have been the object of concerted and systematic protest: for our grandparents' era was not able to create anything much better.

Disaffection becomes real, and systematic—and hence amounts to a sickness in the social organism—only when there is a wide discrepancy between the needs of people and the real possibilities of their age.

Modern denizens of the inner city, it so happens, have at least as many special cultural needs as did immigrant children of eighty or ninety years ago—but they are living in an age of different possibility, hence more galling disappointment.

One cannot be a child of these times—a real child, or adolescent—without sensing the discrepancy between the actual and possible responsiveness of one's environment. If the discrepancy is wide, it is little consolation that, in the old days, what we now have would have been quite enough.

Concrete disaffection builds its nest in the discrepancy between dreary actuality and a quite general possibility that affects not only inner-city dwellers, but all people: the possibility of schools that really are responsive to a multiplicity of people's formative needs in a way heretofore unthinkable.

We may accordingly conclude that, to the degree that our schools are systematically unresponsive to the needs of certain groups, those schools are correspondingly biased in the allocation of formative benefits.

Insofar as this remained true, class, as a material matter of fact, would be a continuing reality.

Let us summarize the flow of the entire argument.

Formative Parity ought to mean parity distribution of actual purchasing power with respect to formative goods and services.

But such parity is only a bogus appearance unless the diverse purchasers can find options in the market corresponding to the defensible educational strategies they have in mind for their children.

Only within such a spectrum of formative options do all people tend to have a meaningful chance to tailor education to their children's specific character, both individual and cultural.

If purchasing such a tailored education is not possible, we have de facto class relations, which are, on this deeper analysis, but another expression of the differences in the degree of alienation people suffer from their formative environment.

But such tailored education can become possible only if parents are in a financial position to procure their children an education which does answer to their family's needs and values.

And this, it seems, can be achieved only if (A) all children are guaranteed a quantitative stipend, corresponding to talent and need, (B) which may be spent in a qualitatively variegated marketplace which contains as many types of school as can answer to the peculiar demands of a clientele.

Private provision of education would create an environment in which a variety of educational options answering to the fluidity and variety of our people could flourish.

Moving toward the solution to the problem of class, one of our age's main forms of cultural disaffection or alienation, therefore requires the establishment of a free-market-cum-stipend form of educational economy.

Though such a private approach would have been unthinkable in the earlier days of our educational system as a means of producing an educated populace, it is—in the world of modern transport and communications—now economically feasible.

Thus, the last remaining significant obstacle in the way of the classless society seems to be something that we now, at long last, can overcome.

9. The Importance of Mandated Stipends

In our conception of a classless society, Formative Parity would be every child's right. The demand that our social institutions facilitate this result would indeed, as we saw in Chapter 5.3, have the status of a social "mandate," a "socialized" guarantee that all children will have access to comparable formative opportunities.

It would in the first place be a mandate upon the state, which would have the task of enforcing this requirement as law and would be charged with supervising the requisite redistribution. (This supervisory charge would exist even if many or even all educational providers were private institutions.)

But it would, just as importantly, be a mandate upon parents and guardians, who would be charged with honoring and fostering this system of formative rights. In a society in which Formative Parity existed as a social guarantee, it would not be legitimate, hence would not be legal, for families to retain the option *not* to provide children with parity educational rights.[27]

This means that Formative Parity would, in one sense of the term, be a "socialized" guarantee in a classless society. This is not the kind of "socialization" that is incompatible with the maintenance of free markets. It must be contrasted with strict socialization in the sense of government ownership—what we may dub socialism$_1$.

One can clearly maintain that we ought to mandate—to "socialize," if you will—formative benefits, even as we permit, or foster, a nonsocialist$_1$, privatistic means of provision. Such a mandate, which we may call socialism$_2$, would be no more nor less than a universal guarantee of a minimum standard of benefit, a benchmark beneath which no member of society would be allowed to fall: that is, what society deems the least tolerable share of various aspects of the social product at a given historical stage.

We have rejected Marx's Promethean argument that alienated labor can be marginalized and the market transcended. We have accepted the conclusion of the Classical Defense of capitalism: that there must always be a strong presumption against socializing$_1$ any given good, that is, against providing it by means of state monopoly. But these arguments do not in themselves impugn the wisdom, which might in either event be acknowledged, of socializing$_2$ access to certain special goods.

For socialized$_2$ mandates are social redistributions in a privatized, market context. It is indeed a truism stressed by the standard economics textbooks[28] that one can insist on various minima while equally insisting that the production and provision of the goods that make it up ought to be made by private firms in mutual competition.

A socialistic$_2$ guarantee insures that, in one way or another, each person has the wherewithal to command a certain minimum value of privately produced goods and services.

If education is to be socialized$_2$, the following minimum condition must be fulfilled: there must be redistributive mechanisms, supported by public resources, guaranteeing that people will have high-quality educational services purchased for them, in case they cannot afford to purchase those services out of their own pocket.

With that assured, education would be a commodity that consumers would purchase, spending their dollars where they judge they can get the most of what they want for the least expense.

Correlatively, schools would engage in earnest competition for those dollars, thus realizing the efficiencies of the market system.[29]

Now within this broad conception, there would of course arise many complex issues of institutional design, and there would be a considerable range of opinions about the most effective strategies.

Some, as we have seen, would suggest a system of "vouchers," where each family would be given a sum of money deemed adequate to the educational needs of each child, and would have direct discretion over that money.

Others, wary of the possibility of parental abuse of a voucher system, would allow families to choose which schools they preferred for their children, but would not allow them to get their hands on the funds, which would be administered by a "Choice Office."

This latter option might give us a way, moreover, of addressing the tricky issue of "add-ons" which seem to leave the door open to an insinuation of class. The question of add-ons is: if a voucher system were adopted, would rich families be allowed to pad the amount of the voucher with their own resources, and so be able to send their children to more expensive schools?[30]

Other options, within this context, would also have to be considered. Instead of a set amount for each child, the dollar value of stipends might be "graduated," with more public funds per child being provided to relatively poor parents than to the relatively well-off, who would be required to provide for at least a large share of their children's formation out of their own pocket. Alternatively, society might directly give all children the same dollar value in stipends, fairly distributing the burden of financing by means of a progressive income tax.[31]

All such redistributive schemes would be in the spirit of socialism$_2$ in the domain of education. But some people would dispute the wisdom of *any* such arrangements. While those of a social-democratic stripe would maintain that mating capitalist production with mandated social minima yields a robust, hybrid economy, many conservatives, by contrast, would argue that such systems are vicious (read, "inefficient") economic mongrels.

For example: we have seen that though the Friedmans support a voucher system as a second-best, interim solution, they believe that such a system should ultimately be replaced by a free-market system in which no vestiges of "socialization" remain—whether on the demand or supply side.

As a general principle, the latter approach can hardly be justified. Here, Hayek has been forthright:

> There is nothing in the basic principles of [free-market] liberalism to make it a stationary creed; there are no hard-and-fast rules fixed once and for all. . . . Probably nothing has done so much harm to the liberal cause as the wooden insistence of some liberals on certain rough rules of thumb, above all the principle of laissez faire. . . .
>
> No sensible person should have doubted that the crude rules in which the principles of economic policy of the nineteenth century were expressed were only a beginning. . . .[32]

Hayek adds that such free-market liberalism "does not deny, but even emphasizes, that, in order that competition should work beneficially, a carefully thought-out legal framework is required. . . ."[33] He gives a particular instance: "it is essential that the entry into the different trades should be open to all on equal terms. . . ."[34]

Which specific guarantees should belong to this "legal framework" underpinning the most efficient forms of competition? The answer, as Hayek would no doubt agree, depends on historical circumstances. What is possible in the nineteenth century will appear "crude" by our own standards.

Too often we make abstract, armchair declarations about this or that "human right"—even though it is out of the question for some cultures, with fewer resources than our own, to guarantee such a "right" to all. We forget that the question of which goods can belong to the least standard of living—can become a human "right"—depends on what a society can produce in relative profusion.

This is consistent with our reflections in Chapter 4.2. There we saw that the social minimum, and therewith the material character of class distinctions, is a historically mobile thing. The increasing inclusiveness of the social minimum is a basic feature of historical development. What is at one stage a luxury becomes, years later, through technological development, a "necessity." And this has profound implications when it comes to the question of social and political rights.

Finally, after a lengthy evolutionary process, the possibility of making certain critical standards of life universally available becomes so insistent as to be formally recognized: defined, enshrined, and protected by all the force and dignity of law. The more regularized the production of this benefit becomes, the greater will be the pressure for society to adopt, as an explicit matter of public policy, the resolve to treat it as the birthright of every member of society.

In our own time, we have seen this happen with respect to specific levels of nourishment, medical care, legal representation, education, old-age benefits, and so on. No candidate for public office—neither Republican nor Democrat, Tory nor Laborite—questions these "rights" any longer.

Formative Parity was unthinkable in an earlier age. But over the course of the past two centuries, it has become thinkable indeed. It is the guarantee of "equal entry," in Hayek's sense, even if it is a more comprehensive and ambitious proposal for our society's "legal framework" than he himself envisages.

On Hayek's principles, Formative Parity could be justified as a legal mandate if and only if it made possible the most productive competitive system. But we ourselves argued, in Chapter 4, that Formative Parity means the optimal preparation—in correspondence with their productive potential—of young people for adult participation in market life.

Thus even—or especially—from a free-market perspective, Formative Parity must be viewed as a prima facie good for which we clearly ought to strive, once we have passed the threshold at which its provision becomes feasible.

Mandated Formative Parity would be nothing more nor less than the comprehensive realization of the "flat playing surface" on which the creative competition of adults can be conducted with greatest effect. And so we may conclude that the reluctance of some free-market theorists—the Friedmans, for example—to accept such a mandate cannot be justified on free-market principles themselves, as plausibly understood.

A system based on "stipends" or "vouchers"—or some other redistributive scheme in the spirit of socialism$_2$—does hold out the promise of achieving this flat playing surface, quite compatibly with the operation of the competitive market. Thus such solutions would not, contra the Friedmans, compromise free-market ideals, but be the condition of their fullest realization.

Thus if Formative Parity has at last become possible, it should have a prominent place among the free market's own mandated ground-rules. In the fullness of time, the classless society and the free-market economy would not be antithetical to one another, but essential to each other's optimal realization.

Notes

1. I bypass here questions which, though interesting, obviously pose no deep difficulties in principle. How, for example, is the distinction between minority and majority years to be defined? One must allow that the borderline is a bit hazy. It is hard to say if we should regard a person as an adult at sixteen, eighteen, twenty-one, or whatever. It follows that, however imprecisely the line be drawn, the concept of class is of analogous imprecision.

   But this only goes to prove that the concept of class, like all concepts, is not of Platonic purity: it is vague, and permits transitional cases. Such vagueness is no objection to the reasonable clarity of a reasonable concept. Everyone agrees that the line between childhood and adulthood is decisively if roughly drawn; and, since antiquity, most have agreed that it is traversed by about one's twentieth year.

2. The 1642 law said that every town with more than fifty families had to have an elementary school teacher. The law of 1647 said that, in addition, every town with more than a hundred families had to build and keep up a grammar school. Education was compulsory not in the sense that children had to attend school, but in the sense that parents were charged with the obligation to make sure literacy was attained in one way or another.

3. Mann, Horace, Tenth *Annual Report*, excerpted in Binder, Frederick M., ed., *Education in the History of Western Civilization: Selected Readings* (New York: 1970), p. 330.
4. Mark Blaug is perhaps the most prominent. See the work edited by Blaug, *Economics of Education*, 2 vols., 1968, as well as his *An Introduction to the Economics of Education* (London: 1970).
5. The "ladder" idea was first proposed by John Amos Comenius as long ago as the seventeenth century.
6. Pounds, R. L., *The Development of Education in Western Culture* (New York: 1968), p. 199.
7. Jencks, Christopher, et al., *Who Gets Ahead?* (New York: 1979), especially chapters 3, 4, 8, and 12. These empirical findings do show up the imperfect results of our vaunted meritocracy, but they show that impressive inroads have been made.
8. Pounds, *The Development of Education*, p. 199.
9. See for example the report of the Coleman Commission appointed by President Lyndon Johnson: Coleman, J. S., et al., *Equality of Educational Opportunity* (Washington: 1966).
10. The Jencks group is careful to note that this measure is hard to make, since it rests on "the dubious assumption that test performance measures 'ability.' . . ." See Jencks, Christopher, et al., *Who Gets Ahead?*, p. 230.
11. Jencks indeed believes that "middle class pupils have retained, almost intact, their historic advantage over the manual working class." Jencks, Christopher, et al., *Inequality* (New York: 1972).
12. Bowen, James, *A History of Western Education*, vol. 3 (New York: 1981), p. 531.
13. Chubb, John E., and Moe, Terry M., *Politics, Markets, and America's Schools* (1990). Chubb and Moe summarize their conclusions in a shorter article, "Choice *Is* a Panacea," *The Brookings Review* (Summer 1990), pp. 4–12.
14. Even those who do not own property would suffer such double jeopardy, since landlords must always factor *their* school tax burden into the pricing of rentals.
15. *Time* magazine has lately made this claim with characteristic cuteness: "Dick and Jane [are] well on their way toward becoming free-market conservatives." 3 September 1990, p. 72.
16. Friedman, Milton and Rose, *Free to Choose* (New York: 1980), p. 169.
17. Ibid., p. 158.
18. Ibid., p. 151.
19. Thus Milton and Rose Friedman remark: "The National Education Association and the American Federation of Teachers claim that vouchers would destroy the public school system, which, according to them, has been the foundation and cornerstone of our democracy. Their claims are never accompanied by any evidence that the public school system today achieves the results claimed for it—*whatever may have been true in earlier times.*" Ibid., p. 170; emphasis mine. The Friedmans, unfortunately, do not dilate upon this potentially profound historical insight: it is made in passing.
20. There were those who, in the name of competition and free enterprise, thought it was a mistake to consolidate New York City's three private subway companies into a single system. The day was won by their opponents: given the finitude of underground space and the advantages of a single interlocking system, the IND, BMT, and IRT were absorbed into one monopolistic, city-administered system.

21. Friedman, Milton and Rose, *Free to Choose*, p. 151. The phrase is Walter Lippmann's.
22. Ibid., pp. 161–62.
23. Ibid., p. 162.
24. "When we first wrote . . . on this subject, we accepted the need for [compulsory education] laws on the ground that 'a stable democratic society is impossible without a minimum degree of literacy and knowledge on the part of most citizens.' We continue to believe that, but [further] research . . . has persuaded us that compulsory attendance at schools is not necessary to achieve that minimum standard of literacy and knowledge" (ibid., p. 162).
25. Quoted in *Time* magazine, 3 September 1990, p. 72.
26. Friedman, Milton and Rose, *Free to Choose*, p. 160.
27. As in the case of our present compulsory education laws, which forbid parents from keeping children ages 6–16 out of school, there would be an analogously compulsory aspect to Formative Parity, though the latter is of course a more radical conception of children's educational rights.
28. See for example Samuelson, Paul A., *Economics: An Introductory Analysis*, 5th ed. (New York: 1961), p. 183.
29. This is certainly not to say that the private provision of medical service is defensible as it stands. It is always the prerogative of sloppy minds, especially those with lots to gain from the confusion, to justify any degree of gouging of the public in the name of "free enterprise."

    The relevant principle here is this: whatever arguments can be mustered in defense of the private provision of medicine extend insofar as the circulation of medical capital really is such as to return, in something resembling a corresponding degree, investable funds into the hands of those who are making contributions to medical development. Defenses of capitalist methods extend that far, but only that far; and, as all good legislators know, the rules underpinning the market must be continually adjusted with this rational constraint in mind.

    The broad defense of private provision rests on the claim that insofar as social investment *is* rationalized, there will typically be significant scope for private appropriation and investment. If the public and its elected representatives notice that the rules allow some doctors to reap the benefits of cunning and greed, rather than Edisonian perspiration and inspiration, the rules that undergird our particular brand of medical capitalization ought of course to be revised.
30. My own opinion is that the "add-on" issue is not as crucial and vexing as some seem to think. Thus Chubb and Moe argue that add-ons "threaten to produce too many disparities and inequalities . . ., and many citizens would regard them as unfair and burdensome" (*The Brookings Review* [Summer 1990], p. 9). But if the stipends are set at a fairly high level, such problems might be of marginal significance. If, by contemporary standards, an impressively high level of education is guaranteed to each child, wealthy parents would, to that degree, lose much of their motivation to send their kids to expensive places. An analogue to this already exists: insofar as fine state universities provide an education that really is of comparable quality to that provided by the ivy-type places, we should expect the children of the rich to take advantage of the bargain thus afforded. More and more, that is precisely what we do find.
31. There is, of course, a considerable gap between the general notion of Formative Parity and specific strategies of implementation. It is the job of the legislator to be attuned to the countless difficulties involved in putting any new distributive

scheme in place. General considerations in favor of parity must, within the four walls of the legislative committee room, be translated into the language of statute. Here there can be no avoiding the myriad intricacies of actual and possible tax law and what not. Legislation, to be effective, must be detailed, clear, and enforceable.

Even the best philosopher cannot be expected to address the implementation problem on this level of detail—any more than the legislator can permit herself the luxury of speculating into forms of law that may turn out to be useful a century into the future. This is not to denigrate either task. Without some philosophical sense of far-ranging social possibility, the legislator's work may lose all sense of aspiration—may become a matter of holding together, with strips of statutory scotch tape, a vague and mediocre status quo. Perhaps this is an occupational hazard of legislators. But the social philosopher has occupational hazards of a complementary kind: an aspect of utopianism, a tendency to neglect the nuts-and-bolts problems of institutional design.

Ethicists and social philosophers who fail to keep at least one eye on the question of implementation—and too many do—run the risk of asserting proposals that are "radical" only in the sense of being impracticable. This book, given its ambitious ideals, certainly does run this risk.

32. Hayek, Friedrich, *The Road to Serfdom* (Chicago: 1944), pp. 17, 18.
33. Ibid., p. 36.
34. Ibid., p. 37.

6

Classless Capitalism: Problems in Interpretation

We may develop the argument by considering some difficulties that will no doubt be on the mind of the careful reader.

1. The Marginalization of Formative Disparities

We have argued that a classless society, in the most robust sense, would be one in which the various formative predilections of various families could find agreeable forms of education available in the market. The values of classlessness and diversity are not casually, but intimately, bound up with one another.

Construed as a worthy candidate for a basic constitutional right, Formative Parity is most closely approximated when families have great freedom to select the form of education they wish for their respective children—the kind of freedom, as I have suggested, that can only be provided by market methods.

Marx maintains that the hazards of birth privilege can be eliminated only when we "replace home education by social" and "the care and education of the children becomes a public matter."[1] In extremis, the achievement of parity requires, he thinks, that family influence upon the educational process drop to the vanishing point.

We, to the contrary, wish to vest in a diverse range of families the right to choose among a diverse range of educational options. The abolition of quantitative formative disparities should occur in the context of the continuance of qualitative differences in familial attitudes, practices, and life-styles.

This necessarily produces a tension between the legitimate effects of adult performance in the marketplace and the formative rights of the children of those adults—a tension that defines the reasonable limits of the concept of Formative Parity itself.

Once we understand the nature of this tension, we see that the concept of Formative Parity is not an expression of pie-in-the-sky utopianism, but is a specific economic goal that is both reasonable and achievable.

There are those who would say that Formative Parity could never be achieved in full purity. The point is well taken and has some interesting implications, but it does not show that we are wrong to conceive Formative Parity as a good candidate for a "basic right."

For *no* basic right can ever be achieved in full purity. Every such right always exists in an environment of rights equally fundamental, by reference to which its range of application will always be delimited. This phenomenon of mutual delimitation does not imply that any one of these claims is bogus.

In our political system, for example, there is a strong presumption in favor of unrestricted religious practice. But that does not mean that there is a pure and unqualified right to religious expression. It does not mean that the Supreme Court cannot delimit that right by reference to other claims of similar stature.[2]

That, despite such delimitation, religious liberty is quite genuine, follows from the fact that the Court will allow it to be abridged *only* insofar as it runs afoul of other presumptions having an equally profound constitutional status. And this is a very powerful claim. Absent any proof that a given religious practice does violate some other basic claim or right, we must allow it to be, no matter how repellent we personally find it.

If Formative Parity were to acquire constitutional status, it would have comparable power, but no more. It would necessarily have its claims delimited by other principles. This would be just one more region in which competing basic rights would exist in a somewhat delicate social balance. The existence of one sphere of rights would assure that the other can never be "purely" achieved.

If we take a backward glance at the entire argument of this book, we can see just where this "delicate balance" lies: at the intersection of three principles which, far from being peculiar to our concerns here, lie close to the heart of our form of culture.

The first is that of the market: adults who perform well in competitive economic activity have a right to greater returns than those who do not.

The second is that of the family: adults have the right to bring up their children as they choose.

The third is that of Formative Parity: each child deserves to be educated commensurately with his or her talent.

The first principle ensures that there will be some semblance—historically relative, to be sure—of the distinction between the "rich" and the "poor."

This, in conjunction with the second principle, implies that some children will be born into relatively affluent families, and others not.

But this result seems to run afoul of the third principle. For it is impossible for us to believe that the wealth of one's parents will have no influence on one's life prospects.

For surely, whatever directly benefits the parent will at least indirectly benefit the child. If, as a result of fair and legal behavior in the marketplace, my adult income is twice yours, will not our children be implicated in this differential outcome? How could it *not* be the case that my children will have corresponding formative advantages, advantages that will indeed, in time, redound to the greater success of the former once they become adults?

But, bearing in mind the mutual delimitation of rights, we must beware drawing the unjustified conclusion that Formative Parity would in that event be "violated." All that follows is that this claim cannot be "purely" realized in the environment of the other two principles. And this does not prove that it cannot function as a claim both basic and powerful.

The question is this: can we, despite the mutual delimitation that characterizes all rights, nonetheless design a system that guarantees Formative Parity in a robust sense—as robust, say, as religious freedom, despite *its* "impurity," is in our culture?

If this can be done, it will clearly involve the same kind of tension as characterizes the competition of all basic claims.

That would mean: while the retention of the family in the market context would no doubt imply some incidental formative disparities, these could be reduced to negligible significance.

Hence the delicate balance.

On the one hand: in the context of market and family, "birth privilege" is not totally eliminable. Formative disparities between children will, in the environment imagined, always be *at least* of an incidental character.

But on the other: if Formative Parity is to be treated as a meaningful right, it must be possible for these three claims to be mutually adjusted so that formative disparities are reduced to what is *at most* an incidental level. The idea that disparities must be at most "negligible" emerges as the key to the requisite equilibrium among competing claims. Here as elsewhere, we must distinguish between *basic* and *incidental* infringements.

In the case of Formative Parity, that means: even if children of successful parents necessarily enjoy some incidental advantages, these must occur in a context in which basic benefits—the benefits most pertinent to what is reasonably meant by economic class—are indeed granted on a parity basis.

The basic/incidental distinction is itself quite meaningful. It may be illustrated by a simple example.

Suppose our society has decided that all children are to have equally impressive rights to medical treatment. No matter who your parents are, you have the same claim on such resources as any other child.

Suppose now that some physician were to exclaim, "This degree of 'socialization' of medical rights means that I am in effect forbidden to give any preferential treatment to my own children, as contrasted with anybody else's. But this is naive—and indeed impossible. The mere fact that my daughter lives under the same roof means that if she should come down with some acute infection in the middle of the night, she will be given more immediate treatment than the stockbroker's son. The offspring of doctors must always have some medical advantages over the offspring of nondoctors. Strict parity treatment is therefore out of the question."

The point is well taken—but of little consequence. All the doctor can prove is that his offspring will, comparatively, have some incidental medical advantages. No doubt these cannot be avoided. But if, aside from her dad's immediate availability in the middle of the night (and the like), the doctor's daughter is in no further respects medically privileged, we are entitled to say that there is no distinction in *basic* benefits.

For the rules of the system may still demand that all children have equal claims on quality medical treatment as quickly as it can be made available. Thus, though it is absurd to pretend that the offspring of doctors have *no* medical advantages, it is not absurd to think these could be confined to the unavoidable incidental effects of the fact that medical treatment is, in that case, necessarily very close at hand.

The question of Formative Parity is ultimately one of "inheritance" in the very broadest sense of the term. If both the family and the market are retained, there will be *some* residue of "heritable" advantage, and classlessness will be no more than approximated. But in many respects, the fate of the parents need not, except in a residual sense, be visited upon the children.

Examples abound. Thus there are some incidental educational advantages enjoyed by the offspring of reading teachers, but it hardly follows that there need be any basic advantages in reading. In a society as advanced as our own, we do not expect the children of such parents to be privileged in anything more than a marginal sense, if at all.

These remarks are intended to reduce the utopian savor of the idea of Formative Parity. We must bear in mind that all measures taken to secure

Formative Parity, as we conceive it, must be consistent with, and delimited by, the legitimate diversity of families. Any mandate of Formative Parity must be so administered that families have extensive discretion over the way in which their children are educated.

If the importance of the family principle is kept in mind, we can see that Formative Parity, far from being an impossibly "pure" or pie-in-the-sky formulation, is (for all its power) a very specific ideal, suited to the resolution of a determinate range of economic problems—problems which, it just so happens, we increasingly have the material ability to resolve.

Formative Parity should in no event be construed as the final solution to all the world's problems, or the end of all contingencies of social existence. It is an ideal pertaining to economic opportunity in a far-reaching and robust way, but it certainly does not spell the abolition of all forms of disappointment, bitterness, and contention.

For we have seen that the idea of overcoming classes is rooted in a quantitative abstraction. Money, the root of that abstraction, is the key measurement of economic opportunity in a very robust sense: children must be given a degree of abstract purchasing power over formative goods that is on a par with their respective abilities.

But the very fact that this conception is governed by this sort of *quantitative* abstraction, means that families retain the right to determine the *qualitative* path their children will take.

And there is nothing in the idea of parity of abstract market command—of economic opportunity as such—that can guarantee any results when it comes to actual quality of life. Quality of life depends not only on one's opportunities, but on the specific ways in which people exploit them. And this is clearly not an economic matter.

In the context of Formative Parity, some parents may invest less wisely than others. Alternatively, some children, the ingrate beneficiaries of wise and caring parents, may squander the opportunities given them.

These are real human problems, but they lie outside the range of economic analysis and critique as such. When, from an economic perspective, we say that classes might be overcome, we mean *only* that there no longer need be formative differences between people with respect to the principal goods and services that those responsible for their upbringing have been able to command.

If such an ideal were achieved in the society of the future, we would still face manifold conflicts and vexations. There would be only one big difference: we could no longer lay the blame for these problems at the feet of "the class system."

2. Distortions in the Determination of Talent

The argument of this book has largely turned on the economic rationality of a correlation between talent and investment. But however clear the rational connection between talent and investment may be in some abstract sense, it is plain that the determination or measure of such talent is no easy matter.

This is an especially acute problem in a market context in which (a) the family is assumed to remain with us, and in which (b) some people are, at least in their majority years, able to win privileges not attained by others. These two conditions do underlie the perennial possibility of abuses and ideological distortions.

It is no part of my argument to deny that, "in the real world," such distortions can—and indeed will—always exist. There will, perhaps, never be a time when society can reasonably relax its vigilance when it comes to the measurement of human talent. We may consider, very briefly, three ways in which this problem may be addressed.

First: there can be little doubt that—as long as there are any persons of privilege at all, and as long as these persons can be expected to have some natural favoritism toward their own offspring—society will need to protect itself against such abuse by means of a strong "civil service" orientation or dimension: those entrusted with the measurement of talent must be hemmed in and delimited by "checks and balances" powerful enough to insulate such determinations from undue influence by those who have attained the greater share of wealth and power.

Second: we see here one more reason why the privatization of education may be a socially progressive step for us to take. For let the point be granted: whatever "structures of domination" exist will tend to exert at least *some* undue influence in determining how talents are measured. All too often it is the case that supposed "natural differences in talent" are overrated—and even sometimes fabricated out of whole cloth—in order to serve special interests.

This adds fuel to the argument that it is important for there to be no effective public monopoly in education: so that no particular ideological conception of how children's talents are to be esteemed, estimated, and developed can hold monopolistic sway.

Third: just because ideological bias in the "mismeasure"[3] of talent is a pervasive problem, I myself am personally inclined to side with those who, when pressed, would wish to interpret "Formative Parity" so as to bring it quite close to a pragmatic assumption of the de facto near equality of children's talents and intelligence.

Granted, for example, that some differences in talent are biologically based, in practice it may be true that, except in some narrowly and carefully circumscribed instances, society will probably do more harm than good by trying to gauge these, than by resolving to invest in our children on a more or less equal basis.

Such a pragmatic tendency to equalitarianism would be reinforced by two further considerations.

The first is that, in those restricted cases in which biological differences *do* exist—perhaps in some cases of "retardation," etc.—offsetting ethical considerations tend to become as prominent as the factors of efficiency that drive our own argument. As I have stressed so often, this study's emphasis on productivity is intended to show that transcending classes can be justified on the basis of a dispassionate calculation of efficiency alone. In cases where talents do manifestly differ, we may nonetheless—on grounds of compassion—demand "equal treatment" for all persons.

The second consideration is that families, given their different values, may differ in their estimation of what "talent" consists in. When it comes to the very notion of what an impressive performance is, big-city African-Americans and rural Baptists may be depended upon to have very different judgments of intelligence itself.

For both these reasons, many of us will have little trouble in interpreting the demand for "Formative Parity" as—by and large, in practice—a demand for equalitarian treatment, a presumption that can be overridden only in uncontroversial cases.

3. Education and Domination

We must also face the difficulty that the educational process itself inevitably seems to involve forms of domination. As radical critics of education[4] have said, the very nature of the teacher-student interaction seems to enforce and reinforce the power relations at least largely constitutive of class.

This is, insofar as it goes, a powerful critique, rooted in some of the penetrating insights of the anarchists of the nineteenth century. But it can be made fully plausible only when we disentangle one sense of "authority" from another.

As an anarchist like Bakunin himself stresses, we may challenge the domination-servitude nexus without questioning the importance of a *non*-coercive sense of "authority." The latter would obtain in the case of one who preeminently possessed some skill, whether it be scientific acumen or great musicianship, which those just starting out would—quite voluntarily—wish to acquire.[5]

"Authority" in this latter sense seems inherent in the very dynamic of experience and inexperience, age and youth. But *coercive* forms of authority do not thereby stand justified.

We can agree with all this, and indeed can argue (again in the spirit of Bakunin, who in this respect learned much from Marx) that much of the problem of coercive authority is rooted in the fact that, historically, ruling elites have had to face the task of maintaining privileges that are, to some significant extent, *not* grounded transparently in such preeminent skill.

Parents or teachers who do not have some real ability or insight to impart to the child will to that extent have nothing stronger with which to back their "authority" than "you must do it (or believe it) because I said so": hence, ultimately, they will be supported by no more than the threat of raw and arbitrary force.

Whereas if, by hypothesis, people have reached positions of "authority" in a system driven by Formative Parity, this latter sort of "authority" would, to that extent, bear a much closer relation to actual skills, and not have to resort to extraneous threats in order to justify itself. To this extent, Formative Parity would at least largely attenuate the "classist" forms of authority educational radicals rightly worry about.

But there is another dimension to this problem, one which "postmodern" radicals have called to our attention. From this perspective, as long as there are *any privileges at all* enjoyed by one subgroup of society, there will be some tendency for those thus privileged to defend their advantages as essential—that is, eternally necessary—conditions of social existence, when in fact these privileges can claim to have only a limited and temporary range of historical justification.

The problem here, of course, is that according to our own "dialectical" treatment of social stratification, the phenomenon of social privilege is itself never-ending. The case here is strictly parallel to our earlier treatment of "alienation" as something incessantly sublimated but never eliminated. In just the same way, it seems we should admit (or rather, insist) that social stratification is never flatly eliminated: that one regime of privilege is always replaced by another; and that each such regime, while free from some of the shortcomings of its predecessors, may be expected to have features that would be found objectionable—hence tend to be felt as "coercive"—by the measure of the revolutionary project of the coming age.

Though, for example, it may be granted that the feudal relation between lord and serf was an advance on the prior relation between master and slave, the relation between bourgeois and proletarian was—in its time, and just as clearly—an advance on *it*. Analogously, the elimination of the birth privileges that characterize capitalism in its present form would be the end of "class" in the strict and narrow sense adopted in this study; but this would not amount to the overcoming of all criticizable forms of privilege.

For, on our own understanding, if Formative Parity were achieved, this would mean that privileges would be allowed to emerge only on the basis of the competitive vicissitudes of adult life. Relative to the initial resources (hence possibilities) of our own time, this is a highly significant restriction in the field of privilege: the entire argument of this book has revolved about its importance. But even if such an ambitious goal were achieved, this could not claim to be the social revolution to end all revolutions, the end of the struggle against privilege *tout court*. For the forms of *adult* privilege that would thereby be legitimated would no doubt bring new horizons of possibility into view: some nascent culture, standing on the shoulders of the society of Formative Parity, would no doubt have even more radical and robust demands to press, a sense of which privileges countenanced by Formative Parity would have to be (in that future age) challenged, and hence a more far-reaching notion of "abuses" and "injustices" that ought to be corrected.

It is in this sense that the ideal of Formative Parity will, virtually as soon as it is realized, begin to appear, by the measure of ever-nascent ideals, an abstract and minimal—that is, insufficient—demand.

It would have to be admitted, in this spirit, that any regime of privilege—the culture of Formative Parity as well as any previous social order—is in this historical sense shadowed by at least some tendency to "arbitrary power." To say, as we do, that there will always be some tension between present privileges and nascent standards of emancipation, is to admit that there will always be some tendency for those who enjoy advantages to think them reasonable and just even after such privileges have become historically obsolescent.

Because of this incessant historical dynamic, those who benefit from a certain regime of privilege, no matter how far advanced it is, will be subject to their own peculiar form of myopia: they will always have some tendency to take their prerogatives fully for granted, as "only natural" and indeed absolute, when in fact there are always respects in which that system of prerogatives can be criticized and improved.

One need not assume any especial ill intent or ruthlessness on the part of the privileged in order to expect such a result. It can often be attributed to the more "innocent" fact that those whose lives are determined by a certain paradigm of authority will simply be unable to appreciate any other way of doing things.

There will in this dialectical sense never be an end to the problem of "arbitrary authority." Rather we should say: we will always, at best, be faced with the task of freeing the present age from forms of privilege that are arbitrary by *its* standards. Each age, in achieving the ideals that form its own prior horizon, may be expected to project even newer horizons of ethical accomplishment, ad infinitum. Hence the criticism of privileges never comes to an end; rather it is forever taking on new forms, insofar as progressive revision is possible, hence justifiable, in terms of established values, and emergent possibilities, of a time.

This will be preeminently so in the sphere of education. To say that there are challengeable modes of authoritarian behavior characterizing a society as a whole, is to say that such behavior will be found in all theaters in which authority is primarily or paradigmatically expressed: in the relations be-tween parent and child, between public official and private citizen—and, of course, between teacher and student.

There is no good reason to believe that pedagogy will ever be free from the hazards of dubious authority. Because authority itself is at best subli-mated, never eliminated, there will never be an end to our need for radical critics. There will likewise always be the need for incessant vigilance, on ever new dialectical levels, regarding the way in which we educate or—as radicals must always tend to put it—"indoctrinate" our children.

There will always be a general need to criticize forms of privilege that are, at a given moment, uncritically taken for granted, and it goes without saying that this will be so in the case of education. All this is entirely compatible with the thoroughgoing dialecticism of this study.

But, just for that reason, it is important always to look at the dynamics of this situation in a two-sided, dialectical way. There will always be a prob-lem of authority, but that does not mean that there is no such thing as revolutionary progress with respect to authority.

Far to the contrary: there could not be a problem unless it were the case that the accomplishments of one period, in any given arena, were always subject to further improvement and refinement. Just as the perenniality of scarcity is a consequence of the fact that ever new frontiers of plenty are conceivable and expectable, the incessancy of the authority problem is a result of the fact it makes little sense to think that amelioration in this sphere, even when it does occur, ever reaches full ethical or normative closure or finality. It is the assumption of progress itself that implies that forms of authority which start off justified must end up, in their historical dotage, the proper object of radical critique and attack.[6]

The radical critique of authority in general, and education in particular, must always be with us. Those of us who now fight for Formative Parity must bear in mind that this—like all revolutions before it and all that remain to come—is "only" one struggle for one time, not the onset of the Millennium.

From a dialectical perspective, we must nonetheless also insist that it is possible to eliminate the obsolescent privileges and disparities which have outlived their usefulness during *our* phase of history. The call for the abolition of birth privilege can never be the last word in the critique of privilege in general; but, relative to the possibilities and resources of our own age, it is a claim that is ambitious, radical, and defensible.

That is all we have ever claimed for Formative Parity, and all we need to claim.

4. *Ecological Dialectics*

Though we have supported a version of the ideal of the classless society, we have also attempted to vindicate the society of commodities and capital. But our defense of commodity culture will be incomplete if we do not devote some space to an important worry on the mind of some contemporary ecological radicals.

According to a critique that comes from various quarters today— postmodernist, radical feminist, "New Age"—one might wonder if the time is not upon us when the commodity form has outlived its usefulness altogether. Such a critic might well be willing to grant that human wants are always dialectically developing. Hence she might allow that scarcity (in one form or another) is with us to stay. But she might wonder whether the logic of the marketplace ought not to be entirely dispensed with.

Such suspicions are especially deeply rooted in the ecological crisis we now face. Given the spoliation and depredation of the environment, some have begun to suspect that the continuance of the logic of commodification is the path to utter catastrophe—not only for our species, but for the entire planet.

Might it not be the case that man's and woman's fate depends on our making a transition to a "communistic" form of culture, even in a context of presumed scarcity? Have we not reached the point at which the commodity form as such has become a deadly peril?

Marx seems to believe that the maturation of our technical intelligence underlies a "total revolution" in which full human emancipation is won. He never seems to doubt that the species is on the verge of liberation made possible by the achievement of fully adequate "science," a breakthrough on which a transparently "dialectical" form of existence will be founded.[7] This can occur because the species is finally able to extricate itself from its initial bondage to nature. Though we begin "immersed in nature," the growth of freedom is the story of increasing sophistication in our grasp *of*, and control *over*, the nonhuman world.

Today, we postmoderns are more apt to find this entire conception of the "conquest of nature" as the misconceived legacy of the metaphysical attempt to put human existence on a fully adequate scientific footing. We tend to read the technological story of human emancipation, favored by Marx and others, as a one-sided narrative, one that remains within the confines of a particular and peculiar view of the relation between human culture and nonhuman "nature." Indeed, the very idea that nature *might* be "conquered" seems a token of the odd idea that nature is, as an objective matter of fact, nothing more than a stockpile (as Heidegger has termed it) of potentially manipulable and useful "mere things."

No longer can we uncritically regard the stockpile-status of nature as an "objective fact." This appearance is now seen as a historical artifact: as the way things began to look, about a half millennium ago, when (for reasons still somewhat obscure) European culture launched its project of techno-logical domination. What we modern Europeans find in apparently objec-tive nature is what we ourselves have put there through our own fateful and tendentious act of "reification."

As long as we are able to treat nature as a noncreative, passive object of technological manipulation, mute and purposeless, there seems no limit to our right to ravish her. This does not prove her to be the mere congeries of inert stuff we think she is, but it does prove something quite impressive: that the ideology of domination, ruthlessly pursued, makes European hege-mony awfully hard to resist.

The postmodern critique of "instrumental rationality" leads to an inter-rogation of this very tendency to treat "nature as such" as spiritless, insen-sate, dead. Attention turns to the possibility of a restoration of *inspirited nature* to the role it held long ago, in the days before the mythos of modern scientism took hold.[8] The following remarks from the work of the pagan feminist Starhawk (Miriam Simos) are representative:

> . . . [W]e see the world as being made up of separate, isolated, non-alive parts (not even dead—since death implies life—but inert matter), which have no inherent value.
> . . . But when nature is empty of spirit, forest and trees become merely

timber, something to be measured in board feet, valued only for its usefulness or profitability . . .

. . . [T]he rise of modern science . . . shifted the "normative image" of the world from that of a living organism to that of a dead machine, which supported exploitation of nature on a scale previously unknown.

. . . [A]nother form of consciousness is possible. . . . This is the consciousness I call *immanence*—the awareness of the world and everything in it as alive . . . and interacting, infused with moving energies: a living being, a weaving dance.[9]

In this spirit, the critic might say: the approach taken in this very study is too "scientistic." For our argument has been based on hard-boiled considerations of "usefulness"—of "economic efficiency." On that basis we have concluded, contra Marx, that the logic of incentives and private appropriation—of the commodity-based capitalist system itself—is with us to stay.

Since, that is, our own commitment to the logic of commodities is rooted in this efficiency calculus, one might object that we ourselves are guilty of the "reificatory" tendency that the critics of instrumental rationality have exposed. Reduced to its simplest terms, this objection comes down to two basic assertions.

(1) If our species is to stop ravishing the planet, we may well have to overcome "scientistic" civilization's tendency to reduce nature to an inert "stockpile" of "mute and purposeless" objects ripe for conquest and manipulation.

(2) The capitalist nexus of cash and calculation—what is sometimes called "commodification"—necessitates just such a scientistic attitude, despite all noble intentions and pious pronouncements to the contrary.

Proposition (1) may well be true. We may agree with the postmodernists that, if we are to solve some of the most pressing ecological concerns of our own period, we may have to put behind us the preponderant "reificatory" bias of modern European culture. We may conclude that a solely technological assessment of culture is one-sided at best. We have stressed that our endorsement of the "Productivity Principle" is only "strategic": intended to imply not that efficiency is the only valid critical perspective, but that it is *one* valid perspective.[10]

But, for our postmodern critic, this is not enough. Our commitment to a criterion of economic efficiency, even if qualified, bars (she might say) an appreciation of the fact that the ecological crisis of our age can be met only if we eliminate efficiency accounting—the logic of the commodity—altogether.

From such a perspective, it is beside the point to object that a culture not based upon commodities would not be "maximally efficient." For it is those very considerations of efficiency that lead us to "reify" nature, and if such reification leads us in turn to ravish—and perhaps fatally undermine—the nonhuman world, then clearly it is the logic of efficiency itself that ought to be dispensed with.

Our quarrel concerns proposition (2) above. It does not follow from the fact that a certain kind of commodification, during a certain period of human history, threatens the ruin of the planet, that commodification as such—if suitably constrained and restrained—is the villain in the piece.

No doubt a single-minded mania for efficiency would—were such a thing possible—be utterly catastrophic. If a cult of cold-blooded calculation ever were to achieve predominance, we may grant that the result would be an Orwellian anti-utopian nightmare, and the fulfillment of the ecology movement's worst dreams.

But to suggest that the commodity form of economic mediation may, in point of efficiency, have an enduring logic, is not at all to imply that efficiency calculation is the only logic which our society ought to obey. Indeed, as things are in our own culture, all calculation of efficiency occurs within an assumed framework of basic values, "inalienable rights" which specify the "boundary conditions"—the limits—within which commodification must operate, and thus define the terms in which efficiency itself is to be understood.

The point is formally analogous to that made with respect to the dialectics of class in Chapter 4.2. In our society today, for example, one cannot be deprived of an education, medical treatment, or legal representation on grounds of indigence: and this implies that the sphere of commodification has "boundary conditions" or limits. It is no part of my argument to deny this. To the contrary, I have emphasized that human history is marked by the incessant "socialization" of certain minima which accordingly are, insofar, insulated against the vagaries of a pure market calculus.

But now we must note: it is possible for a shift in the nature of commodification to be manifest not only in the case of interpersonal relations—as what we regard as a more "humane" standard of "human rights"—but also in the form of a more humane conception of acquisition and "exploitation" with respect to the nonhuman world.

Thus, just as our epoch can come to view previous forms of society as having an impoverished sense of human relations, we can also begin to see previous attitudes toward the nonhuman world as impossibly crude by contemporary standards. That commodification is never eliminated, does not mean that the specific, qualitative character of such commodification is not itself subject to a potentially endless process of refinement.

We need to achieve a more balanced view. Saying that "development" is essentially ongoing, and hence that commodity production is with us to stay, is not at all the same as saying that everything should be subjected to efficiency accounting. There clearly comes a point at which certain forms of human exploitation and environmental spoliation must be ruled flatly impermissible and not subject to laissez-faire market administration.

The postmodernist objection we have been entertaining goes much farther than this more balanced view. The critic wonders, in effect, if our future does not depend on the *total* elimination of the commodity form. It is this idea that I find radically implausible—and entirely unproved.

It is beyond the scope of this book to give this many-sided issue the full-dress consideration it no doubt deserves. I am convinced, however, that the controversy will ultimately be resolved on the basis of an exposure of a crucial non sequitur. It is illicit to move *from* the fact that our culture treats the environment as a commodifiable means of human enrichment, *to* the conclusion that it must treat it *merely* as a means to such enrichment.

The point is analogous to one made by Kant in the sphere of ethics. It must be granted that human life would be unimaginable if human beings did not treat each other as usable (and in that sense "exploitable") "means": that is how I treat the waiter or plumber—or any functionary—in the social division of labor. But, as Kant rightly stressed, it does not follow that I must, in "using" the waiter for my own purposes (in this case, the delivery of food to my table), treat him *merely* as such. It is also possible to treat him as an "end in himself." That means: my "exploitation" of the waiter must be limited to forms of treatment that do not negate his own moral autonomy.

While using another person *merely* as a food deliverer would be unethical, I fulfill my moral duty insofar as I always *also* consider his essential humanity, and hence refuse to use him in any ways that violate the precept that he and I have equal rights, and equal claims, within the same "kingdom of ends."

It does not follow from the fact that I am "using" you to the satisfaction of my desires— indeed, buying your labor power, as a commodity in the strictest sense—that *all* I am doing is using or commodifying you.

Analogously, it does not follow from the fact that we are using and commodifying the nonhuman environment for human purposes, that we cannot limit such "exploitation" to forms of activity that *also* pay due regard to the sanctity—and indeed the "autonomy"—of the natural world.

Admittedly, Kant did not have a place in his ethics for such an attitude toward nonpersons.[11] The latter expansion of ethical consciousness may well be one of the great achievements of our own time. We may nonetheless say, in the same Kantian spirit, that while treatment of the environment as *mere* means would be the path to disaster, the idea that such a reductive attitude is necessary is unproved and, to all appearances, implausible.

In avoiding the Scylla of "instrumental rationality," we must be wary of a Charybdis: the idea that we might possibly do without technical intelligence as such. There are indeed dangers in allowing an excessive scientism to seize exclusive control over the center of our culture. But there are equal dangers in a "backlash" that would attempt to discredit this perspective entirely.

Granted, the technological dimension of emancipation is at most one of several avenues of revolutionary practice. But the legitimacy of a nontechnical, nonreificatory "moment" of analysis does not prove the illegitimacy of the technical moment in itself. It is possible to insist on the limitations—and the potential distortions—of technical intelligence, while remaining convinced that it will indefinitely remain a fertile emancipatory force.

In the field of revolutionary thought and practice, the danger exists that we will begin talking as though such techniques lacked emancipatory relevance altogether. Marx may be one-sided in addressing only those dimensions of revolution which lie within the bounds of technical-productive intelligence. But it is equally one-sided to treat technological civilization as a prison from which we must try to escape.

That our culture "privileges" the technical moment is a fact that has, for those of us who have become aware of it, two diametrically opposed consequences.

The first is that we must indeed be suspicious of our culture's tendency to "reify," to suppress nontechnical styles and approaches, to treat things as manipulable objects.

But the other consequence is that those of us who have, for these five centuries, inhabited a culture built upon science and technology can no longer assign much meaning to the claim that technical progress has no relevance whatever to our emancipatory concerns.

I have argued that the realm of scarcity is always being displaced, and that, in those specific, historically restricted regions where scarcity does by hypothesis exist, *there* commodification will continue to prove a productively useful dimension of social mediation.

No one has ever given cogent reasons to conclude that we cannot reap the benefits of a kind of commodity production that is suitably constrained. And this casts radical doubt on the contention that the commodity system per se is the *bête noire* of our age.

The commodity system has been, and can continue to be, ever revised in the light of emergent human needs. In this dynamic context, why should it not be possible for the environmental challenges we now face to be appropriately addressed?

5. Formative Parity as a Rational Historical Trend

Whereas Marx tended to treat his economic projections as "predictions" of "inevitable" developments, most theoreticians of our own time would be more inclined to substitute a far-reaching sense of historical *contingency* for any such talk. This has been a familiar aspect of the philosophical critique of Marxism for quite a few decades, forming (for example) the backbone of Karl Popper's critique of Marxian "historicism"[12] as well as of Sidney Hook's exploration of the decisive role the contingent intervention of individuals plays in history.[13]

It has left its mark in Marxian circles as well. Even those who continue to favor some form of "communism" or "proletarian revolution" now tend to treat these objectives as, at most, desirable and feasible, rather than necessary and unavoidable. Progress—by anybody's standards—is itself by no means assured. Regression, and even the wholesale destruction of the human species, are entirely possible.

In the same spirit, I do not claim that a movement toward Formative Parity is an *empirical* trend. As a matter of rational economic organization, a social form may become decreasingly useful and yet not, in empirical fact, decline to a comparable degree. One can indeed be empirically skeptical about a future path of development—can wonder if it really will occur—and still believe that the conditions exist that make it the rational road to travel.

Thus even if there were less evidence of a decline in class discrepancies than there in fact is, the more important question would be whether ongoing formative disparities contribute to the productivity of our society. That we have often failed to seize the day, does not prove that the day was not worth seizing. Plenty of things that ought to happen are much too long in getting started. And this is sometimes so in much more than some moralistic sense of "ought." Some things ought to be as a matter of hard-headed economic good sense.

We must not be browbeaten by excessively positivistic souls who think that the heaping up of mounds of data about dreary reality is somehow more "scientific" than the attempt to come to grips with rational possibilities. If anything, it is less so: if we are ever to have some prospect of making rational social projections into the future, empirical "facts" about how society is now organized are hardly the essential thing.

An analogy: it may make a lot of sense for women to have equal economic opportunities. Feminists who call for such a step build their case at least partly on the conviction that human progress would thus be served. And yet one can believe this (as many of us do) and still worry, on the level of empirical fact, whether humanity will "get it together" to take such a step—despite that step's eminent reasonableness.

Thus if we confine ourselves to the trends suggested by empirical data alone—what the current situation regarding women and salaries actually is—we would be forced to admit that it is anybody's guess if society is on the way to sexual parity. In the case of overcoming discrepancies in pay between women and men, there really is no very clear contemporary empirical trend.

But all this shows is that feminists should not build their case on merely empirical trends. The only useful "prediction" of sexual parity would have the cash value of the following hypothesis: "If human society is to develop in the most rational and creative way, parity treatment of the sexes will have to occur."[14]

Analogously, the question before us, when it comes to comprehensive Formative Parity, is not whether classes *will* be abolished, but whether, given the present state of productive resources, the continuance of classes is the best way, under conditions now emerging, to make use of our developing human resources. We might have good reasons for supposing that social classes are losing their rationale, and yet bemoan the degree to which, in empirical fact, they manage to hang on.

If at times the actual decline of class does not keep pace with what is possible, perhaps all we can say about this is that many practices, even after they have outlived their usefulness, are, for various reasons, quite tenacious. Marx said it best: "the tradition of all the dead generations weighs like a nightmare on the brain of the living."[15] People can persist in their fondness for the institutions in which they were reared, long after these practices have, in functional terms, become obsolete.

There is no question of "inevitability" here. We *project* a classless form of capitalism. We do not *predict* it. We agree with Marx that the material conditions for the overcoming of class exist in the sense that real *possibilities* "exist," but, for us, the material possibility of cultural stagnation or even degeneration equally "exists."

Here is another aspect of Marx's excessive "scientism" that must be jettisoned. Social progress cannot be forecast in the way communism's founder seems to have conceived. It is entirely up to us whether we take the proper steps to institutionalize our revolutionary potential.

6. Living up to Our Rhetoric

In trying to assess the rational potential of our age, we must obviously not limit ourselves to asking what has already been done. We must also consider what we are tangibly close to achieving.

"Tangibly" because, with a kind of vague insistency, the ideal of the classless society is being more and more widely *felt* to be reasonable. This is in itself significant. For, realistically, we who have lived in a market society will tend to entertain classlessness seriously only to the extent that formative disparities are beginning to seem less and less admissible by the standards imposed by our own enunciated principles, our own rhetoric.

The rhetoric of parity is beginning to become familiar to us.[16] Today, if asked whether a child able to maintain a good record all the way through college should be allowed to do so, on public support if need be, I daresay many people, even in our own hard-hearted times, would say yes. Just decades ago, such a vision would not have been beyond our wildest dreams.

Such incipient rhetorical acceptance of Formative Parity must of course be taken with a large pinch of salt. That a principle has begun to be treated with respect, does not mean that its implications have been thought through. But endorsement of such formulae may mean that we are in the process of committing ourselves to a journey from which we can scarcely turn back.

The thesis of this book occupies the site of a fundamental tension. On the one hand, Formative Parity will lack plausibility with modern readers unless it is a principle whose time is, if not come, perhaps dawning. On the other, this ideal will lack the dramatic force of a revolutionary demand unless we are still a good distance from realizing that principle—as of course we are.

But as all dialecticians, Marx included, have seen: it is in this very gap between dawning recognition and explicit realization that we find so much of the dynamic of world history.

An analogy may prove instructive. Though our society did, in its Bill of Rights, commit itself more than two centuries ago to the basic protections of "due process," it was only in our own century that the logic of these rights begot the principle that courts must guarantee all people a good defense lawyer, regardless of indigence. But however long this development took, the result does seem, at least in retrospect, a logical outgrowth of those initial "due process" principles. The ideal of court procedure with which we began entails a conception of legal rectitude which, in the normal course of events, will create pressures, and define a trajectory, in the direction of ably-staffed public defenders' offices.

It is a poignant circumstance. The new rhetoric of universal parity reveals our own self-imposed commitment. We experience this as the rift between ideality and reality. This tension underlies much of the dynamic of social life. Only out of such tension, over the course of generations, do our revolutionary dreams come true.

Will we, and our children and grandchildren, realize this goal? This is, in the very nature of the case, and for better or worse, an unanswerable question.

One can only hope that we will be able to put together the best aspects and insights of the world's two most dominant economic systems, and so transcend both of them; so that, like all else in this world of unceasing change, Marxian communism and class-riven capitalism can pass—or should we say "wither"?—away.

Notes

1. Quoted above in Chapter 4.3.
2. In this spirit, the Court has indeed ruled against religious polygamy and ritual use of certain drugs. It would a fortiori be the case if, absurdly, some religion tried to justify child sacrifice on a First Amendment basis.
3. The term is Stephen Jay Gould's. See his *The Mismeasure of Man* (New York: 1981).
4. Paulo Freire has made an outstanding contribution in this area. See his *Pedagogy of the Oppressed* (New York: 1970) and *Education for Critical Consciousness* (New York: 1980).
5. This treatment of the distinction between what Bakunin calls "natural and beneficial authority," on the one hand, and imposed authority, on the other, runs through his works, and indeed is a familiar theme in all the anarchist literature. But see, for example, Bakunin, Michael, "Social and Economic Bases of Anarchism," in Horowitz, Irving L., ed., *The Anarchists* (New York: 1964), esp. pp. 133ff.
6. There are of course those who would question the concept of "progress" itself. The only sense of "progress" needed by the argument of this book has at least an

important dimension of historical relativity: (1) the relevance of considerations of efficiency may be taken for granted *in the context* of a culture, like our own, which is built on technological foundations; while (2) in such a context, Formative Parity is inescapable, since it involves, all other things being equal, the more efficient use of human resources.

7. That is: a form of human existence that knows that incessantly creative dialogical social activity is its own purest essence. The forms of opposition that remain do not constitute "alienation," but are forms of benign provocation required by the dialectical character of fulfilled human rationality itself.

8. This recurrent—though necessarily heterodox—theme has been sounded by visionary souls still able to speak on behalf of possibilities that Europe, caught in a frenzy of "modernization," was bent on suppressing. Wordsworth, for instance, in his sonnet "The World Is Too Much with Us" (1803), can complain of our having "given our hearts away" to a utilitarian world of "getting and spending" in which the gods themselves can no longer be seen and heard:

I'd rather be
A Pagan suckled in a Creed outworn;
So might I, standing on this pleasant Lea,
Have glimpses that would make me less forlorn;
Have sight of Proteus rising from the sea;
Or hear old Triton blow his wreathed horn.

In our own century, this Wordsworthian longing for a reopening to inspirited nature appears in various (sometimes overlapping) quarters. It shows up today in the recent women's movement, as an entire research project centered on the idea that goddess-worship, in contrast to now-dominant patriarchal religion, treated the natural world as alive and addressable. It even finds a voice in popular culture, as a basic dimension of "New Age philosophy."

9. Starhawk, "Consciousness, Politics, and Magic," in Spretnak, Charlene, ed., *The Politics of Women's Spirituality* (New York: 1982), pp. 174–77.

Habermas, in summarizing aspects of the thought of Herbert Marcuse, has lucidly summarized this entire "inspirited nature" tendency, though we must be careful to add that he does not seem to accept it himself: "Instead of treating nature as the object of possible technical control, we can encounter her as an opposing partner in a possible [dialogical] interaction. We can seek out a fraternal rather than an exploited nature. At the level of an as yet incomplete intersubjectivity we can impute subjectivity to animals and plants, even to minerals, and try to communicate with nature instead of merely processing her under conditions of severed communication. . . ." Habermas, Jürgen, "Technology and Science as 'Ideology,'" an excerpt from *Toward a Rational Society*, in Seidman, Steven, *Jürgen Habermas on Society and Politics*, p. 241.

10. See section 6 of the Introduction.

11. It might be argued, however, that Kant did as much as anyone in his time to laying the foundation for such a "revaluation," by means of this treatment of the latter in the last volume of his great trilogy of Critiques, *The Critique of Judgment*.

12. Popper, Karl, Sir, *The Poverty of Historicism* (New York: 1961).

13. Hook, Sidney, *The Hero in History: A Study in Limitation and Possibility* (Boston: 1955).

14. In the economic sphere, this is to assert a *correlation* between increasing

productivity and sexual equalization. Like other scientific projections, it is of the form, "If P is to occur, Q must occur." One can have very good reasons—as "scientific" as a reason could be—for asserting such a *hypothetical* linkage between P and Q, and still wonder about the (always dubitable) *categorical* proposition that P itself, and hence its consequence Q, will really come about. And so one can have solid grounds for maintaining that there has, in recent times, been an ongoing *rational* trend in the direction of sexual equality, and yet note that *actual* historical progress in this direction has been, at best, uncertain and choppy.

15. Marx, Karl, *The Eighteenth Brumaire of Louis Bonaparte*, in *The Marx-Engels Reader*, ed. Tucker, Robert (New York: 1978), p. 595.
16. One of our great state universities has as its motto: "Let each become all he is capable of being." Advertisements for that great equalitarian institution, the U.S. Army, counsel us: "Be all that you can be."

Conclusion
Beyond the Ideology
of the Age: The Nature
and Limits of the
Contradiction between
Capitalism and Communism

1. Why Have "Capitalism" and "Communism" Been Opposed?

We must now briefly consider the "ideological" context in which the battle for Formative Parity is being fought.

For such a transformation—even if conditions are ripe for it—will not take place unless we are able to raise our consciousness to the point of critically reexamining the assumptions that define the limits of our age. Truly revolutionary changes can be brought about only if a culture is able to bring to light—and to question—the unchallenged "paradigm" that underlies it.

This need is preeminently acute in the case of Formative Parity as I have conceived it. To appreciate the full import of this ideal, one must interrogate the very antithesis between "capitalism" and "communism" as it has been understood to now.

This study has been a promarket transcription of some themes that remain, nonetheless, of recognizably Marxian pedigree. We have attempted to "reinsert" Marx into a more consistently "dialectical" framework, and this has led to the clarification and defense of two basic hypotheses.

The first is that alienated labor, though it can and does change its form from one epoch to the next, is, as such, with us to stay. It would follow that capitalism as such—in particular, the market recirculation of investment decision—is not the merely temporary phenomenon Marx thought it was, destined to "wither away."

But since alienation does indeed change its form as society moves from one stage to the next, we cannot evade the burden of overcoming the specific obsolescent types of social alienation that typify our own time. This occasions our second hypothesis: that Marx may be right in thinking that social classes are fast becoming obsolete. We have, to this end, defended the ideal of Formative Parity. Classlessness in this sense would be the fulfillment of the reasonable ideals of the "socialists" of the past two centuries.

Such a system would rest on "socialized" guarantees. But these would be, contra Marx, consistent with capitalistic ideals, and could indeed largely be produced and supplied in the private sector. The noblest goals of communism, and the noblest ideals of capitalism, could be conjointly satisfied.

Were such a "utopian" vision to become a reality, it would involve both capitalistic and socialistic elements. Such a society would no longer bear witness to some absolute difference between capital*ism* and social*ism* as forms of economic organization. Thought and practice governed by such "isms"—attempts at institutional and ideological purity of one type or the other—would have given way to a practice founded on the recognition that a rational advanced economy must partake of the methods of *both* socialization *and* capitalization.

Socialization: the "social minimum" must, as a matter of political mandate, come to include sweeping guarantees of parity investment—expenditures in proportion to talent—effective during our children's entire formative period.

Capitalization: the marketplace—based upon monetary exchange, individual initiative, and the reaping of profits (and the taking of losses) in case of successful (or unsuccessful) investment—must continue to be the main theater of economic operation, into which one would enter in one's majority years. We would regard it as axiomatic that our most precious resource—human intelligence—is best fostered by benign competition among vying creative conceptions.

Why then—if these two moments ought to conspire rather than oppose one another—have we had the historical dichotomy between capitalism and communism at all?

For, plainly, the "Western" and "Eastern" systems have been systems indeed. They rest on disparate theoretical and ideological bases which determine opposed forms of social practice. Indeed the partisans of both systems have, for a century and more, agreed about this much: the differences between capitalism and communism are fundamental and irreconcilable.

In view of the fact that East and West embody complementary half-truths, are we to say that apologists on both sides have been "confused"? Is a failure of "insight" responsible for the fact that each system captures an important truth but overlooks another? Have all these decades of strident opposition—which for a good while threatened global devastation—been rooted merely in a mutual failure to grasp the necessary "synthesis" between the rationality of the market and fundamental formative rights? Has the conflict between capitalism and communism been in this sense an avoidable tragedy? Or does it have a "logic" in the peculiar circumstances of our time?

No doubt, history *has* had its share of large-scale stupidity: days that could have been saved if our leaders had been just a little brighter or more conscientious. But the struggle between capitalism and socialism has been no mere confusion or mistake. Rather it is inherent in the nature of the transition problem: the formation of a world in which the ideals embodied in both systems can be realized.

The conflict itself has a logic. There is a certain "inevitability," if you will, about the dichotomy. Far from being a mere "error," it is just what one must expect to characterize the epoch in which the conditions for a new "synthesis" are in the process of formation, but are not yet fully formed.

It is a struggle inherent in the transition from class-divided "bourgeois capitalism" to a classless form of capitalism. During this transition, the species begins to take the abolition of classes as a serious goal, but cannot yet achieve that goal within the bounds of capitalism in its existing, class-divided form: what we may dub "bourgeois capitalism."

This means, on the one hand, that as our wealth increases, classes should begin to seem—at least to some—an increasingly intolerable burden; and so they will increasingly come under attack. If the impressive achievements of bourgeois capitalism are undermining the logic of classes, it is only to be expected that, as this proceeds, people will increasingly feel the discrepancy between the *potentiality* of such emancipation and the *actuality* of a society still mired in old, nonemancipated ways.

This is just the newest instance of an old story: when a form of emancipation is just beginning to appear on the horizon, there will be those—we call them radicals—who begin to think and act in its name.

But since a rationally administered market system cannot afford to complete the historical movement to classlessness until relatively late in its history, it is only to be expected that, during the entire lengthy prethreshold period we have been passing through, the inability of the market system to transcend social classes will seem to all—on both sides, East and West—to be no temporary aspect of the market, but eternally essential to its operation.

When it comes to the emancipatory potential of the market society, the striking fact is that, under capitalism as we have so far known it, classes have indeed been an irreducible and indispensable aspect of social existence. So it is no wonder that people have uncritically assumed that the market society is flatly incapable of transcending social classes.

In the present instance, neither side can see that this is not an eternal truth, but is of more restricted application: to the range of problems typical in industrial societies up to the present.

And so it has seemed to both that we must have either class-divided capitalism or a society that can achieve classlessness only by means of the supersession of capitalism.

So important is this dichotomous assumption, that it deserves a name of its own. I will call it the *Bourgeois Principle*.

The Bourgeois Principle is but one instance of a general kind of ideological distortion that haunts periods of social revolution. Radicals and conservatives tend to agree about at least this much: the existing system obeys a conservative logic; it itself cannot accommodate the changes that radicals demand. Any characteristic that has *to now* been inconsistent with the system will "naturally" tend to be treated as incompatible with it *in principle*: as being achievable only if the system is abolished.

This conviction is by no means groundless, but rather follows from a correct perception, by all concerned, of the actual existing regime. That is why the idea that the system itself cannot accommodate the demands of radicals acquires the status of an apparently "empirical fact" that can be confirmed "by inspection." It amounts to a "paradigm" admitted on all hands, an assumption which, far from being merely of an intellectual or conceptual character, governs the most automatic, prereflective, immediate behavior of all who work within the system's confines.

Both "East" and "West" prereflectively accept the Bourgeois Principle as paradigmatic, and this common premise lies at the heart of the dichotomy between them.

Partisans of the Western model, pointing to hard historical example, argue (A) that optimal productivity can never be achieved outside a market context. But when assertion (A) is taken in conjunction with the Bourgeois Principle, we get the apparent implication (B) that classes are the price we must pay to live in the most productive society. The result is the nexus of attitudes that define class-divided, bourgeois capitalism.

Proponents of the Eastern model, pointing to the possibilities of emancipation made possible by the bourgeois order itself, assume (A') that optimal productivity in the next epoch can be achieved by a society that has eliminated classes. But when (A′) is taken in conjunction with the Bourgeois Principle, we get the further apparent implication (B′) that human emancipation requires the elimination of the market system.

Because capitalism has to now been inconsistent with classlessness, it has seemed opposed to classlessness in principle. That bourgeois capitalism might give way to a "postclass" capitalism—this will remain beyond the imagination of either camp until, through a "paradigm shift," the Bourgeois Principle itself is called into question.

The call for Formative Parity involves just such a paradigm shift. Only when we escape the confines of the Bourgeois Principle that has dominated our time can we see that there is in fact no ultimate inconsistency between the retention of the market and the overcoming of class distinctions.

The idea that capitalism and classlessness are inconsistent will inevitably be socially dominant so long as the material conditions for classless capitalism have not yet evolved. This paradigm cannot achieve ideological dominance—cannot become the "conventional wisdom"—as long as the conditions for classless capitalism have not yet ripened.

That they are ripening has been one of the main contentions of this book. This may indeed be the extraordinary prospect of our own time. The only credible outcome of my argument is the adumbration of a new "paradigm" able to accommodate the chief aims and insights of both the communistic and capitalistic worldviews.

If the argument is sound, this is no mere synthesis of ideas. Rather it is an anticipation of the joining of the trajectories of two leviathan economic systems. Though market societies up to now have operated below the threshold at which Formative Parity at last becomes feasible, this condition need not be forever: we are approaching the threshold at which classes, within the market context, are becoming dysfunctional.

But if a transition to a classless society is finally becoming feasible, it is also possible that, through ideological and theoretical reflection, the dominant form of consciousness of our epoch—according to which capitalization and socialization are ultimately antagonistic—will undergo a correspondingly profound sea change.

2. *Toward a New Social Paradigm*

The question of Formative Parity cannot reasonably be considered within the boundaries of any individual nation. A truly classless society can be achieved only on a global scale.

Here, again, Marxism has a contribution to make. Marxists have astutely observed how wealthy nations can imperialistically "export the proletariat." The apparently "universal" rights of our own people are sometimes gained through the exploitation of those who toil in obscurity, in less developed places. It goes without saying that in this case the rights would not truly be universal. Class distinctions would be pushed from view, not eliminated.

This underscores the immensity of the task before us. We can attack the problem only if we see in it an issue confronting the "global village" as an integral phenomenon. I have argued that approximating Formative Parity means the increasingly rational use of human resources. For this reason, one hopes it will become an explicit and indeed axiomatic item on the species's agenda as we inaugurate the Third Millennium.

If this is to occur, one of the main dogmas that has divided the world must be decisively jettisoned.

We have, till quite recently, thought of our world as divided into "capitalist" and "socialist" camps. The terms themselves are misleading in the extreme. For neither of these tendencies can forever resist the pull of the other. Each rages against an insuperable adversary. Together they constitute a false antithesis. Assuming that this antithesis can be resolved, each of these forms will be remembered as a mixed blessing.

Bourgeois (class-based) "capitalism" will be remembered as the system that unflinchingly committed itself to the preservation and refinement of the market system.

And yet it will also be remembered as the system that put up resistance to the constant upgrading of the social minimum—and which opposed the attack upon classes, denigrating this as an idea of obviously communistic pedigree.

The West has not yet fully grasped that the establishment of such universal guarantees does not threaten market processes. But just because such guarantees do serve the interests of the increasing productivity of the market society itself, the West, despite all its ideological resistance, may not, in the end, be able to resist the tide of such progress.

"Communism" will be remembered as the system that took up the banner of the overthrow of classes when the conditions of such an overthrow were beginning to develop in the womb of bourgeois capitalism.

But it will also be remembered as the system that fought for a form of "total socialization" of the economy, the thorough transcendence of the market, the abolition of individual, "private" appropriation.

We have agreed that historical progress involves the upgrading of the guaranteed "social minimum" even up to the point of Formative Parity. In that sense, it is the limitless march of "socialization."

Yet we have also seen that the communist conception of social*ism*, as an economic and political doctrine, means much more than this: it stands for the conviction that the time is coming when rational economic organization dictates all-encompassing politically administered monopolies in essential areas of production. We have seen that, in reality, the competitive market is warranted in all but some rather special cases.

An incalculable price has been paid in the attempt to do away with market methods as such. It may be an even greater price than has been paid in the Western world for the error of thinking that steps toward classlessness are necessarily "communistic." The very reasonable idea of the constant upgrading of the social minimum has been deformed into a tyrannical ideal: that of totalistic, monopolistic economic planning.

"Totalistic"—that is, *totalitarian*. The term is apt in a straightforwardly descriptive sense: centralized planning does indeed put the political mechanisms of the unified, single political totality ahead of the economic pluralism embodied in the decentralized, competitive marketplace. And that is what is wrong with it.

Marx thought human progress would consist in the formation of an economy beyond the bounds of the market. Pursuit of this will-o'-the-wisp has caused the human species a good deal of grief.

But Marx also thought that progress would bring about a classless society. This ideal—the most revolutionary dream of the modern epoch—may be far more practicable than most of us have dared to think.

Index